CNUT

CNUT

EMPEROR OF
THE NORTH

M.J. TROW

SUTTON PUBLISHING

First published in the United Kingdom in 2005 by
Sutton Publishing Limited · Phoenix Mill
Thrupp · Stroud · Gloucestershire · GL5 2BU

British Library Cataloguing in Publication Data
A catalogue record for this book is available from the British
Library.

ISBN 0-7509-3387-9

Typeset in 11/14.5pt Sabon.
Typesetting and origination by
Sutton Publishing Limited.
Printed and bound in England by
J.H. Haynes & Co. Ltd, Sparkford.

Contents

List of Illustrations

One, by God's grace, will overcome
all the hardships that bedevilled his youth
and achieve happiness in old age:
he will welcome the rising sun, and receive
riches, treasures and the mead-cup from his people
as much as anyone can own in this life.

The Fortunes of Man

Acknowledgements

Cnut, Emperor of the North is the work not just of the writer, but of many whose efforts and talents have gone before.

I would like to take this opportunity to thank: my editor, Jaqueline Mitchell and her unflagging staff at Sutton; my agent, Andrew Lownie, for his tireless work behind the scenes; Dr John Crook of Winchester for his expertise and photographic input; to the vicar of Deerhurst Church; to J.M. Dent, a division of the Orion Publishing Group, for permission to quote from the *Anglo-Saxon Chronicle*, translated by Professor Michael Swanton; to Boydell and Brewer Ltd, for permission to quote from Kevin Crossley-Holland's translations, detailed in the notes; to all others who have given me permission to quote from their works and to those who we were unable to trace; to all who have given permission to use picture sources and to those we were unable to trace; to my son, Taliesin, whose 'mastery' of archaeology is far beyond mine; and, as always, to my long-suffering wife, Carol, who is endlessly having to put her own books on hold because she is typing mine!

Cnut's England

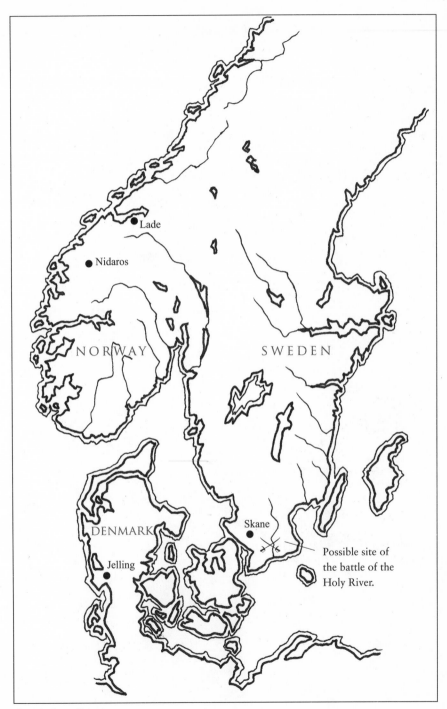

Cnut's Scandinavia

ONE

The Fury of the Northmen

The waters ferment,
sea-horses foaming . . .
The whale-mere roars, fiercely rages . . .
The Exeter Book, 1072

It was the chronicler and archdeacon Henry of Huntingdon who first put the story on parchment in 1154. His *Historia Anglorum* was one of several histories of England compiled in the Middle Ages; and on the subject of King Cnut, he told the tale of the waves.

So powerful is this image that the philosopher and historian David Hume was to record Henry of Huntingdon faithfully six centuries later:

Canute, the greatest and most powerful monarch of his time . . . could not fail of meeting with admiration from his courtiers; a tribute which is liberally paid even to the meanest and weakest of princes. Some of his flatterers breaking out one day in admiration of his grandeur, exclaimed that everything was possible for him. Upon which, the monarch, it is said, ordered his chair to be set on the sea-shore, while the tide was rising; and as the waters approached, he commanded them to retire, and to obey the voice of him who was lord of the ocean. He feigned to sit some time in expectation of their submission, but when the sea still advanced towards him and began to wash him with its billows, he turned to his courtiers, and remarked to them, that every creature in the universe was feeble and impotent, and that power resided with one Being alone, in whose hands were all the elements of nature; who could say to the ocean 'Thus far shalt thou go, and no further'; and who could level with his rod the most towering piles of human pride and ambition.[1]

Today, this is about all most people know about the Viking king of England and worse, since Huntingdon's and Hume's time, the king's piety and humility has vanished and he is portrayed as a stupid and arrogant megalomaniac who believed he had greater powers than God. The 'Canute Syndrome' of self-delusion is regularly applied to politicians and economists in the modern world in a way completely opposed to the intentions of Henry of Huntingdon.

Who was this man, at once an arrogant overlord and a humble Christian, whose life and message is today so seriously misunderstood? To answer that question, we have to go back in time . . .

The dragon-ships came out of the mists again that summer of 980. Laconically as always, the Anglo-Saxon chronicler at Abingdon recorded what happened: 'and in the same year Southampton was ravaged by a raiding ship-army and most of the town-dwellers killed or taken prisoner. And the same year the land of Thanet was raided; and the same year Cheshire was raided, by a northern raiding ship-army.'[2]

'Northern raiding ship-armies' had been the bane of Englishmen for nearly two centuries and the chronicler who catalogued, with his quill scratching on vellum, the events of the 980s, was more prosaic and perhaps resigned than his counterparts in Canterbury and Peterborough in 793 who had written: 'Here, terrible portents came about in the land of Northumbria and miserably afflicted the people. There were immense flashes of lightning and fiery dragons were seen flying in the air and there immediately followed a great famine; and a little after that in the same year, on 8th January, the raiding of heathen men miserably devastated God's church in Lindisfarne through looting and slaughter . . .'[3]

The heathen men were back in 980. The word 'Viking', variously translated as inlet-dweller or pirate, struck terror into the hearts of Franks, Goths, Russians and innumerable racial groups around the Mediterranean. Without doubt the best and most fearless sailors in the world, their famous long-ships sheared through waters as distant as the North Atlantic and the mouth of the Volga. The fanatical rantings of their *berserker* warriors and their indiscriminate slaughter of men, women and children persuaded defenceless priests that the legions of Hell had risen against them and they ascribed non-existent diabolical horns to their helmets.[4]

The ships that furrowed into the sand in Southampton Water in the summer of 980 were the largest of the *drakkar*, the serpents or dragon-ships, 90ft long with twenty oarports and capable of carrying a hundred men. Such ships were once thought to be the hyperbole of the Viking saga writers, but giant ships excavated at Hedeby and Roskilde fjord in Denmark since the 1960s have lent the weight of archaeological support. They were the galleons and Dreadnoughts and aircraft carriers of their day – fast and deadly, with a speed of 7 knots under oars. Men's hearts sank when they saw their square sails clutter the horizon.

The dragon-ships were built for speed and manoeuvrability. Sliding up the shingle at Sandwich, anchoring on Northey Island, patrolling the Solent or negotiating the Holy River, they had to get their raiding-party crews back to sea quickly after an attack. Their thirty-four oars on each side were designed to be independent of the wind, and for long journeys or naval battles there would have to be changes of rowers.

Oak was the timber of choice, but beech, alder, ash, lime, willow and birch all had their uses. Oak logs were split radially, using metal or wooden wedges to create 'slices of a cake'. Saws were never used, because the strength of a piece of wood lies with the grain, not against it. Hemp was used for ropes, willow and lime bast for rigging. Sails were woven with wool by the women who could do little, in the Viking age, as Rudyard Kipling said, but watch their men 'Go with the old, grey widow-maker' [the sea]. Pine tar was smeared on all timbers to preserve against the corrosion of wind and water.

A whole range of woodworking tools was used: axes, adzes, hammers, tongs, knives and augers all played their part in building the most advanced killing machines of their day. Their performance was awesome. Their sleek lines meant that they could ride the waves, rather as a modern catamaran does, terrifying watching ceorls on headlands throughout the known world. They had no compass and no timepiece, but Cnut's helmsmen could steer by the stars, the direction of the sea's swell and the feel of the various winds on their faces. The height of the sun could be calculated by fingers, fists or a notched stick. We do not know exactly how the

Vikings did this, but they probably used skills we no longer know we have because we are never called upon to use them.

Southampton in 980 was a cluster of 150 hides[5] comprising about 15 acres. It was the third settlement in the area since Roman times, since Clausentum had been abandoned for Hamwise around the year 700. That thriving port had been hit by Viking attacks so many times that it too had been abandoned and the 'new' town was built on higher ground overlooking the River Test and Southampton Water. Despite its being declared a royal mint in the reign of King Athelstan fifty years earlier, the site seems to have been only partially populated in a large area that made a nonsense of its protective rampart and ditch defences. Clearly the Viking raiders of 980 saw it as a soft touch. Not until after the Norman Conquest of 1066 would the area be repopulated.

The same raiding party took their captured slaves, their wine and their livestock and left Southampton burning. Then they sailed north-east, hugging the coast and looking for somewhere else to lay waste. The abbey at Minster, visible from what is today Pegwell Bay, would have been irresistible to them. In 980, the River Wantsum was still wide enough to make Thanet an island, and the old Roman forts of Richborough and Reculver had long since ceased to defend it. The scattered villages there, of wattle, daub and thatch, were put to the torch as their inhabitants fled inland.

The attacks in Cheshire are more vague. The *Anglo-Saxon Chronicle* gives us no place names and no timescale. Was the Cheshire raid a later one by the same fleet? Or are we looking at two different attacks by two separate bands? And if so, were those attacks coordinated or coincidental? As always, the *Chronicle* throws up more questions than answers.

Nor can we be sure that the raids of the following year were the work of the Southampton/Thanet fleet. Whoever the attackers were, their targets were further west: 'Here, in this year, Padstow, was raided,' railed the Abingdon *Chronicle*, 'and the same year great harm was done everywhere along the sea coast, both in Devon and in Cornwall.'[6] St Petroc's church in Padstow (called Lanwenehoc in the eleventh century) had been founded by the saint in the sixth century as part of a monastery. By definition, the core of the

Chronicle's cataloguing of events lies in the church. The *Anglo-Saxon Chronicle* is not a continuous history composed by one hand, as earlier historians believed, but a fragmentary record of certain events begun in the ninth century and ending in 1154. The earliest entries go back to the birth of Christ – 'Octavian reigned for fifty-six years, and in the forty-second year of his reign, Christ was born.'[7]

There are actually four chronicles, known today as Ā, C, D and E, and another three – A, B and F – which are copies of the other four. Ā, known also as the *Parker Chronicle* after its sometime owner, Matthew Parker, Archbishop of Canterbury and Master of Corpus Christi College, Cambridge, was probably written at the Anglo-Danish capital of Winchester. Soon after the Norman Conquest it was taken to Christchurch, Canterbury, and is the oldest manuscript, covering 60 BC to AD 1070. A is a copy of the latter made at Winchester, but it was badly damaged by fire in 1731 – the same fire that damaged the original text of the Anglo-Scandinavian poem *Beowulf* – and only fragments remain. B and C include the Annals of Aethelflaed and the Mercian *Chronicle* and are eleventh-century copies of earlier originals. D, the Worcester *Chronicle*, was probably sent to Ripon or York for safe keeping. E was written at Peterborough and appears to be a copy of D, with the addition of various charters and monastic matters. A serious fire at Peterborough in 1116 probably destroyed most, if not all, of the monastery's books. F was written in both English and Latin in the twelfth century, by which time Latin had returned as the 'official' language of law and the Church. It causes a certain ambiguity with its bilingual terminology. For instance, the English *ealdorman* meaning nobleman appears as *dux*, leader, a specifically Norman addition.

With all the copying and transposition and interpolation that went on, we are left with a sometimes infinitely vague and often contradictory narrative which does not answer our questions. The chroniclers themselves were clerks, churchmen whose literacy and livelihood lay in the church's bounty. Inevitably, Church matters loom large. So, in 981, along with Viking attacks, 'Aelfstan, Bishop in Wiltshire, passed away and his body lies in the monastery at Abingdon; and Wulfgar succeeded to the bishopric. And in the same year, Womaer, Abbot in Ghent, passed away.'[8]

It is not merely this obsession with Church events that leads the *Chronicle* to single out attacks on monasteries. They had been known to the Vikings for two hundred years as easy meat, housing rich collections of plate and other valuables whose guardians, the monks, did not fight back. As we shall see in a later chapter, the Vikings of the late tenth century were not quite the 'heathen men' of earlier generations, but they still had no qualms about burning Christian churches or hacking down Christian priests.

The attacks continued sporadically throughout the decade. In 982, according to the *Chronicle*, 'Three ships of Vikings came up in Dorset, and raided in Portland. The same year, London too burned . . .'[9] The Isle of Portland was an invasion site waiting to happen. Dorset's 'Rock of Gibraltar', as the guide books call it, still carries traces of Saxon strip farming, an indication that this was rich agricultural land. It was also studded with wealthy churches not far inland.

London however was a different proposition. Known to the Saxons as Lundenwic, the post-Roman settlement had been attacked by Vikings many times since the 820s. Such was the ferocity of these raids (the long-ships easily rowed upriver from the Essex marshes) that the place became largely depopulated until its refounding under Alfred the Great. In 886, says the *Chronicle*, 'King Alfred occupied London fort and all the English race turned to him . . .'[10]

Lundenwic was in no sense Alfred's capital, but there was probably a settlement in the precincts of St Paul's Cathedral and perhaps a royal palace on the site of the old Roman fort at Cripplegate. By the time of the 982 attack, there were at least three centres of high population – Cheapside and East Cheap, the two markets, and a third on the site of the old Roman basilica. Archaeological finds in recent years indicate that the port was as bustling in the late tenth century as it had been under Roman occupation. Viking homestones have been found along the waterfront, yards from the remnants of silk from Byzantium and from China. Copper, gold and silver were presumably worked here, although the evidence is sparse. The fact that the city could withstand a major assault by the Vikings in 1013 and 1016 suggests that the burnings of 982 were only partial and the damage soon rectified.

Watchet in north Devon was ravaged in 988 in what was the last of the foraging raids of the decade. Until this point, the attacks had followed the pattern of the centuries in lightning hits, largely on undefended coastal areas, so that retreat was easy. Such were the communication problems of the tenth century that no force of any strength could be gathered before the raiders had come and gone. All that such a force would find would be bodies, smoking buildings and the horror-stories of the survivors.

What happened in 991 was entirely different. 'Olaf came,' says the *Chronicle* ominously, 'with ninety-three ships to Folkestone, raided round about it, and went from there to Sandwich, and so from there to Ipswich and overran all that – and so to Maldon.'[11]

Olaf was Olaf Tryggvason, who would be king of Norway four years later. The great-grandson of Harald Halfdanarson (Fine Hair), Olaf was about thirty when he landed in Kent. Described in *Chambers' Biographical Dictionary* as 'the most spectacular Viking of his time', he was brought up in Novgorod at the court of Prince Vladimir I of Russia. By the age of eighteen he was fighting as a mercenary (a common Viking occupation) in the Baltic. His ship in the raid of 991 would be eclipsed seven years later by the *Long Serpent*, with thirty-four benches.

'The head and coils of the dragon's tail were all ornamented in gold. The Long Serpent was the finest ship built in Norway, and the most costly', wrote the anonymous creator of *Olaf Tryggvason's Saga* in the thirteenth century. Ships of the time possibly carried a crew of three hundred which means that, allowing for the fact that the *Chronicle*'s fleet of ninety-three includes support vessels, not merely warships, we can estimate a Viking army of at least 2,500 men and quite possibly twice that number. A man of Olaf's status leading an army that size could only mean one thing; this was not a raid – it was an invasion.

The *Chronicle*'s curious phrase 'raided round about it' may imply that Folkestone itself was too strong to attack. This is a possibility, although its geography, with its towering cliffs, probably made it appear more formidable than it actually was. Certainly, low-lying Sandwich along the coast would have offered no serious challenge to Tryggvason's troops, and the hearts of the men of Thanet must have sunk anew at the appearance of so large and terrifying a force. Avoiding the Thames estuary, the Vikings sailed north, following the coast as always, and landed on the banks of the Orwell to overrun the area around Ipswich.

How seriously the town itself was damaged is not known. It was a major port and commodity centre in the Saxon kingdom of East Anglia by the late sixth century. Bronze, iron and bone had been worked there for centuries, but by the time of the Viking attack, Ipswich pottery was famous throughout England and may have been centred on what is today St Stephen's Lane, with cluttered shops and houses along the street edge. A sparser settlement along Foundation Street indicates a rural centre and it was probably this area that formed the target for Tryggvason's men. The fortifications of the town were, ironically, Viking, in that Ipswich was in the area of England known as the Danelaw, occupied by the Vikings for over a century.

Tryggvason was virtually a king and his raiding party an army. No self-respecting king of England could sit idly by while the Vikings chose to attack wherever they liked. Unfortunately, the king was Aethelred Unraed and the man he sent against them Ealdorman Byrhtnoth.

A number of revisionist historians have tried to reassess the reign of Aethelred, pointing quite correctly to the achievements of the early years of his reign and his grasp of the *realpolitik* of his situation – he did, after all, reign for an astonishing thirty-six years. They accuse the major sources of his day, the various manuscripts that make up the *Anglo-Saxon Chronicle*, of painting a one-dimensional character that misses the king's subtleties. That is as may be, but kingship was measured above all in terms of military ability and decision-making. And Aethelred, it seems, was the wrong man for the job. Election to kingship, being born to kingship, taking the crown by force – none of these guarantees the essentials of a 'good king'. Nicholas Romanov, the last Tsar of Russia, was famously described as making an excellent turnip-farmer. The best epitaph that the *Anglo-Saxon Chronicle* could give Aethelred on his death in 1016 was that 'he ended his days on St George's Day, after great trials and difficulties in his life'.[12]

Later generations interpreted Unraed as Unready, although the philosopher David Hume in his *History of England* [1792] unwittingly gets the original meaning right: 'In this extremity, Ethelred . . . instead of raising his people to defend with courage their honour and their property, hearkened to the advice of Siricius, archbishop of Canterbury, which was seconded by many of the degenerate nobility . . .'[13] Unraed means ill-counsel or badly advised and in respect of Aethelred is *exactly* like Nicholas Romanov and many rulers between them.

All the advice in 991, however, was unanimous and sound; make a stand. And it was just bad luck perhaps that Ipswich lay in the territory of Byrhtnoth, who, with Custer-like bravado, seems to have underestimated his enemy when he met them at Maldon. Ealdorman is a complex term, deriving from the Latin equivalent of *princeps*, *comes* and *praefectus* under the Romans. By the time of the Norman Conquest, the vernacular version of Earl had replaced it in England, with heavy borrowings from the Danish *jarl*. In the reign of Aethelred, an ealdorman was a substantial landowner and military leader, but essentially, the king's man (which had not been the case in the earlier Saxon period). A man like Byrhtnoth, whose only mention exists in connection with Maldon, would have wielded considerable power on Aethelred's behalf. The attendance in his army of Aescferth of Northumbria implies that Byrhtnoth's status was substantial. He either held lands in Northumbria or Aescferth was sent to Byrhtnoth's 'court' as a youngster who could learn from the great man. Ealdormen were generals in time of war, signatories of charters and other documents in time of peace. As overlord in Essex, it was Byrhtnoth's duty, as well as his right, to face Tryggvason.

The account of the battle of Maldon is one of the most heavily debated of the period because it is the subject of one of the few surviving poems of Anglo-Saxon literature. Only *Beowulf* is better known and the debate inevitably arises out of how much is fiction and how much fact. *The Battle of Maldon* itself has survived by sheer luck. Written on three bifolia which may have been used as book-binding in the Middle Ages, it was first catalogued in 1621 in the collection of Robert Cotton, one of the founding members of the Society of Antiquarians. Although this original with a fragmentary beginning and end was destroyed by fire in 1731, it had been copied line by line by David Casley, deputy keeper of Cotton's library. All modern versions are based on this:

> Bold seamen have sent me to you, and
> told me to say that you must send
> treasure quickly in return for peace,
> and it will be better for you all to buy
> off an attack with treasure, rather than
> face men as fierce as us in battle. We
> need not destroy each other, if you
> are rich enough. In return for the gold we
> are ready to make truce with you.[14]

We do not know when the poem was written, but its 325 lines probably belong to late in the reign of Aethelred, when Maldon was seen as a great, lost opportunity and a Viking darkness had descended on the land.

In the August of 991, Tryggvason's fleet, laden with plunder from Ipswich, sailed up the Blackwater in the direction of the burh at Maldon. Forts like this were dotted all over England. Often built over Roman fortifications or Celtic hill strongholds, they were timber and earth walls and ramparts enclosing a small settlement. By Aethelred's time, some of these were actually manor houses of the type that would become far more common after the Norman Conquest. The Vikings beached on the low island at Northey, most likely on the east coast for a fast getaway. They probably built a defensive wall and ditch, as was their custom, to protect the fleet as best they could. Across what today is Southey Creek, called the Pante in Saxon times, they were jeered and taunted by the thegns and levies of Ealdorman Byrhtnoth's army.

In the poem, Byrhtnoth orders his cavalry to dismount and drive their horses away; it was the English way. He unleashes his favourite falcon from his wrist and watches it fly to the safety of the forest. The slave Spartacus was reported to have dismounted similarly at his last battle with the Romans; so did the outnumbered Henry V at Agincourt:

> Can you hear, you pirate, what these people say?
> They will pay you a tribute of whistling spears,
> Of deadly darts and proven swords . . .

Such was Byrhtnoth's version of the Danegeld Tryggvason had demanded. His words are almost Churchillian in their defiance:

> Listen, messenger! Take back this reply:
> break the bitter news to your people
> that a noble earl and his troop stand over here –
> guardians of the people and of the country, the home
> of Aethelred, my prince – who will defend this land
> to the last ditch.

We have no realistic idea of the number on either side, and if the English were regarded as underdogs in the poem and the historical sense that followed, it was probably the result of hindsight. The fact was that the Vikings were willing to be bought off with gold as the lines above indicate, perhaps because they knew themselves to be outnumbered and likely to lose. Vikings, contrary to common preconception, would usually rather be paid than fight. They were fierce warriors, but large-scale pitched battles were not their style. Byrhtnoth's arrogant defiance may merely be poetic heroism, but it may have been born of an over-confidence resulting from superior numbers. Northey Island is very flat. The English could have seen the whole of Tryggvason's force at a glance and the fleet that brought them. In high summer, it is likely that visibility would have been good.

All that separated the armies was a narrow causeway, then only negotiable at low tide, and it meant that the Vikings had a small time frame in which to operate. The poem tells us that Byrhtnoth faced the raiders with that most famous of Saxon battle-tactics, the shield wall. This undoubtedly suited the Viking force. There *are* known examples of the Vikings using horses successfully in battle – at Sulgit in Ireland in 968 for instance or Montfaucon in the Frankish kingdom – but they instinctively preferred to fight on foot. The poem implies that Byrhtnoth made the decision to dismount so that his men could not escape so fast, but footsoldiers were the norm in English armies too, so we need not look for a gutsier motive.

The shield wall which both sides presented was literally that – a line of men with their circular wooden shields overlapping to about half their width, giving a frontage of less than 2ft per man. This front line was composed of the biggest, best-armed warriors, tall men with fearsome iron swords and axes. Behind them, second, third, fourth and fifth lines formed a solid phalanx. The problem at Maldon was the narrowness of the causeway which would allow only three or four men abreast to cross it. Tryggvason's Vikings *could* have made use of the second commonly used tactic – the *swynfylking* or 'swine-array', a wedge-shaped formation reputedly devised by Odin, the Norse god of war. The *Flateyjarbok*, a fourteenth-century Icelandic chronicle, describes the wedge as having two men in the front rank, three in the second and five in the third, and multiples of this could be formed and re-formed all over the battlefield.

Byrhtnoth allowed the Vikings to cross the causeway at low tide and has been criticised for it ever since by, among others, that creator of ludicrous battle scenarios, J.R.R. Tolkien.[15] The fact was that if he had not, Tryggvason's Vikings would have rattled their *rangels* (iron rings whose noise frightened away evil spirits) and roared their defiance before embarking in their ships again and destroying who knew how many homesteads anywhere along the coast. The pirates must be taught a lesson – England was Aethelred's not theirs, and at Maldon enough was enough. So this was not an example of the Ealdorman's *ofermod* (pride) but common sense. He had to give the Vikings room to force a battle. The poem blames Byrhtnoth's excessive pride for this, but the mood of the entire English army was probably summed up by a young soldier who yelled:

> Now the way is clear for you. Come over to us quickly,
> warriors to the slaughter. God alone can say
> who will control the field of battle.

From then on, it all went badly for the Essex *fyrdmen*. We shall see later how English armies fought, but their backbone, by the time of Aethelred, were the thegns, local noblemen to whom training in arms was a way of life. Far more numerous and far less trustworthy were the rank and file of the *fyrd*, peasants armed with slingshots, spears and staves, men forever torn between defending their hearths and homes from a foreign invader and the vital, driving need to get the harvest in. There is probably no finer description of a battle than that given in the poem – the 'slaughter-wolves' waded across the Pante to face men already marked for death –

> the ravens wheeled, and the eagle circled overhead,
> craving for carrion.

In the poem, Byrhtnoth dies early, hacking down his assailant as he falls. '. . . one will be spear-slain,' prophesied another poem, *The Fortunes of Men*,[16] 'one hacked down in battle.' His bondman Godric, terrified in the face of the clashing, writhing shield wall, scrabbles backwards to find his lord's horse and gallop away, leading others to believe that Byrhtnoth himself was fleeing.

Historians today doubt the poem's defiant rhetoric and the single-minded will with which Byrhtnoth's thegns stood and fought to avenge him, knowing full well he was dead. But similar stands were made at Senlac years later when William the Bastard's mailed knights thundered over the crest, crushing the dead body of Harold Godwinesson. And such doubters should read their Tacitus. Watching the Vikings' ancestors, the tribes of Germania, in action nine centuries earlier, he wrote:

> As for leaving a battle alive after your chief has fallen,
> that means lifelong infamy and shame.[17]

One by one, thegns and thegns' men came forward to make the Vikings pay at Maldon:

> Aescferth . . . did not flinch in the battle-play
> but fired arrows as fast as he could . . .
> . . . Aedweard, the tall, eager and ready,
> did not stray from the line of the battle.

> . . . The brother of Sibyrht . . . split the hollow shields and
> warded off the sea-farers.
> . . . Strong men fell
> drained by wounds; the dead dropped to the earth.

As in all battles, some men held their nerve and their ground; others cracked and ran. Either way, the result was the same – a Viking victory which heralded a new age. 'And afterwards,' wrote the Chronicler, 'they made peace with them . . . by the advice of Sigeric, Bishop of the inhabitants of Kent and Aelfheah, Bishop of Winchester.'[18]

The treaty, known by historians today as II Aethelred, was drawn up by Sigeric, who was actually Archbishop of Canterbury, and Aelfric and Aethelweard, the two ealdormen of Wessex. The prominent name on the Viking side was Olaf Tryggvason. The terms of the treaty were sensible enough, covering the treatment of merchant ships in English or Scandinavian ports, their cargoes, rights of salvage and so on. In the matter of relations between the Vikings and the English, all depredations before 991 were to be overlooked, in a sort of slaughter amnesty. What outraged contemporaries and has continued to give Aethelred a bad press is the demand for tribute in the treaty, usually known as Danegeld.

The poet Rudyard Kipling had his tongue firmly in his cheek nine centuries later when he wrote:

> It is always a temptation to an armed and agile nation
> To call upon a neighbour and say:-
> 'We invaded you last night – we are quite prepared to fight,
> Unless you pay us cash to go away.'[19]

The 'geld' was actually largely paid in silver and the amount was frightening. Allowing for the tortuous changes in the value of money, an estimated £10,000 was paid in the year of the treaty, £16,000 three years later (by which time Tryggvason was once again raiding England with impunity), £24,000 in 1002, £21,000 in 1014 and £72,000 in 1018. The fact that Aethelred's kingdom could stand the loss of an extra £143,000 speaks volumes for its wealth and the administrative and financial organisation of the ill-advised king. We do not know enough about the economics of the first millennium to compare the paying of the Danegeld with, say, the reparations loaded on to Germany by the Treaty of Versailles in 1919, but what we are left with in 991 is a sense of humiliation and bad psychology.

Even if we see the payments of tribute as some revisionist historians do, as a form of protection money by effectively paying Vikings to defend Aethelred's realm as mercenaries, the psychology simply did not work. By 994, Tryggvason was back, not as a treaty co-signatory, but as a raider once again. And this time he was not alone. According to the *Chronicle*:

> Olaf and Swein came to London town on the Nativity of St Mary [15 August], with four and ninety ships, and then they were determinedly attacking the town and they also wanted to set it on fire . . . And they travelled from there and wrought the greatest harm which any raiding-army could ever do, in burning and raiding and slaughter of men, both along the sea-coast, in Essex and in the land of Kent and in Sussex and in Hampshire.[20]

There is little doubt that the invasion of 994 was more serious than most men could remember. The size of the fleet rivalled that of 991, but this time it was an allied effort. Swein was Swein Haraldsson, known as Forkbeard. In the days before accepted primogeniture, Swein had rebelled against his father Harald Gormsson, called Bluetooth, nine years before he sailed to England. It is not clear that he was actually the king of Denmark when his levies torched the outlying hamlets around London, but his presence, rather than Tryggvason's, seems to have signalled panic in some of the English thegns.

Aethelred's policy of appeasement had clearly failed and at least one of his noble subjects, Aethelric of Bocking, planned to accept Forkbeard as king in Essex. In the event, the rather unlikely alliance between Forkbeard and Tryggvason did not hold and clutching the £16,000 given to them by Aethelred, the Vikings wintered in Southampton before sailing home. Tryggvason behaved rather differently. Already a Christian, he was brought to Aethelred at

Andover and confirmed in a solemn ceremony. 'King Aethelred received him at the bishop's hands,' says the *Chronicle*, 'and gave to him royally: and then Olaf promised him . . . that he would never come back to the English race in hostility.'[21] We need not see a new devotion or sense of honesty in Tryggvason. He simply had other designs and within four years would make himself king of Norway.

The mid-990s, in the various editions of the *Chronicle*, are occupied by ecclesiastic events, and apart from the appearance of Halley's comet – 'the longhaired star' – in 995, we see none of the hysteria and foreboding which other sources imply accompanied the first millennium. But the Book of Revelation had prophesied it accurately enough:

> And he laid hold in the dragon, that old serpent, which is the Devil, and Satan, and bound him a thousand years. And cast him into the bottomless pit, and shut him up, and set a seal upon him, that he should deceive the nations no more, till the thousand years should be fulfilled; and after that he must be loosed . . . .[22]

And let loose he was in the summer of 997, out of the abyss of the North Sea. Not one devil, but thousands. And were there not horns on their heads?

TWO

Forkbeard

Then the grizzled warrior, giver of gold, was filled with
joy; the lord of the Danes, shepherd of his people . . .

Beowulf

While Cnut was growing up, his father, Swein Forkbeard, was busy in England. 'The raiding-army travelled round Devonshire,' lamented the *Chronicle*, in 997, 'into the mouth of the Severn, and there raided, both in Cornwall and in Wales and in Devon.'[1] Watchet, Land's End, the Tamar, Ordulf's monastery at Tavistock – 'indescribable plunder' was the order of the day everywhere in the West Country. The following year, Frome and Dorset were the targets and the Vikings wintered in the Isle of Wight, striking out suddenly into Hampshire and Sussex. Each time local levies went against them they were either too slow and missed the raiders altogether or, as at Rochester in 999, were deserted by their allies. A concerted effort in that year seems to have fallen apart because of English incompetence. A fleet, fitted and waiting to challenge the Vikings at sea, failed to sail because of unspecified delays.

Unaccountably, the year of the millennium saw King Aethelred himself campaigning in Cumbria, 'the motive for which,' wrote Sir Frank Stenton, the doyen of Saxon experts, two generations ago, 'is part of the lost history of the north'.[2] It meant that the king knew the Vikings had turned to raiding Normandy that summer, giving his thegns a breathing space. It also meant that he intended to consolidate his power in their absence and could afford to look north because the south was secure. This is the first recorded military campaign by Aethelred himself and even though bad weather probably prevented his army from joining forces with his fleet and finishing the campaign, it may have been designed to do no more than restore the king's reputation and perhaps even steady a populace convinced the devil was unleashed.

But the following year, the Vikings were back: 'There was great hostility in the land of the English race, through the raiding ship-army; and they raided and burnt almost everywhere . . . until they came to Devon. Then Hampshire came out against them . . .'³ The *Anglo-Saxon Chronicle* lists the dead in a battle which must have been the largest since Maldon a decade earlier: 'there Aethelweard, the king's high-reeve, was killed and Leofric of Whitchurch, and Leofwine, the king's high-reeve, and Wulthere, the bishop's thegn, and Godwine of Worthy, the son of bishop Aelfsige's – in all eighty-one men.'⁴

The loss was pointless because, yet again, in a phrase that runs throughout the various versions of the *Chronicle*, the Vikings 'had the power of the battlefield'. In Devon, there was defection by some of the fleet under a leader called Pallig, 'because he had deserted king Aethelred, contrary to all the pledges which he had granted him'. Teignton was burned along with so many estates the Chronicler could not name them. Another battle, near Pinhoe, resulted in a Viking victory and a desperate Aethelred offered Danegeld once again: 'That year [1002] the king commanded killed all the Danishmen in England on St Bricius Day, because he was informed that they meant to beguile him out of his life, and then his counsellors and so have his kingdom afterwards.'⁵ This outrageous act of what today we would call 'ethnic cleansing' has no parallel in English history until later pogroms against the Jews, for instance their systematic weeding out by Edward I in the 1290s. It was an extraordinary measure, impossible to implement fully and almost guaranteed to invite Viking reprisals. The extent of the massacre has sparked fierce debate among historians. The day itself was that of a fourth-century bishop of Gaul, Brice, and in 1002 it fell on a Friday, not the *lauear-dagr*, the bath day of the Vikings, which was always a Saturday. The image of all the Vikings in England being simultaneously slaughtered while naked, defenceless and wet, is dramatic, but highly improbable. St Brice's Day was probably the date of Aethelred's writ, the butchery itself to be carried out as soon as possible after that date. Why did Aethelred institute such an outrage in the first place? The answer to that belongs to the dilemma that is Aethelred. The 'do-nothing' king may have been an earlier clone of James I, terrified of daggers, tobacco and witches and convinced that the latter intended to kill him. Alternatively, he may have seen such a move as a popular one to fan local racial hostility and again bolster a reputation that desperately needed all the help it could get. The second problem lies in the intended targets. Did Aethelred mean the second- or third-generation inhabitants of the Danelaw, who were, to varying degrees, 'English'; or did he consider first-generation Viking interlopers as suitable for the slaughter? The only hard evidence we have of killing taking place is in Oxford, then a 'frontier' town on the edge of the Danelaw. A royal charter of 1004 describes the rebuilding of the church of St Frideswide in the heart of the town. Danes in the area two years earlier had rushed to the sanctuary of the church, pursued by a mob, and the place was destroyed in the ensuing riot. The charter is concerned with the church property rather than the Danes inside, but the likelihood is that they died in the flames or under the cudgels of the mob. The charter reads: 'it will be well known that a decree was sent out by me with the counsel of my leading magnates, to the effect that all the Danes who had sprung up in this island, sprouting like weeds amongst the wheat, were to be destroyed by a most just extermination.'[6]

Some historians today accept the tradition that one who died as a result of the St Brice 'pogrom' was Gunnhild, the wife of the duplicitous Pallig. This woman, apparently a hostage of Aethelred's, was the sister of Swein Forkbeard. There is a real possibility that Pallig and his child died too.

The furious Viking was back the following year. The *Anglo-Saxon Chronicle* tells us that Exeter was sacked and a great deal of booty taken. From William I's Domesday Book, compiled nearly ninety years later, we know that Exeter was easily the largest settlement in Devon, with an estimated 1,500 inhabitants. Something that probably escaped Forkbeard's attack was the Exeter Book, with its riddles, kept in the bishop's palace.

From there, the Vikings with their king moved eastward across the rolling plain near Salisbury. They burnt Wilton, with its abbey founded by Alfred the Great, as the English army scuttled before them. Inigo Jones and carpet-making lay centuries in the future; in Forkbeard's day, Wilton stood at the edge of the huge forest that stretched through Wiltshire into Hampshire. Most of the county's villages lay along the banks of the Avon and the Wylie and any number of these, oak-built and straw-thatched, may have gone down before Forkbeard's flames. The Salisbury he attacked was Sarisberie in Domesday, not the New Sarum where the Normans built their cathedral, but the ring of settlements around the Iron Age fort to the north-east.

The sequence of events in the *Anglo-Saxon Chronicle* for 1003 is confusing and no other record mentions Forkbeard's personal presence. What is consistent in all known records is that a French ceorl called Hugh was in charge of Devon's defence and, either through incompetence or treachery, allowed Exeter to fall. A ceorl is actually a peasant and it is most unlikely that such a man would conduct a defence of anything other than his own plot of land. It is probably a mistranslation of eorl (earl). Hugh seems to be the king's reeve appointed by Aethelred to oversee Devon, and as he was French he may have been the choice of the king's new Norman wife, Emma. The 'illness' of Ealdorman Aelfric, commanding the English army in Wiltshire, may well have been political. The *Anglo-Saxon Chronicle* graphically describes him as 'retching to vomit'.[7] Historian Ian Howard puts forward the intriguing possibility that some sort of truce was arranged between Aelfric and Forkbeard which the Viking broke, accounting for the scattering of an otherwise strong and undamaged English army. If this is true, it was typical of King Aethelred's defence against the Vikings, falling into trap after trap and constantly underestimating the enemy.

The *Chronicle* tells us that Forkbeard's force 'went back to sea . . . where he knew his wave-stallions were'[8] after attacking Salisbury. The shortest route would have been due south to reach the coast in Dorset, but whether the entire fleet set sail for home or whether all or part of it wintered, as they often did, in the Isle of Wight, we do not know.

'Swein came with his fleet to Norwich,' says the *Chronicle*, 'and completely raided and burnt the town.'[9] Norfolk's capital, once the tiny Venta Icenorum of the Romans, had grown dramatically to be home to an estimated 5,000 inhabitants. Its defences, ditches and wooden ramparts clearly posed no serious problem. A stand was made by Ulfkell Snilling (called Ulfcytel in the Abingdon manuscript of the *Anglo-Saxon Chronicle*). His order seems to have been to destroy Swein's ships on the coast or along the banks of the Wensum wherever they were moored. This did not happen (why is not recorded) and Ulfkell had to make a fight of it. He lost, but the strength of opposition rattled Swein. The Vikings, said the Chronicler, 'had never met with harder hand-play in England than Ulfcytel gave them'.[10] For years afterwards, East Anglia was still called Ulfkell's land. The Ealdorman wisely decided, with his witan, to pay the Danegeld. Forkbeard broke the truce that resulted, probably not for the first time, and attacked Thetford. This religious centre had been the local capital of the Danelaw since the ninth century. It probably had about 4,000 inhabitants.

Forkbeard's campaigns of 1003–5 were not as successful as earlier raids, and the unnamed battle between Ulfkell and the Danes, in which many Vikings died along with the 'senior men' of East Anglia, sounds like a draw. It may well have been the famine of 1005 – 'such that no man remembered it ever being so grim'[11] – that drove Forkbeard home. Slim pickings in the campaign season could not sustain a large army throughout the winter and there is evidence that the problem of a particularly poor harvest was affecting Denmark, too. In the 1150s the chronicler Henry of Huntingdon wrote colourfully of the 1006 invasion: '. . . the audacious Swein reappeared off Sandwich with a powerful fleet. He was accompanied by his three usual attendants, fire, slaughter and pillage; and all England trembled before him, like the rustling of a bed of reeds shaken by the west wind.'[12] However, Forkbeard was probably not there at all. The likely commander was Tosti, perhaps a cousin of the king. His name occurs on a rune stone at Yttergärde in Uppland, Sweden: 'Ulf [clearly a Viking mercenary] took three gelds in England. The first was the one that Tosti paid, then Thurkel, then Knutr.'

If Forkbeard was not present in England at this time, it is unlikely that Cnut was either. Where was he? One vague possibility is that he stayed briefly with the fleet anchored off the Isle of Wight, or in one of the Island's harbours – St Helen's or Brading. Perhaps he accompanied Thurkil's army which reached Kent in the summer of 1009. This force was exceptionally large according to all contemporary sources, and throughout 1008–9 Aethelred was building an equally impressive navy to counter it. He ordered that every 310 hides (a slightly bizarre number, the explanation of which is now lost) should provide a warship. Eight hides had to provide a helmet and coat of mail. Earl Eadric Streona was appointed to command forces in Mercia and the English fleet assembled off Sandwich: 'there were so many of them that never before have there been accounted to us so many in books, in any king's day in England.'[13] This fleet was destroyed by the piratical activities of Wulfnoth, the South Saxon, and a particularly bad storm that smashed an unknown number of warships commanded by Brihtric. Aethelred ordered those that remained to London.

It is also possible that Cnut was present in Thurkil's huge fleet of Lammas (1 August) 1009. This still seems unlikely. Thurkil the Tall is described in Latin by the chroniclers as *comes* which loosely translates as war-leader. With him were Eglaf and Heming, both called *duces*, implying a higher social status than Thurkil, but there is no mention of Cnut. By this time, by our reckoning, the boy would have been fourteen, and, as Forkbeard's heir apparent, would surely have merited a mention. Once again, the mercenary Ulf received his share of the geld – the total £36,000 this time, an unprecedented amount of blood money.

The other possibility for Cnut's whereabouts during his teens, and the more likely scenario, is that he was in Denmark with his father. That, too, gives us an infuriating blank, because we know so little of events there in this period.

There is an intriguing chance that Cnut was back in England by 1012. In the previous summer, a Viking force had attacked Canterbury. St Augustine had, some centuries earlier, made this town one of the most famous in the country. Its holiness had established an international reputation long before the death of Thomas Becket in 1170 made it especially hallowed. The territory ravaged by the Vikings in 1011 made depressing reading for Aethelred and his advisers. East Anglia, Essex, Middlesex, Oxfordshire, Hertfordshire,

Cambridgeshire, Buckinghamshire, Bedfordshire, half of Huntingdonshire, much of Northamptonshire, all Kent, Sussex, Hastings, Surrey, Berkshire, Hampshire and much of Wiltshire had all been overrun, according to the *Chronicle*. In fact, a casual reading of the list entitles us to ask which of Aethelred's counties had *not* had a visitation from the raiders! Again, as so often, it was the duplicity of an Englishman, Aelmaer, that got the Vikings into Canterbury. A number of key players fell into the raiders' hands, including Aelfheah, the Archbishop, who was taken to London in April 1012, in time for Easter. Some sort of dispute seems to have broken out; perhaps the Danegeld was late, perhaps the Vikings were inflamed, as the *Chronicle* says, 'because of the southern wine that had been brought'. On Easter Sunday, the arrogance of Aelfheah seems to have caused some of the Vikings to snap: 'They seized the [Arch]bishop . . . and pelted him there with bones and the heads of cattle and one of them struck him with the back of an axe on the head, so that with the blow he sank down and his holy blood fell on the earth and sent forth his holy soul to God's kingdom.'[14] According to the chronicler John of Worcester, writing about 1130, the murderer was Thrym, a Viking who had been baptised by Aelfheah the day before. As such, it was a *coup de grâce*.

In true Christian martyr tradition, Aelfheah went on to perform miracles long after his bloody death. The Anglo-Saxon Chroniclers were in no doubt that his tomb in St Paul's minster in London was already a shrine – and that 'God now makes clear the holy martyr's power'. His power may nearly have killed Forkbeard and with him, Cnut. In 1023, Cnut ordered the reburial of Aelfheah's bones in what may have been more an act of guilt than routine piety. Osbern, the preceptor of Christ Church, Canterbury, remembered the ceremony vividly as a boy and his subsequent life of St Aelfheah recounts the dead man's revenge on his murderers. Those who killed him were hit by a sudden storm at sea, losing 160 ships with a further 65 blown off course to far-off lands where their crews were butchered. We know from the *Annales Cambriae* that Forkbeard was shipwrecked in 1012, but this may be a coincidence. One of the killers of Aelfheah was Hákon, the son of the Norwegian Yric of Lade, and we know that he fought at the battle of Ringmere in

1001. Cnut's recent biographer M.K. Lawson reasons that because Yric and Forkbeard were allies against Olaf Tryggvason and that Yric was later made Earl of Northumbria by Cnut, it is likely that all three men were present in England at this time.

There is no doubt, however, about where Cnut was in 1013. Forkbeard 'turned southward,' says the *Chronicle*, 'with his whole army, and entrusted his ships and his hostages to his son Cnut'.[15] Just as Forkbeard may have invaded England in 1002 as a result of Aethelred's attack on 'English' Danes on St Brice's Day, so now, in the summer of 1013, it may have been to teach a lesson to Thurkil the Tall. At some point in the previous year, the Viking commander and possible foster-father to Cnut had gone over to Aethelred, although precisely why is unclear. It may simply be that the English king paid him handsomely to lead a formidable force in protection of his country; in other words, Thurkil became a mercenary. This was, after all, standard practice among the Vikings as far east as Byzantium. On the other hand, Bishop Thietmar of Merseburg, who was also Cnut's contemporary, implies that Thurkil was opposed to his men's killing of Archbishop Aelfheah and that they lost confidence in him as a result. The Encomiast has a very unlikely theory that this was a cunning plan on the part of Forkbeard and Thurkil so that the Jomsviking could *pretend* defection to Aethelred and wait for the chance to show his true colours. Whatever the reason, Thurkil took between forty and fifty ships with him, leaving a sizeable hole in the Viking fleet.

In the *Encomium*, the anonymous writer describes how Forkbeard organised the invasion. This was a period of his growing personal power and the establishment of royal control. In his raids of the early 990s, Forkbeard led a lið, that is a private army of freebooters numbering hundreds. By 1013, he was probably commanding a *leding*, a national force of many thousands raised under a social and military obligation to their king. This raising of armies reached its full strength under Cnut and was an exceptional achievement. The *Encomium* has Forkbeard asking Cnut his views on the invasion: 'He, questioned by his father, fearing to be accused if he opposed the proposal, of wily sloth, not only approved of attacking the country, but urged and exhorted that no delay should hold back the undertaking.'[16] The Encomiast is a fascinating writer, as important for what he does not say as what he does. This invasion by Forkbeard was, according to the crafty monk of St Omer, his first and he was urged to it by Thurkil.

We do not know the size of the fleet that Forkbeard and Cnut sailed across the North Sea, with a bearing on the Kent coast, but it was once again formidable. The Encomiast delighted in his dazzling descriptions of Viking fleets. We have seen nothing like them. Even Kirk Douglas's spirited re-creation in *The Vikings* only boasts three ships. Managing an astonishing 7 knots under oars and nearly 2 under sail, Forkbeard's ships must have terrified Aethelred's sorely pressed people:

> On one side, lions moulded in gold were to be seen on the ships, on the other birds on top of the masts indicated by their movements the winds as they blew, or dragons of various kinds poured fire from their nostrils. Here there were glittering men of solid gold or silver nearly comparable to live ones, there bulls with necks raised high and legs outstretched, were fashioned leaping and roaring like live ones. One might see dolphins moulded in electrum and centaurs in the same metal . . . The blue water, smitten by many oars, might be seen foaming far and wide, and the sunlight, cast back in the gleam of metal, spread a double radiance in the air.[17]

In July, the fleet reached Sandwich, a base well known to the father, if not to the son, and they stayed there for a few days before sailing up the Channel for the broad mouth of the Humber. It may well be that Forkbeard's plans this time were for invasion and he may have found the south-east initially too well-defended for this purpose. His dragon-ships' oars dipped in the river that no one had yet bridged and, unchecked, went on up the Trent until they reached Gainsborough.

They were now in the heart of the Danelaw, Lincolnshire, the second most populous county in the country. The land was endless and flat, crossing it made difficult by miles of undrained fenland, but the scattered villages contained peasants descended from the

Viking raiders of the first 'invasion' and they may have been delighted to see Forkbeard, Cnut and their red shields. The town of Gainsborough was a large, industrial settlement by the standards of the time, able to cater for Forkbeard's men as long as they did not overstay their welcome. 'All Northumbria' went over to the Danish king, led by their Earl, Uhtred, 'and all the people in Lindsey, and afterwards the people of the Five Boroughs and quickly after, all the raiding-army to the north of Watling Street; and he was granted hostages from each shire.'[18] The *Anglo-Saxon Chronicle*, usually quick to condemn treacherous Englishmen, makes no judgement of Uhtred or any of his people. It is a reminder of how 'separate' the Danelaw still was at this time.[19] Earl and ceorl alike were Viking in origin. Throwing in their lot with Forkbeard was not so much treachery as perfectly natural. The Five Boroughs were: Leicester, Nottingham, Derby, Stamford and Lincoln and the land surrounding each. Leicester had its own mint from the 970s and by the time of Domesday, six churches and 2,000 inhabitants. Lincoln was the centre of the now vanished province of Lindsey, and had a larger mint than Leicester. It was the largest town in the Midlands by 1087. Stamford was probably the richest of the five, producing large quantities of yellow, glazed pottery sold prolifically in the richer south. 'They turned to Oxford,' recorded the Chronicler, 'and the inhabitants of the town immediately submitted and gave hostages.'[20] The town had spilled beyond its fortifications by Domesday and there were many commercial properties with cellars. The Burghal Hidage, a list of English defences probably compiled a century before Forkbeard's arrival, says the town had 1,300 or 1,500 hides. As such, it was rich and had a great deal to lose, all the more so because this was one town, we know from the charters of Aethelred, that complied with his slaughter of Danes on St Brice's Day. We can be sure that the townsfolk bowed before Forkbeard faster and lower than most!

The fact that the Danelaw succumbed to Forkbeard so quickly has led historians to speculate that he had sent some sort of diplomatic mission there in 1012, preparing an alliance with the men who could have tried to stop him. Earls Morcar and Sigefirth both professed loyalty to Forkbeard and in their attitude we catch a glimpse of the tangled internal politics of Aethelred's reign. If Forkbeard's emissaries had told these lords that the Viking came not as a raider bent on pillage, but as a wise and just ruler to oust the incompetent and unpopular Aethelred, then they would no doubt have been assured greater roles in the new king's reign. These two earls were the cousins of Aelfgifu of Northampton who had no reason to love Aethelred either. Her father, Ealdorman Aelfhelm, was murdered on the orders of the king's right-hand man, Eadric Streona of Mercia, seven years earlier and her brothers, Wulfheah and Ufegeat, had had their eyes gouged out on the orders of Aethelred himself.

Perhaps before Forkbeard marched south into the Five Boroughs, or at any rate before he reached Oxford, Aelfgifu the orphan was married to Cnut, destroyer of the chariot of the sea. Marriage in both Viking and English society was a family contract, strengthened by a financial promise from the groom of the 'bride-price', a non-returnable gift. On the morning after the marriage was consummated, the eighteen-year-old Cnut would have given his new wife the 'morning gift' (*morgengifu*) which would be passed to her own family if she died childless. That Cnut took his vows seriously is echoed in several laws relating to marriage that he passed during his reign. That said, this was clearly a political match and it is unlikely that Aelfgifu, at least, had any say in the matter. It is also unlikely that any form of religious ceremony took place, which put Cnut at possible odds with his Christian Church in the years to come. The ever-careful Encomiast, employed to write an account of Cnut's reign by his *second* wife, Emma of Normandy, never refers to Aelfgifu by name, nor that Cnut underwent a previous marriage. She is casually called his concubine, possibly because the Encomiast had no choice, in his narrative, but to acknowledge her existence.

The status of women in English society at this time is hotly debated. It seems generally that they enjoyed greater freedom from their menfolk than at any time after the Celts until the twentieth century. They could buy and sell property, had places named after them and were personally accountable under the law. They witnessed charters and wills and by the time of Domesday (1087) some were major landowners. We know from various sources that they owned expensive clothes, jewellery, slaves, livestock and books. Women of Aelfgifu's rank were particularly articulate and if she had little choice in her marriage to Cnut, this does not imply a doe-eyed Dora Copperfield, but a realist with her eye to the main chance. If Forkbeard's venture came off, she would one day be queen of England and her sons kings. She may have been more literate than Cnut and possibly just as tough. Her role here, however, in an age when the loom was the heart of the family, was of 'peace-weaver', a bridge between two peoples whose common purpose was to build an empire. It was just her bad luck that her husband and her place as his queen would be usurped by an even stronger woman, with, ironically, the same name.

If the marriage really happened early in Forkbeard's march south, there was little time for nuptials, let alone a full-blown honeymoon. From Oxford, the Viking army, with its king, its prince and his new bride, marched to Winchester where Cnut's body would lie twenty-two years later. Witnessing a spurt of development in the late ninth century, the old Roman street plan of Venta Belgarum had vanished. Monastic reforms in the century before Cnut had seen extensive ecclesiastical building, centring on the minster with its associations with St Swithun. Twenty years before Cnut's birth, the old church was greatly extended and a new minster created alongside it. Already, by the year of Forkbeard's attack, the streets reflected their manufacturing centres – Goldestrete, Tannerstrete, Sildenwerkerstrete (Silversmith Street).

The Vikings then moved on to London and, not for the first or last time in its history, London proved awkward. 'Many of [Forkbeard's] people drowned,' crowed the *Anglo-Saxon Chronicle*, 'because they did not look for a bridge.'[21] This is hugely confusing and one of the many non sequiturs that the *Chronicle* throws up. There may have been two bridges across the Thames by 1013 – the updated version of the Roman London Bridge and a second upriver near Staines. Either way, the Vikings could have avoided the problem. Coming from Winchester, they could have crossed at any of the fording places higher up, back into the 'friendly' Oxfordshire countryside. Whatever the reason for the drowning of Forkbeard's men, Aethelred himself was in the city, along with the treacherous Thurkil, and they fought back.

Forkbeard wasted no time here but swung south-west into Berkshire. At Wallingford, a sizeable market town with its own mint, he decided to strike further west, to Bath, the old Aquae Sulis of the Romans. This was as well defended as Wallingford with ramparts, ditches and palisades, but there was no resistance. 'Ealdorman Aethelmaer came and the western thegns with him and all submitted to Swein and gave hostages.'[22]

Aethelmaer was a leading light at Aethelred's court until 1005, when he seems to have retired. The circumstances of his going are not recorded, but the English king appears to have had something of the Saxon equivalent of a cabinet reshuffle at that stage and it may be that the Ealdorman left under a cloud. That a number of thegns followed him over to Forkbeard speaks volumes – his influence was still great and as far as Aethelred was concerned, the writing was on the wall.

The Viking king went 'northward to his ships and all the nation had accepted him as full king'.[23] Cnut was at Lincoln, only a few miles away, presumably holding all the hostages the shires had sent to him and enjoying the company of his new wife, who was probably pregnant by Christmas of 1013. While Thurkil sulked at Greenwich with a fleet and an army, London thought better of its hostile stance and offered hostages as well as provisions. Thurkil demanded the same, so that some hapless thegns and their peasants were no doubt torn as to whom they should revictual for the winter and how.

Aethelred was now a king with a price on his head. Forkbeard had ousted him without a major battle, and the English king dithered for a while with Thurkil on the Thames then sailed for the Isle of Wight. Here, he spent Christmas while his family fled into exile. Emma Aelfgifu, his queen, sailed home to Normandy to her brother Richard in the company of Aelfsig, the abbot of Peterborough. His sons, the athelings Edward and Alfred, were sent subsequently under the protection of Bishop Aelfin. It was not until early January that their father joined them at the Norman court.

'Swein ended his days,' recorded the *Chronicle*, 'on Candlemas, February 3rd and the fleet all chose Cnut as king.'[24] The boy was a boy no more. By our reckoning, he was nineteen, a young man with a crown. Now he would have to fight for it.

THREE

The Boy who Would be King

The dank earth, wondrously cold,
first delivered me from her womb . . .
The Exeter Book, 1072

Denmark lies on the same latitude as Scotland, and even though its west coast is lashed by the same tempestuous North Sea that hammers bleaker Norway, the land is altogether more hospitable. And it was here that Knutr, Swein Forkbeard's son, was born. The terrain is surprisingly flat, with Yding Forest Hill rising a mere 568 feet above sea level. The highest waterfall in Denmark is only 56 feet above the sea. The beaches from which Forkbeard's dragon-ships were launched at the time of Cnut's birth are flat and sandy, with gentle undulating dunes behind them. Over four hundred islands lie to the north of Jutland, their topography marked by rich, green hills, unexpected lakes and dark forests, redolent of the fairy tales of Hans Christian Andersen.[1]

When Cnut was born, the earth was warmer. Some historians go so far as to point to the 'Little Optimum' of early medieval warmth to explain Viking exploration in the first place. The melting of the polar ice cap which sends a frisson of fear through global warming fanatics today, was a commonplace between the eighth and twelfth centuries, removing the pack ice which would otherwise have crushed the dragon-ships bound for 'Vinland' and the far west. In Britain, there would be thirty-eight vineyards listed in William I's Domesday Book, fifty years after Cnut's death, and they reached as far north as Ely. The south of England, where Cnut would be buried in the Old Minster at Winchester, had temperatures not unlike those of the South of France today.

The topography of the Denmark of today dates only from the eleventh century. Before that, the whole of the Jutland peninsula and most of its outlying islands were covered with dense deciduous forests and pitted with lakes, water-meadows and bogs whose peaty depths have revealed astonishingly preserved sacrificial bodies from the time of Christ to the centuries after Cnut.[2]

The vicious winters of Norway and Sweden created an equally savage economy, in which food was scarce and meat supplemented by hunting walrus and elk. In Denmark, arable farming was the norm, with the best soil in Scandinavia providing oats, wheat and barley. Its rich meadows provided grazing for cattle and sheep and the inland waterways teemed with fish and waterbirds.

The islands of the Skaggerat were more remote. Ideas and news spread more slowly here and the more easterly of them came under Slavic influence, from their ships to their pottery. Gotland and Oland, despite being part of the Danish kingdom of the late Viking period, were more properly Swedish; Bornholm had a rugged independence born of its lying midway between Sweden to the north and Wendland to the south.

Exactly when and exactly where Cnut was born are both vexed questions. His first biographer, Laurence Larson,[3] refused to speculate at all on Cnut's boyhood because of the complete lack of evidence. Cnut's pedigree was impeccable however; he came from a line of powerful rulers of Denmark who had spent the previous century stamping their ideals on their people and turning the country into a strong, centralised and even Christian state.

British historians of earlier generations seemed to accept that 793, the year of the first recorded Viking attacks on the English coast, marked the beginning of the 'Viking Age'. It is more rational to see this date as the culmination of half a century or more of development and to see it, moreover, as a defence mechanism against the expansionist activities of kingdoms to the south. The 'German' empire of Otto I, the growth of Slavic Poland, even the establishment of a rudimentary England – all these were a reality by the mid-eighth century. The other threat to the Scandinavian world was that these new states were Christian and the evangelising drive of Christian missionaries from Augustine onwards to convert the pagans found another point of contact.

These influences showed themselves in art and archaeology from the eighth century onwards. The swirling plant and animal motifs

characterised by the Mammen, Borre, Jellinge and Ringerike styles
of art clearly owe a great deal to the Celtic designs of La Tene,
further to the south and a thousand years earlier.[4] 'Alien' finds of
glass and pottery in Denmark clearly establish evidence of an
increase in trade, and the use of coinage was unknown in the area
before the encroachment from the south.

What characterised the Viking Age in the first half of the ninth
century was piracy. In their sleek dragon-ships, the Vikings carried
out lightning raids along the English, Scottish and Irish coastlines,
robbing, butchering and running. The second half of the century
saw a marked change. The dragon-ships carried kitchen utensils,
house-building tools and supplies to last for longer expeditions
than the hit-and-run tactics of piracy would suggest. The reasons
for this are complicated and debatable. Did the Vikings, especially
of bleak and inhospitable Norway, long for a softer life in the fertile
fields of the west? Was this homeland's economy too febrile to
support them? They sailed towards the sunset, to settle in the
Shetlands, the Orkneys, Greenland, Iceland and probably America.
The Finns turned east, into slowly developing Russia and as far as
Byzantium, where units of them formed the Varangarian guard[5] of
the Eastern Emperor and one of them carved his runes in the
marble of the great basilica of Hagia Sofia; only his name –
Halfdan – is still legible.

It was largely the Danes who turned south, to raid and settle in
England and the Frankish lands of today's Normandy. And they
probably had a single dynasty even before the Viking Age. At the
beginning of the ninth century, the first of these kings was Godfred
and his successors were Heming and Horik. Their names appear like
ghosts in the tantalisingly fragmentary records of the time. Godfred
was the leader of the 'wild Danish people' mentioned in 808 in the
Royal Frankish Annals. He rebuilt the Danevirke, the line of
fortifications across the base of the Jutland peninsula and settled
Hedeby as a Danish town. Almost nothing is known of Heming, and
Horik is not one man but two, the Elder and Younger, who appear
to have ruled together. Under them, the Christian missionary Ansgar
from Germany was allowed to build his churches in the Danish
towns of Rike and Hedeby in the 850s.

Laurence Larson put the Danish kings into some sort of context when he wrote: 'In the legendary age a famous dynasty known as the Shieldings [Scyldings] appears to have ruled over Danes and Jutes. The family took its name from a mythical ancestor, King Shield, whose crossing to the Daneland is told in the opening lines of the Old English epic *Beowulf* . . .':[6]

> Listen!
>   The fame of Danish kings
> in days gone by, the daring feats
> worked by those heroes are well known to us.
> Scyld Scefing often deprived his enemies,
> many tribes of men, of their mead-benches . . .
> He prospered under heaven, won praise and honour,
> until the men of every neighbouring tribe,
> across the whale's way, were obliged to obey him
> and pay him tribute.[7]

Larson admitted that the exploits of the Scyldings are far from established history and belong to that same school of antiquarianism that once had Joseph of Arimathea walking on England's green and pleasant land and London founded by survivors of the Trojan war!

The first Danish king about whom we know anything with certainty is Gorm, often referred to as Gorm the Old. According to the Danish chronicler Saxo Grammaticus,[8] the scholar, born in Zealand about 1150 and clerk to Bishop Absalom of Roskilde, Gorm was tall and stately, but dull and bone idle, lacking any elements of true greatness. Grammaticus is rightly regarded as Denmark's first historian, writing with power and imagination and especially at pains to explain and place in context early legends. Historical and archaeological evidence from Gorm's reign, however, seems to prove the scholar wrong on the king's laziness. His burial chamber at Jelling in central Jutland implies a man of great power, respect and even adoration among the people who placed his body there. Larson contends that in the 'Shielding Age', the royal palace was at Lethra in Zealand, but he believed that Jelling was Gorm's headquarters. Jelling is a necropolis, a city of the dead, and there is no hard evidence that Gorm or any of the Danish kings actually lived there. The originally prehistoric mounds are divided by a Christian church, still in use today, and two of the most fascinating rune stones from the Viking period. Runes themselves are Scandinavian letters comprising a *futharka* or alphabet of sixteen letters. There are two variants; one used in Sweden and Norway to the north, the other in Denmark to the south. The tradition was to carve these letters on hard surfaces like wood, stone or bone using a knife or chisel. The curves possible with a medieval quill on vellum are difficult to obtain, so the *futharka* is composed of stilted, sharp-angled letters. The shortage of letters in the tenth century led to mutations. So Gorm's name on the Jelling stone is spelt KurmR. His grandson, Swein Forkbeard, has his name spelt Suin. And when Cnut had his name written, it would appear like this: ᚴᚿᛏ, Knutr in his own language.

The massive stone, with its inscriptions curling from the bottom, reads 'King Harald had this monument made in memory of his father Gorm and his mother Thyri . . .' The smaller of the two stones has an older inscription: 'King Gorm made this memorial to his wife Thyri, the glory of Denmark.' It is likely that the memorial was not merely the stone itself, but something altogether more worthy of a woman who was Denmark's glory. It has not survived. The history of Denmark – and England – in this period is riddled with powerful, dynamic women. Working from suggestions in the *Danmarks Riges Historie* (The History of the Kings of Denmark), Larson conjectured that Thyra was the daughter of a jarl, a major landowner in Holstein to the south. When Larson was writing, Danes still knew this woman as Thyra Daneboot – the Dane's defence.

The North mound probably housed the body of Gorm and perhaps his wife. Excavation into the centre of the mound in 1820 revealed a low-ceilinged burial chamber containing wooden fragments that may have come from the royal palace and a magnificent silver goblet, decorated with curling monsters, which has given its name to a whole school of Viking art. The planking in the chamber has been ring-dated to the winter of 958–9 and if Gorm died then, he was still a pagan king who was taking the grave furniture (and probably much else, now gone) into the afterlife with him.

More recent excavations in the vicinity of the church have brought to light what may be the king's body. The disarticulated bones with silver-gilt strap-ends and gold-thread textile fibres lying nearby were those of a middle-aged man. From what we know of Danish history after 960, it seems plausible that when Gorm's son, Harald Bluetooth, became Christian, he ordered the removal of his father's body from its pagan site in the North mound to one in front of God's altar.

The Jelling stone's runes continue: 'this was the Harald who won for himself all Denmark and Norway and made the Danes Christian.' Harald Gormsson, known as Bluetooth, seems to have ruled a larger province than that of his father, including what is today Skåne in Sweden. Impressed by the miraculous performance of the missionary Poppo who underwent the ordeal of the hot iron probably just to convert the pagan king, Bluetooth may have been a vassal of the far more powerful German Emperor Otto I, who died in 973. The story of Poppo's performance in which he bore no blistering wounds at all was first recorded by the chronicler Widukínd of Corvey less than a decade after the event allegedly happened in about 960. The king's relationship with the Germans to the south was never good and it was perhaps because of this that he married Tufa, the daughter of Mistivoj, of the Slavonic tribe of the Abodrites. Tufa seems to have been a faithful wife to him, embracing her new country by adopting the Danish name of Gunnhild. Since the Slavs and Germans were ancient enemies, here was a chance for Bluetooth to defend his southern frontier.

Most of what we know of Cnut's grandfather comes from the much later German chroniclers Adam of Bremen, Widukind of Corvey and Thietmar of Merseburg. Adam was writing the history of the Archbishopric of Hamburg-Bremen in the years immediately after the Norman conquest of England, but he knew Swein Estrithsson, Cnut's nephew, and could be reasonably accurate on the king's family. Whereas Widukind is incredibly obscure, Thietmar was Bishop of Merseburg and died in 1018, two years after Cnut became king of England. He would have been a boy during Bluetooth's reign and, like Adam of Bremen, can be expected to have picked up elements of the truth.

We know from the archaeological record that Bluetooth was an inveterate builder. It is likely that the South mound at Jelling was his work, although its purpose remains unknown. Like the second Jelling stone, larger than its earlier equivalent, it may be that part of the purpose was to build bigger and better than his father. For all the apparent honour given by Bluetooth to Gorm, the father–son relationship of Danish kings was not always a smooth one and the Jelling stones and mounds may be evidence of a deep rivalry. There is no sign of a burial chamber at the heart of the South mound, although there was clearly once a wooden building on its top. Tree-ring dating ascribed this mound to 970, but when Bluetooth died in 986, he was buried, according to his own wishes, in his new cathedral at Roskilde on the island of Sjaelland to the east.

It is on Sjaelland that one of the other great engineering feats of Harald Bluetooth's reign has been found and it is one of four. Historians and archaeologists cannot agree on the precise purpose of the fortresses built at Fyn, Sjaelland and in Jutland, but they are without parallel in the history of the Viking Age. Each of the four fortresses, often named after that built at Trelleborg, follows the same basic plan. That at Fyrkat, on a ridge in an otherwise marshy valley, was levelled and extended to make a firm ground. An astonishing 353,000 cubic feet of earth and stone were used to create circular ramparts with an internal diameter of 394ft. The height of the earth wall is 11ft and it probably had a wooden palisade above that when Bluetooth had it built. The four gateways stood at the points of the compass, dividing the circle into quadrants. In each of these were built four bow-sided block houses around a central courtyard, each building 96 Roman feet long, probably with curved shingle roofs and wooden buttresses to support them. One rather fanciful notion in interpreting these buildings is that they were built to resemble warships, rather as some Viking graves are constructed, with stones pegging out the ghost of a hull. In fact, the buildings at Fyrkat, Trelleborg, Aggersborg and Nonnebakken have raised more questions than answers. Archaeologists of the post-Second World War era assumed they were huge holding camps, rather like those dotted over southern England in readiness for D-Day in 1944, and that they had housed the 'great army' that Swein Forkbeard brought with him in his invasion of 1013. Yet Fyrkat in particular has produced domestic and craft finds, making it clear that women and children lived there, along with smiths, carpenters and jewellers. Beyond Fyrkat's outer ring, the cemetery has yielded thirty or more graves, some skeletons in coffins, others in carts. Both sexes and all ages are buried there and the community seems generally to have been wealthy. Intriguingly, there are no signs of repair and no timbers or debris later than the eleventh century, as though the four fortresses had a brief existence that spanned no more than three kings' reigns and were then abandoned for reasons that remain unknown.

Whatever they were for, the Trelleborg-style fortresses are not the only example of the extent of Bluetooth's power. We know from tree-ring evidence that the much earlier defences around Hedeby and Birka were extended and strengthened under Cnut's grandfather. The Danevirke is first recorded in 808 under Godfred, but archaeology proves a constructional date around the 730s. Nineteen miles long, it provided a defensive barrier against marauding Saxons to the south and its third phase of development was carried out in Bluetooth's reign. The sections known as the Crooked Wall, the Main Wall and the Connecting Wall all date from the late 960s and are clearly more massive than anything attempted before. Bluetooth's defences would not be seriously challenged until Bismarck's Prussian army batted them aside in 1864.[9]

Roads and bridges, probably with a military rather than a trading purpose in mind, were being built and extended in the late tenth century, although some of these had a religious significance in that they led to the newly built Christian churches of Bluetooth's Denmark. A bridge at Ravning Enge, nearly half a mile long, had 2,500 posts to support it, with a walkway of 16–20 feet in width. The ambitious nature of this construction, along with the Trelleborg fortresses, implies that in Bluetooth, Denmark had a remarkable king – able, centralist, determined; a man with a clear view of his role and perhaps, too, the destiny of his country. He commemorated his work, Ozymandias-like, on the rune stones at Jelling. He was proud of himself and he had reason to be. All that he had, he passed on to his son.

Cnut's father was Swein Haraldsson, known as Forkbeard. Like Gorm and Bluetooth before him, details of the man's life are sketchy and much of what we know comes from the thirteenth-century Saga of Olaf Haraldsson, itself part of an epic history of the kings of Norway written by Snorri Sturluson. This is the *Heimskringla* and some of it is collated from the skaldic poems written by Viking bards, which are difficult to translate and interpret. The sagas are a fascinating source in their own right. Unique in many ways to Scandinavia and dating from the twelfth and thirteenth centuries, they were the first examples of literature to portray Vikings as heroes. In all the English, Frankish and Arab chronicles, they are villains and vandals, intent on nothing but raiding and destruction. To the saga writers, as much as to us, the Viking Age was a golden one, of warriors and epic voyages. Historian and archaeologist Julian Richards[10] likens these stories to the Hollywood version of history – based on fact, but manipulated for the sake of a storyline.

Snorri Sturluson was an Icelander and he probably produced his work between 1220 and 1241. He in turn was quoting from earlier Icelandic historians whose work is lost to time, but one major source for him was Ari Thorgilsson the Wise, living in the late eleventh century. Despite Sturluson's own background and the theme of his work, it is likely to be more accurate in some ways than the German chronicles mentioned above. He knew Norway intimately and sailed extensively; he did not suffer from the age-old problem of the hack historian – he was a political figure in his own right and not beholden to any sponsor who might be looking for a partisan angle.

Swein Forkbeard was born about 960 and although there was as yet no primogeniture among the Danes, he would inherit, all things being equal, the whole of Jutland and the large islands off its eastern coast, like Sjaelland and Fyn, as well as Norwegian coastal areas like Skåne, Halland, Greenland and Vestfold. His father may have been a king, but his mother was Saum-Aesa, a servant girl, and there is no evidence that Bluetooth took the boy seriously as his successor. Forkbeard married in his teens a sister of the Polish king Boleslav Chobri, re-cementing the alliance with the Slavs that was so crucial to an encirclement of the German Saxons. By the time he was twenty, Forkbeard had a daughter,

Gytha, but this was possibly by a former marriage. The Polish princess, like other royal brides before her, changed her name to Gunnhild – far more acceptable and pronounceable to Viking society – and was almost certainly Cnut's mother.

When he was twenty-seven, Swein Forkbeard became king of the Danes. Bluetooth's legitimate sons had died before him and in 987 there was a rebellion against the old king in which Forkbeard certainly played a part, even if he did not engineer it. It is possible that Bluetooth's massive building operations had led to high taxation and the inevitable resentment that followed, fuelling revolution.

The account, written about 1042 by the anonymous monk of St Omer whom for convenience's sake we call the Encomiast, is altogether more positive on Forkbeard: 'When he grew to be a young man, he increased daily in the love of his people, and accordingly, his father's envy increased more and more, so that he wished, not in secret, but openly, to cast him out, affirming by oath that he should not rule after him.'[11]

Shortly before Cnut's birth, Forkbeard led an expedition against the jarl Hákon of Lade in Norway. Central to his force were the fearsome Jomsvikings, a military brotherhood whose very existence is bound up inextricably with legend. Their leader in Forkbeard's reign was Sigvaldi Strut-Haraldsson and the group was in effect an artificial 'tribe' raised under strict elitism to inflict the maximum damage on defending armies. Under its rules, no man was to run from an opponent; each man was to avenge his brother on the battlefield; booty was to be shared out equally; no one was to spread rumour or dissatisfaction – only Strut-Haraldsson disseminated news; no women were allowed in the Jomsviking fortresses and ties of actual kinship were irrelevant.

Although the Jomsvikings' austere organisation has led to exaggeration of their prowess akin to that of the later Templars or even the modern SAS, there is no doubt that they were a formidable force as their Saga makes clear. Against Hákon, however, they made little headway and the invasion was a failure. Legends abound that Swein Forkbeard was captured during the campaign, but there is no evidence that he actually attended in person.

By 990, the Danes faced a more serious threat. Yrik of Sweden, named the Victorious in later years, probably invaded Forkbeard's kingdom (details are virtually non-existent) and drove the king out. Gunnhild fled separately to Pomerania on the shores of the Baltic. And perhaps, in the year that Forkbeard lost his crown, his son Knutr was born.

We have no hard evidence of the date of the future king's birth. The *Knútsdrápa*, written about 1017 by the skaldic poet Ottar the Black, paints a savage picture of Cnut, the young warrior, in action:

Destroyer of the chariot of the sea, you were of no great age when you pushed off your ships. Never, younger than you, did prince set out to take his part in war. Chief, you made ready your arrowed ships and were daring beyond measure. In your rage, Knutr, you mustered the red shields at sea.[12]

Given the probable date of authorship, there is no reason to doubt that Cnut was very young when he went to war. The problem arises because the campaign above is undated. Was Ottar writing about Cnut's invasion of 1016, Forkbeard's of 1013 or earlier forays in the 990s? There are two possibilities. Forkbeard 'married' twice. His first 'bride' was probably the Slav who renamed herself Gunnhild, Saum-Aesa, who was the sister of Boleslav of Poland. How many children the pair produced is uncertain. Most genealogists today plump for an oldest son, Harald (named, as was usual, in honour of the boy's grandfather, Bluetooth), with Cnut as the second born. The *Encomium Emmae Reginae*, however, an account written in 1042 on the orders of Cnut's wife, Emma, states boldly that Cnut was older than Harald, so it may be that there were two Haralds who were the sons of Gunnhild and that one died before his father, leaving Cnut as the eldest boy. The story in the *Encomium* that Cnut and his brother returned later to bring their mother home from exile in Pomerania has no other source to support it.

What makes it so difficult to establish the year of Cnut's birth is the extraordinary events of the 990s. We know that his father, Forkbeard, was with Olaf Tryggvason in the serious raids on England in 994–5. Having plundered the south-east, the invaders wintered in Southampton and collected Aethelred's £16,000 Danegeld. The story, from Adam of Bremen's *Gesta Danorum* in the 1070s, of Yrik of Sweden's invasion of Denmark and Forkbeard's meek disappearance into exile makes little sense. If it is true, then Gunnhild, with the little Cnut, fled home to Pomerania, leaving Forkbeard to wander, cap in hand, to seek support from a *rex Scotorum* who may actually have been an Irish ruler. According to Adam, Forkbeard waited there until Yrik of Sweden's death and then returned to marry his widow, Sigrid. This was in 995, so Forkbeard's exile was short-lived. Beyond the possibly incorrect interpretation of the later chroniclers, two runestones near the town of Hedeby may leave vague, tantalising clues from this period. One reads 'King Sven set this stone in memory of Skarthi, his man, who had travelled in the west but now met his death at Hedeby.' If 'the west' means England, then perhaps Forkbeard and Skarthi came home to find Hedeby in the clutches of the Swedes and Skarthi died trying to retake it. Adam of Bremen says that Yrik's son, Olaf, with a force of Slavs and Swedes, drove Forkbeard out again, but he later gave the Dane his kingdom back, perhaps under pressure from Sigrid. Sigrid the Haughty was the daughter of a Viking adventurer named Tosti. Stories of her choice of suitor to replace him smack of pure folklore, but those of her aversion to Christianity and fierce defence of the old panoply of Norse gods which resulted in Forkbeard's smacking her in the mouth with his glove are probably based on reality.

The other possibility concerning Cnut's birth is that his mother was not Saum-Aesa/Gunnhild, but Sigrid, which would place his birth around 999. If Ottar the Black was referring to Cnut's actions with his father in 1013, it would still fit with his reference to the boy's youth, as he would have been only fourteen at the time. Several historians today simply take an average, claiming that the king was born in 995. This is actually very neat, explaining why Cnut made little headway in England in 1016 – he would only have been twenty-one and perhaps a less well-tried option than the far older Aethelred to whom the English turned. I am going with this option, not because an average is a convenient exercise in fence-sitting, but because a number of events later in Cnut's reign fit well with the supposition. Certainly, Larson had no problem with opting for it and in this, as in other important areas, he actually makes more sense than some modern historians.

The contemporary anonymous poem *The Fortunes of Men* has its usual words of wisdom:

> Often and again, through God's grace,
> men and women usher a child
> into the world and clothe him in gay colours;
> they cherish him, teach him as the seasons turn
> until his young bones strengthen,
> his limbs lengthen. So his father and mother
> first carry him, then walk with him,
> and lavish gifts and garments on him. Only God
> knows how years will use the growing child.[13]

Not knowing exactly when Cnut was born or who his mother was is irritating, but does not alter in essence the kind of upbringing he would have had. If he was in exile with his mother in Pomerania, the boy's lifestyle would have been curtailed, but he was still the son and probably the eldest surviving son of a king and that gave him an edge over contemporaries, which mattered. After Cnut, the next invader who took the crown of England for himself was Duke William of Normandy and his boyhood too was fraught with the need for self-preservation. We know very little about Viking birth customs, but it is likely that when Cnut was born they were still throwbacks to a pagan age. He was not baptised a Christian, but the tribal obsession with water as a sacred element may have taken his mother to a holy well where she drank or bathed. If that mother was Gunnhild, then Slav custom would have played a part here.

Slavonic mythology, with its rustic gods of barn, field and forest, was already Christianised by the time of Cnut's birth, but the belief in the power of water was easily absorbed into a faith that accepted baptism. Examples of holy wells are found extensively in that part of England called the Danelaw, implying a Viking overlay of ritual over the earlier Saxon and Celtic practices. In peasant communities, the 'hagtesse' was a cunning woman or witch, who would attend on the pregnant mother about to give birth. Only later Christian generations demonised the woman into 'hag', whose magic lore threatened the Church's control of society. Merely because Gunnhild was a queen and the baby Cnut a prince did not mean that the 'hagtesse' was not vital. Assisting the birth in a practical way, the wriggling, slimy child struggling in air for the first time, the 'hagtesse' also no doubt prophesied the boy's importance. Did she tell the exhausted mother, one wonders, that the helpless little one would one day be the king of Denmark, of Norway, of parts of Sweden and of England?

Perhaps the Dance of the Mothers followed. A barely Christian people laughed and clapped and sang, all the women of the court, as of the village, blessing the goddess Frigg whose star was waning in the brightness of the most famous mother of them all, Mary the Nazarene. We know that in Schleswig, near the Danevirke, shrieking women ran amok through the countryside, smashing farm carts and uncoupling horses. They stole food and drink and whipped off passing men's caps and filled them with dung. In Cnut's Denmark, even three centuries after his birth, 'the women gathered together in the house and sang and shouted while they made a manikin of straw which they called the Ox'.[14] They danced erotically, grunting a guttural, rhythmic song which was much older than they were and very definitely un-Christian!

One of the poems of the *Edda*, a thirteenth-century collection of Scandinavian literature, though couched in terms of Norse mythology, could well be a description of Cnut's birth:

> Then was Heigi, the huge-hearted
> Born in Bralund to Borghild.
> Night had fallen when the Norns came,
> Those who appoint a prince's days:
> His fate, they foretold, was fame among men,
> To be thought the best of brave kings.
> There in Bralund's broad courts
> They spun the threads of his special destiny:
> They stretched out strings of gold,
> Fastened them under the hall of the moon.[15]

Of Cnut's boyhood we know practically nothing.

> Then a son was born to him, a child
> in the court, sent by God to comfort
> the Danes; for He had seen their dire distress,
> that once they suffered hardship for a long while,
> lacking a lord; and the Lord of life,
> King of Heaven, granted this boy glory . . .[16]

These are lines from the best known of all the Scandinavian poems, *Beowulf*, and were written first in the early eighth century. The only surviving copy, however, dates from about 1000, when the Prince of Denmark was probably five. The thirteenth century *Flateyarbok* recorded that little Cnut was 'fostered' by the powerful Viking leader Thurkil inn hávi, the Tall, the brother of Sigvaldi Strut-Haraldsson who commanded the Jomsvikings at their fortress at Jomsburg on the Vistula. This source is not always accurate, but there is nothing improbable about it. Forkbeard would have wanted his son brought up in the Viking tradition and placing sons of titled men with other noble households was already commonplace. Such an upbringing would explain Cnut's reputation for battle as well as the extraordinary love–hate relationship he had with Thurkil. Historians since Laurence Larson have doubted this situation, largely because the *Flateyarbok* is demonstrably wrong on other details. This does not seem a good enough reason to damn it all however and it is difficult to explain the yo-yo nature of Thurkil's career between 1016 and 1023 in any other way. By now, Cnut could possibly read and write, certainly the runic letters of the *futharka*, perhaps even the Slavic language of his mother. Whether he had yet met and mastered the gerundives of the Latin of Christendom to the south we do not know. He would have known the games of childhood – nine men's morris and fox and geese. In particular, a future king and warlord would have learned *hnefatafl*, a chess-like game in which two players contested a board, one with a small force, the other with a large. It was a game he would one day have to play for real.

Outdoors, Cnut would have learned to practise with his wooden sword and shield, hacking and parrying with heavier equipment as his strength grew. He threw spears, shot arrows, played a rough kind of football. Perhaps he watched and cheered at horse-fighting contests, in which stallions, within sight and smell of tethered mares, were goaded to fight each other. The boy would have been taught swimming from an early age – a Viking's destiny was to sail and the sea was in his blood. He hunted, chasing wild boar through the reeds of Jutland's fens and sending his hawk hurtling to the sky in search of prey. By the time he was eleven or twelve, he would have been introduced to the feasts which were such a vital part of Viking life.

Feasts were the occasion of celebration among the Danes as they were among most ancient peoples. Drink was the mainstay, but wine was a rare commodity, not laid down to age as now, but drunk newly harvested, light and fruity. Beer was not as alcoholic as it is today. In England, to which the young Cnut would sail perhaps before his fifteenth birthday, the hops that were grown were used for cloth-dyeing. So the beer of the Jomsviking halls was probably sweet and thick, like porridge. Mead was more plentiful, sweeter than today, brewed from honeycomb. The Exeter Book, which carries the riddles that form some of the chapter headings of this book, spoke mockingly of alcohol in the 1070s: 'I am a binder and a scourger and soon become a thrower, sometimes I cast an old fellow right to the ground.'[17] The Vikings had not perfected distillation by Cnut's time, so most wine was made from fruit. The more alcoholic beers were thought to be dangerous. An old Viking collection of poems, the *Hávamál* or Words of Odin, warns 'be cautious with beer and another man's wife'. Drinking was done largely from cow horns, often richly decorated with silver or even gold. These had no flat bottoms so the contents had to be downed in one or at least quickly, which may well be the origin of the 'yard of ale' contests so beloved of student bars the length and breadth of central Europe today!

The sagas of the skaldic poets, recited on grand occasions to extol the courage of heroes living and dead, often describe feasts and their ritual significance among the Vikings. By Cnut's time, barrels of costly wine were imported from the Rhinelands, along with glasses to drink from. Food in Viking communities, especially among the rich, was varied. Men took their own knives to the feast, to hack their meat. Hare, rabbit, duck, chicken, goose, elk, venison, lamb, beef, veal, pork, horse and wild boar could have been found at the Jomsvikings' groaning tables. Bread was unleavened and eaten newly cooked and still warm. Some of this, especially in the north of Denmark, was made of pine bark and dried peas, heavily laced with the grit of the stone querns that ground them. However, most of the Jomsvikings' bread would probably have been of finer quality than this. Fish would have been on the table too – cod, haddock, eel and herring being the most common. The *Rispula*, a tenth-century Icelandic poem, tells of silver-mounted dishes and linen tablecloths. The Vikings were famous plunderers and the feast was a time to display the exotic acquisitions, which themselves extolled the prowess of Forkbeard's forebears – not unlike the regimental silver on British army mess tables to this day.

Forkbeard and the Jomsvikings would have been expected to have kept a lavish table. Hospitality was a Viking trait. And all his life, his son, the future king of England, would have done the same.

In the epic poem *Beowulf*, the heroes who are the dragon-slayer's companions, the Geats, sit down to feast:

> Then, in the feasting-hall,
> a bench was cleared for the Geats all together,
> and there those brave men went and sat,
> delighting in their strength; a thegn did his duty –
> held between his hands the adorned ale-cup,
> poured out the gleaming liquor; now and then the poet
> raised his voice . . . the warriors caroused . . .[18]

But carousing, practice in the field with sword and axe and bow – these were just games. The games had a real and a deadly purpose. And that purpose – as Cnut was to learn – was war.

FOUR

Ironside

If I can stay still, I'm strong in the fray.
If not, their might is greater than mine:
they'll break me in fragments and put me to flight . . .
                                        The Exeter Book, 1072

W e do not know how or where Swein Forkbeard died, merely
     when. The feast of Candlemas, on 3 February, was one of the
quarter days of the Christian calendar. The pagan Saxons had
known the month as Solmonath, the month when cakes were
offered to the gods, but Christians knew this day as St Mary's Feast
of the Candles, usually kept on 2 February, which marks the fortieth
day after Christ's birth. It was traditionally the day on which Mary
washed herself and presented the child Jesus at the Temple in
Jerusalem. Simon met her there and prophesied that the boy would
be a 'light to lighten the Gentiles', beginning a tradition of candle-
lighting that would last nineteen centuries in England.

The anomaly of the date of the king's death has been variously
explained by serial errors in the copying of the various texts of the
Anglo-Saxon Chronicle or even the imprecision in the period of
exactly when one day ended and the other began.

For Forkbeard to die when he did, only months after declaring
himself king of England, seemed to contemporaries to smack of
divine or supernatural intervention. One version of his death told
how in a bizarre encounter with the ghost of St Edmund, shot with
arrows and beheaded by a Viking army in 869, Cnut's father was
skewered through the neck by the spirit's lance. If, indeed, blood had
accompanied his passing, then the cause was likely to be an
aneurism. He lasted, according to the later chronicler, William of
Malmesbury, 'tormented with great pain until twilight', when 'he

ended his life with a wretched death'. More balanced accounts by Snorri Sturluson in the thirteenth century and the *Encomium* of Forkbeard's future daughter-in-law Emma cannot decide whether he died suddenly in the night or had time to bid his farewells to his nearest and dearest. We do not know, therefore, whether Cnut was actually present and whether Forkbeard died at his Midland fortress of Gainsborough. Neither do we know where he was buried, although York, the Viking Jorvik, is one possibility.

The *Encomium*, written by a man of God for a specific propagandist purpose, has the following:

> Feeling, therefore, that the dissolution of his body was threatening him, he summoned his son Knutr, whom he had with him and said that he must enter upon the way of all flesh. He exhorted him much concerning the government of the kingdom and the zealous practice of Christianity, and, thanks be to God, committed the royal sceptre to him, the most worthy of men.[1]

What we can be sure of, however, is the euphoria that ran through English ranks as horsemen rode south with the news. No doubt Aethelred in his safety at the Norman court raised a goblet to the fates that had brought his enemy down. We need not look, as contemporaries did, for poetic justice – the greedy Forkbeard's demand for an impossible amount of Danegeld. By any reckoning, the man was in his early fifties by 1014 – time, in the eleventh century, for him to go.

There was now a need to move quickly. Primogeniture was not fully established in either Denmark or England in this period. There had to be an election. Throughout Scandinavia, a new king needed to have royal blood, but he also needed to be acceptable to the *Thing*, the free men of their districts who met regularly to decide all important matters. As such, for the whole of the medieval period, the king was not seen as being on a pedestal, but merely *primus inter pares*, first among equals. There were presumably enough free men in Cnut's fleet at Gainsborough to carry out the task and he was duly chosen by them. This had parallels in the English witan, who performed the same duties, and even had earlier echoes in the

Roman habit of the legions electing their emperor from an elite group of successful generals. It would be wrong, however, to see the election of Cnut by his fleet as an example of vestigial democracy. He had to fulfil, in his followers' eyes, the role expected of him. To achieve legitimacy, he had to have shown wisdom, courage and military ability. His behaviour over the next three years in which he fought for his kingdom must be seen in this context.

The year 1014 was a stormy one. According to one version of the *Anglo-Saxon Chronicle*, every counsellor in England suggested bringing Aethelred back from exile rather than submit to Cnut. Further, 'full friendship was confirmed with word and pledge on either side, and they declared every Danish king outlawed from England for ever'.[2] Anglo-Saxon England was never quite as unified as that. Ealdorman despised ealdorman; thegn hated thegn. Like any state at any time, there were rivalries, jealousies, animosities. Large sections of the Danelaw were probably happier to accept the untried Cnut than the ditherer who had, after all, unleashed a pogrom against them only a few years earlier. Leading lights of Aethelred's kingdom, ealdormen like Morcar, Uhtred and Sigiferth, had sworn allegiance to Forkbeard; they now owed it to his son.[3] Since Cnut was married to Morcar's cousin, this alliance was natural, but it also played along with the regional rivalries that saw Mercia and Lindsey at loggerheads and almost everybody at daggers drawn with the hegemony of the Wessex-driven south.

For once in his life Unraed acted decisively. Before he left Normandy, he sent messengers to key players – 'commandeth that all his nation be greeted' is a feat of communication beyond the capabilities of the early eleventh century. The Chronicle tells us that Aethelred's son Edward (later the Confessor) was sent with the messengers as though to reinforce his determination, but even by a generous reckoning, the boy could have been no more than eleven in 1014 and his role must have been severely limited to that of symbolic figurehead. The exiled king's writ promised a new Aethelred: 'that he would be a gracious lord to them and would improve each of the things which they all hated and each of those things should be forgiven which had been done or said against him.'[4] The reciprocal deal was total devotion to Aethelred. He waited until the more favourable campaigning weather of the spring before he returned.

Cnut left his winter quarters on the Trent at Easter and with horses supplied to him by the people of Lindsey, foraged throughout the countryside. No doubt this had the effect of alienating some at least of his supporters, who may have been better disposed to Aethelred's army when it arrived in force. The luckless peasants fared no better here – 'all human kind that could be got at were raided and burned and killed'.[5] The king may have swept past Southampton, picking up a mercenary army on the Isle of Wight as he went and at some point he must have joined forces with the enigmatic Thurkil. They attacked Viking-held London, but the main thrust of the attack on Lindsey was a raid of attrition, punishment for their daring to side with the Danes.

The Scandinavian sources, especially the *Heimskringla*, tell of the future St Olaf leading his Norwegians alongside Aethelred and a major battle being fought in East Anglia against the long-suffering Ulfkell, once again called to defend his flat homeland, this time against his own people. According to the chronicler William of Jumièges,[6] Olaf the Stout, as he was known in life, was in Normandy in 1013–14, fighting for Duke Richard in a family squabble with his brother-in-law, Odo of Chartres, over his sister's dowry. Olaf, very far from the saint he became after death, carried out a series of bloody raids along the Brittany coast and took the Norman castle-fortress of Dol. It was back in Rouen, as hero and guest of Richard, that Olaf and several of his men were baptised by Archbishop Robert. It was here, too, that Olaf met the fugitive Aethelred and lent him his support. The skaldic poet Ottar the Black sang Olaf's praises and Snorri Sturluson quoted him at length in the *Olafsaga* over a century later. In fact Olaf's role was likely to have been limited, but his presence, along with that of Thurkil the Tall, probably gave the young Cnut food for thought.

There is little doubt that Cnut was caught napping by the speed of Aethelred's return. A nineteen-year-old could not be expected to have the experience necessary – he was playing with the big boys now, the battle-hardened veterans of the Jomsburg fortress, the warriors who had just humiliated a count. Earlier, Unraed had flown into exile with his tail between his legs. He would never return, Cnut may have believed, certainly not at the head of an avenging army. Wrong-footed, Cnut sailed away. 'And so', smarted the Peterborough Chronicler piously, 'the wretched people were destroyed by him.'

In 1912, Cnut's biographer Laurence Larson pondered whether help could have come from the Viking community based in Ireland. The raiders had established tiny communities on the Irish east coast as early as the ninth century, but their real strongholds lay in the areas of Dublin, Limerick, Waterford and Cork, and in any case, in April 1014, they had their hands full. It was in that month that Brian Boruma, the half-legendary High King of Ireland, took on the Dublin Vikings and their allies from Leinster in a classic showdown. Various sources refer to reinforcements from all over the Viking world, including presumably the Danelaw and Normandy. Losses were heavy on both sides – Sigurd, Jarl of Orkney and Brodir, Jarl of Man were killed, as were Boruma and his son Murchadh and grandson Tordelbach. The Viking threat was destroyed in this epic confrontation and perhaps none of the survivors was in a mood to aid Cnut in England.

But Cnut's Vikings did not sail far. The fleet hugged the east coast and put in at Sandwich, their well-known harbour in Kent. Here, Cnut put ashore the hostages he had been holding for months on the Trent 'with their hands, ears and noses cut off'.[7] Many historians share the view of Ryan Lavelle: 'hostages were probably adolescent sons [of the nobility] and their mutilation would have been a terrible occasion, traumatizing many of the West Saxon and Mercian nobility for a generation to come.'[8] No doubt this is true and it is evidence, if any were needed, that Cnut was a Viking, a ruler and a hard man, but to see him as a sadistic monster as some historians have is to miss the essential point that the eleventh century was a bloody age. Medieval chivalry and the code of the Geneva Convention lay in the future. Archbishops ordered terrible mutilations and Cnut's Viking predecessors used the appalling blood-eagle torture, in which a prisoner was tied to the ground and his chest slit open before his ribs were snapped off one by one, allowing his heaving lungs to flap like eagles' wings on the ground.

By these standards, Cnut's hostages at Sandwich got off lightly! It is likely that Cnut took with him his wife Aelfgifu and their baby son Swein when he sailed away.

We do not know the exact year of Swein Knutsson's birth. It was a tradition among Vikings to name a baby, even one born posthumously, after his grandfather. It is likely that the boy was no more than three or four months old. If Forkbeard's body was indeed buried in hallowed ground in York Minster, it was destined to find a more permanent home in the church at Roskild in Denmark. 'In the meantime,' said the ever-tactful Encomiast, 'a certain English matron had a ship prepared for her, and taking the body of Sveinn . . . and having embalmed it and covered it with palls, she went to the sea, and making a successful voyage, arrived at the ports of the Danes.'[9] The matron was almost certainly a royal mistress, although her name is not recorded. The exact process of embalming is uncertain, but Forkbeard had already been entombed once and if he was not embalmed soon after death, it is not likely to have been successful.

Sending a message to the two brothers [Cnut was back in Denmark by 1019 with his brother Harald], she indicated that the body of their father was there . . . they came gladly, and received the body with honour, and with yet more honour placed it in the monastery which the same king had built in honour of the Holy Trinity, in the sepulchre he had prepared for himself.[10]

The *Chronicle* talks of a geld of £21,000 as if it was paid to Cnut to make him go away, but it seems equally likely it was the blood-money given to Thurkil's mercenary army, which may have returned to its position with a fleet at Greenwich or perhaps had never even left it. Its presence could have deterred Cnut from harrying in the south. The year 1014 may have seen the end of the Viking usurper to Aethelred's throne, but to those so minded, God's wrath was felt again on Michaelmas Eve (28 September). While in far Scotland, the Michaelmas lamb was being slaughtered and the Struan Michael, the Michaelmas cake, was being baked, and in Lindsey, they lit bonfires and threw seed to the wild birds to bring luck to the farmstead, 'came a great sea-flood widely through this country, and it ran farther inland than it ever did before and drowned many settlements and a countless number of human beings'.[11]

Why did Cnut go so gladly into the dark night of exile? There is no evidence that he personally crossed swords with Aethelred, Olaf or Thurkil at all; in other words, he left without a fight. With Forkbeard's death, Cnut now had claim to the throne of Denmark, along with his sibling Harald. Denmark was a far more stable proposition than England and he needed to establish himself at home. The fact that the first coins struck bearing Cnut's name as king of Denmark were minted in Lincoln in the Five Boroughs, is testimony to the speed at which he moved. Kinsgship in the eleventh century was nothing if not personal. Cnut's brother Harald Sweinsson was a clear rival if Cnut himself were not in Denmark to prevent rebellion. In any case, it is likely that 'Cnut Cyng', as the *Anglo-Saxon Chronicle* now calls him, had no intention of staying away from England for long. One source says that he returned to Denmark with only sixty ships, implying that he either lost some in the hasty retreat or they were destroyed in North Sea storms. By 1015 he was back.

Events in England moved fast. 'There was a great assembly at Oxford,' the *Peterborough Chronicle* tells us and this could only have been called by the newly returned Aethelred. In an age of slow communications, rumour and counter-rumour, the councils were the only way a peripatetic ruler could maintain links with his nobles and keep his grip on government. Two of the thegns, Sigeferth and Morcar, on the way to Oxford from the Five Boroughs, never reached it. Eadric Streona of Mercia 'lured them into his chamber and in there they were killed dishonourably'.[12] This has all the hallmarks of a palace intrigue, and one probably engineered by Aethelred. Certainly the king lost no time in seizing the dead men's lands and he even imprisoned Sigeferth's widow, Aldgyth, in the abbey at Malmesbury, with its silver shrine given to them by Aethelwulf of Wessex nearly two centuries earlier. With Morcar and Sigeferth dead, Streona strong in Mercia and Cnut back in Denmark tending to brotherly affairs of state, Aethelred may have had time to breathe a sigh of relief; but he had reckoned without his own son, Edmund.

We first come across the third son of Aethelred as a witness to a charter written at Winchester in 993. His other brothers Aethelstan, Eggberht and Eadred, were present at this meeting too, and the boy was unlikely to have been more than five years old. His mother was Aelfgifu, Aethelred's first wife, rather a shadowy figure who was never his anointed queen and whose name disappears entirely from the record about 1002. Aethelred's biographer Ryan Lavelle suggests that she died in childbirth or as a result of a complication and this makes more sense than a separation or divorce which would surely have brought some contemporary censure, at least from the Church. Aethelred was probably fonder of her than the records suggest – his second wife, Emma of Normandy, was renamed Aelfgifu, perhaps in her honour. Edmund was probably brought up at the king's estate at Aethelingadene in Sussex by his grandmother Aelfthryth, a redoubtable woman in any age. The daughter of a powerful thegn, her second marriage was to king Edgar in 964. She had two sons, Aethelred and Edmund, but her larger than life reputation rests on her involvement in the murder of her stepson, Edward 'the Martyr' in the 'gap of Corfe' in 978. While Aethelred was a minor, her word was law and even after he married and governed in his own right, there is evidence to suggest that she still wore the trousers at court – something which may explain Aethelred's curious vacillations at various times during his reign. She founded and ran abbeys and was the first consort in the century to be anointed queen. At once the spiritual descendant of Agrippina, the pushy mother of the appalling Nero and the spiritual forebear of Eleanor of Aquitaine, mother of the Lionheart, she raised in Edmund the gung-ho hero her own son was famously not.

On 25 June 1014, Aethelred's eldest son died, adding to his father's woes as Forkbeard and Cnut carved up his kingdom. Although it is not specifically mentioned anywhere, Athelstan was his father's heir and this was recognised by chroniclers like Thietmar of Merseburg as far away as Germany. Whatever illness killed him, he had time to draw up his will, which still survives, with a copy in the archive at Christ Church, Canterbury. The will is a fascinating snapshot of royalty in the early eleventh century. He left considerable estates in ten counties in the south and clearly had close links with abbeys at Canterbury,

Winchester, Shaftesbury and Ely. He left five horses, a silver trumpet, two shields, a drinking horn, a coat of mail and eleven swords, one of which had belonged to Offa, the eighth-century king of Mercia. We even know the names of his friends – Godwine, the Earl of Wessex, Aelfwine, his chaplain who said mass for the dying prince; a stag huntsman and a sword-polisher. With his death, the spotlight now fell on the new atheling, Edmund.

Far from standing beside his father in his attempt to reinvent himself as a benign ruler, Edmund probably despised him. Aethelred was in his mid-fifties by now, an old man, increasingly ill and reliant on Eadric Streona, an over-mighty subject if ever there was one. 'Streona' means the aquisitor and the appellation says it all. Ealdorman of Mercia from 1007, his marriage to Aethelred's daughter Edith was a calculated piece of social climbing. It worked; by 1012 he was the king's right-hand man, a position he clearly intended to hold whoever wore the crown.

The *Chronicle* takes up the tale: 'After a short while, the atheling Edmund travelled [to Malmesbury] and took the woman [Aldgyth] against the king's will and had her for wife.'[13] This act may have amounted to one of civil war. Aethelred lay ill at Cosham at the head of Portsmouth harbour in the south. With the atheling's alliance with Aldgyth, Edmund had secured strong support in the east Midlands, within easy striking distance of Streona in adjacent Mercia. Before the Nativity of St Mary (15 August), records the *Chronicle*, 'the atheling travelled from the west, north into the Five Boroughs and immediately rode into all Sigeferth's territory and Morcar's, and all that people submitted to him'.[14]

The expected clash between Edmund, now called Ironside for his valour, and the ambitious earl never happened: 'When they came together, the ealdorman wanted to betray the atheling and therefore they parted without a fight and retreated from their enemies.'[15] 'Their enemies' were the army of Cnut, newly landed in the south. According to the monk of St Omer, whom we call the Encomiast, Cnut had two hundred ships.

Furthermore, there were so many kinds of shields, that you could have believed that troops of all nations were present . . . Gold

shone on the prows, silver also flashed . . . [and] who could look
upon the lions of the foe, terrible with the brightness of gold, who
upon the men of metal, who upon the bulls on the ships
threatening death, their horns shining with gold, without feeling
any fear for the king of such a force. Moreover, in the whole force
there could be found no serf, no freedman, none of ignoble birth,
none weak with old age. All were nobles, all vigorous with the
strength of complete manhood, fit for all manner of battle, and so
swift of foot that they despised the speed of cavalry.[16]

The situation was now highly complicated. 'At then the same time,'
says the *Chronicle*, 'king Cnut came to Sandwich, immediately
turned around the land of Kent into Wessex, until he came to the
mouth of the Frome and then raided in Dorset and in Wiltshire and
in Somerset.'[17]

It was the age-old tactic which had been consistently repeated
almost every year since the 980s – hit and run with the fleet never
far away. But Cnut had not come to raid – he had come to retake
what he saw as his kingdom and he had two allies which gave him
an edge. First and foremost was Thurkil the Tall, Strutt-Haraldsson.
A well-respected Viking war leader, he had fought with Forkbeard
and invaded England in 1009. It was he who had sacked Canterbury
and presided over, but may not have approved, the murder of
Archbishop Aelfheah. He is inscribed on the runestone in Uppland,
Sweden, as the provider of Danegeld for the mercenary Ulf of
Borresta. His defection to Aethelred no doubt caused raised
eyebrows in some quarters and apoplectic rage in others, but he may
have had personal reasons of which we know nothing. The
Encomiast, remember, believed this to be a game of double-bluff in
which Aethelred was the loser. When Forkbeard and Cnut invaded
in 1013, Thurkil did not waver, holding the large fleet at Greenwich
and exacting a large amount of gold for it. He stayed in England
when Aethelred ran to Normandy. But the succession issue of 1015
was decision time.

Aethelred and his increasingly pushy second wife, Emma of
Normandy, favoured the sons of their union, Edward and Eadwig.
Athelstan was dead and Edmund, the remaining son from

Aethelred's first marriage, was carving out a kingdom for himself in the Midlands. Eadric Streona was driving royal policy-making too and he had his own agenda, physically taking out the leaders of the Danelaw. In this context, Thurkil's position at Aethelred's court was decidedly at risk and at some point in the spring of 1015, he sailed for Denmark and swore allegiance to Cnut. He may only have brought nine ships and he was a traitor, but Cnut was already, at twenty, a shrewd judge of men. Thurkil was a giant in every sense. And he was a leader of the feared Jomsvikings who had taught the boy how to fight. Cnut needed such men.

The *Jomsvikingasaga* has a possible explanation for Thurkil's change of heart and return to Cnut. It tells how Ulfkell of East Anglia carried out two attacks on Viking garrisons, one in London, the other in the still unidentified Slesswick further north. These Vikings were almost certainly mercenary units in Aethelred's service, despised by the English because of the bitter raiding that had now been going on for over a quarter of a century. Among the dead at Slesswick, where the attack seems to have been more successful, was Henning, a chieftain whose name disappears from the record after 1015. And Henning was the brother of Thurkil the Tall.

The second ally that Cnut had in 1015 was less trustworthy, and less believable. Of all people, Eadric Streona 'enticed forty ships from the king [Aethelred] and then submitted to Cnut'.[18] The chronicler John of Worcester says that most of these crews were Danes anyway, so the defection was not as difficult to achieve as it might have been. Streona's motives are unknown. Perhaps he believed that Edmund Ironside could not prevail against Cnut; perhaps he had inside information we do not. Certainly, Aethelred's own days were numbered and in that context it was a straight choice between the atheling and the Danish king. Both were natural leaders of men, decisive, impulsive and of an age. Both were married to women with lands and allies in the Midland shires. It is not likely that a man like Streona would simply have tossed one of Aethelred's silver coins to make his choice, but in the end he went with Cnut and it would cost him his life.

Wessex, its villages burning, submitted to the Viking and provided horses for his army and there Cnut camped 'until midwinter'.

The campaigning season of 1016 began early; as Laurence Larson wrote nine centuries later, 'for the enemy now had a leader who saw no need of rest, who struck in winter as well as summer'.[19] 'Cnut came with his raiding-army and Ealdorman Eadric with him, over the Thames into Mercia at Cricklade, and then turned into Warwickshire during the midwinter season and raided, burnt and killed all that they came to.'[20] Ironside, in the meantime, was joined in the north by Ealdorman Uhtred of Northumbria. This powerful warlord was the son of Waltheof and one of a family who had held the borderlands for generations, endlessly battling with marauding Scots rather as the Percies would centuries later. In 1006 when King Malcolm of the Scots laid siege to Durham, Uhtred had attacked and destroyed his army. The invasion by Forkbeard had seen Uhtred throw in his lot with the Vikings but he returned, as many of the nobility did, to Aethelred in 1013. His switch to Ironside two years later speaks volumes regarding the polarisation of loyalties caused by Aethelred's age, illness and inactivity.

When Cnut and Streona attacked in the north, Uhtred was not there. He and Ironside were raiding in the west Midlands as far as Shropshire and news must have been brought by galloper that the Vikings were back in Northumbria. Perhaps in a panic, perhaps with regret, Uhtred abandoned Edmund and returned to make peace with Cnut. As Richard Fletcher says in *Bloodfeud*, 'Everything we know about Earl Uhtred of Northumbria could be written on a postcard',[21] and that includes his death.

In his murder, we see Cnut at his harshest. But the son of Forkbeard was a hard-bitten realist. He had seen with his own eyes the shifting allegiances of his time; ealdormen with their eyes to the main chance, thegns on the make. Men like Uhtred, men like Streona, men like Thurkil had their uses, but they could never really be trusted; better to keep them at sword's length. Uhtred sent hostages to Kent – and we already know how Cnut treated hostages – and no doubt there were tricky moments of diplomacy. Richard Fletcher has tentatively identified the meeting place of the two leaders as Wiheal (today's Wighill), north of Tadcaster on the River Wharfe in Yorkshire. It was probably the middle of March and the scene unfolded at the manor house at Wiheal, a damp, smoky structure

with oak frame and thatched roof. Whether Cnut was there in person
cannot now be known, but Thurbrand was, and he and his followers
crashed into the hall, hacking down Uhtred and as many of his men
who resisted. This single act sparked an internecine feud among the
families of the north which lasted for three generations, spanning the
death of Cnut and the Norman Conquest before it finally petered
out. It is a reminder, not only of the Anglo-Saxon survival of the
ancient blood feud, where 'an eye for an eye' was the accepted means
of controlling crime, but of the parochialism of English history in this
period. Few men thought in terms of nationalism, of England versus
Denmark, but rather within the smaller framework of their shire,
their hundred, their little plots of land.

In Uhtred's place, Cnut installed Yric of Lade as Earl of
Northumbria. This vassal of Cnut's had been ordered west out of
Denmark early in 1016 although it is not known exactly when he
arrived. He must have been in Northumbria (perhaps at York) by
early April for Cnut and Thurkil to have felt secure enough to
march south on London.

In a rare moment of reconciliation, Ironside galloped to his dying
father's rescue, probably in early April. Easter fell on 1 April in 1016
and Aethelred was in London. Various sources imply that he set out
from Cosham with an army, but the likelihood is that he was too ill
to conduct a campaign and took refuge behind London's defences to
await events. The Encomiast glossed over the king's role entirely.
Because his subject, Queen Emma, wanted to be portrayed as a first
true wife to Cnut, her marriage to Aethelred appeared nowhere in
the *Encomium*. Instead, the English leader, vague and unnamed, was
described as 'a prince'.

The Peterborough manuscript of the *Anglo-Saxon Chronicle* says
that Cnut's advance on London went 'another way, keeping to the
west'. We can imagine this was to gain support, rallying the central
shires to him since he was more confident in allegiance from the
Danelaw in the east. Already, his old supporters, the 'Company of
the Thingmen' were closing in on the city, ready for a final
showdown with Aethelred.

In fact, death claimed him first. Before Cnut arrived, Aethelred
died on St George's Day, 23 April, 'after much trouble and

wretchedness in his life'.[22] It is almost certain that Emma his wife was
with him and that she would have wanted her own son, Edward, to
succeed. Unfortunately for her, Ironside was already in the city and
'all the counsellors . . . and the town-dwellers' elected the older
atheling as their king. Once again, London held a key position in an
invader's plans and it was well defended: '[The Vikings] dug a great
ditch on the south side and dragged their ships to the west side to the
bridge, then afterwards diked the town around so that no one could
get in or out and often attacked the town, and they [the English]
resolutely withstood them.'[23] Among the collection of skaldic poems
of the period is 'The Liðsmens' Song', the story of the shipmen who
attacked the city under Cnut: 'every morning the lady on the Thames
bank sees the sword dyed in blood'.[24]

Thietmar of Merseburg is the only contemporary chronicler to
explain the machinations of the queen dowager in these fraught
days. The Encomiast, who might be expected to have known most,
does not mention her at all, but his account of the war between
Cnut and Ironside is woefully sketchy. Emma/Aelfgifu sent
messengers to Cnut, probably as soon as he arrived. She knew
Thurkil and Streona of old and may have offered a negotiated peace
in favour of herself and her boy, Edward, still only thirteen. The deal
was that London's armoury was to have been handed over to Cnut,
including some 24,000 *byrnies* (shirts of mail) and, more
importantly, the queen's stepson Edmund Ironside, in chains. If this
is true, it explains, no doubt, Emma's omission from the scene in the
Encomium. Whether Edmund discovered all this or realised he could
not withstand Cnut's siege, he broke out of the besieged city and fled
south into Wessex.

Evidently, Cnut detached a part of his army under Streona and
Aelmar Darling and they gave chase. There is evidence in the
fighting that followed, that Cnut led his army in person, although
some accounts have Thurkil in command. The *Knutsdrápa* says:
'You broke the raven's sleep, maker of battle. Bold son of Swein,
you led an attack at Sherstone, further south . . .'[25] The Anglo-
Viking force clashed with Ironside at Penselwood, near Gillingham
'and fought another battle after midsummer at Sherston'.[26]
Penselwood still has its stretch of coniferous forest and symbolically

marked the rallying point for Alfred the Great's defence against the Danes in his own day. It may be that if he had any choice in the matter, Ironside deliberately selected the place to make a stand. The result was inconclusive, as was the clash at Sherston in Wiltshire. The ever bubbly Encomiast has a resounding Viking victory here and pictures a devoutly Christian Thurkil the Tall 'continually sending up silent prayers to God for victory'.[27] 'There,' said the *Chronicle*, 'a great slaughter fell on either side and the raiding-armies themselves broke off the fight.'[28] Exhaustion and darkness had probably intervened at both battles and nothing but slaughter had been achieved. Ironside marched east to relieve London.

The *Chronicle* implies two raids on the future capital by the English army. Aethelred's queen was still inside, Aethelred's body newly interred at St Paul's church. Cnut was outside the city and according to the *Chronicle*, was forced to abandon the siege. Two days later, Ironside crossed the Thames at Brentford and beat Cnut's army back. He lost too many men, however, in the river's marshes in their eagerness to loot and pillage. Again, according to the *Chronicle*, 'the king went after that into Wessex and gathered his troops'[29] but it is unclear as to which king this refers. Technically, both Cnut and Ironside could be regarded as kings, but it makes most sense if this force was Cnut's because it returned to London and 'attacked it fiercely by water and by land, but the almighty God rescued it'.[30] Baulked of London, Cnut turned north, sailing in his dragon-ships up the Orwell into Mercia. This seems to have been a foraging raid, because he returned to the Medway with food supplies, driving cattle before him. Ironside, buoyed up by the inconclusive nature of the Penselwood and Sherston fights, harried the Vikings in Kent and drove them back into Sheppey, the flatlands intersected by estuaries and mudflats: 'the king [Ironside] killed as many of them as he could overtake'.[31] The Encomiast clearly had no sense of the timing of all this. He has Cnut wintering in Sheppey and 'peacefully awaiting the outcome of the matter'.[32]

At this point, the slippery Streona changed sides again. No doubt believing he had hitched his wagon to the wrong star, he bowed the knee to Ironside at Aylesford. 'There was', said the *Chronicle*, probably with the hindsight of a later scribe, 'no more unwise decision than this was.'[33] Streona had probably been playing a waiting game and it is possible that even while the war was raging, Ironside, Streona and the queen may have been in touch with each other by messenger.

Inevitably perhaps, Cnut's damaged troops sailed north into Essex and 'at the hill which is called Assuendun . . . there they came together resolutely'.[34]

With hindsight, the third battle of 1016, at Ashingdon – the hill of ash trees or *mons fraxinorum* as the Encomiast calls it – was the decisive one which gave Cnut his kingdom. At the time, it could have gone either way. Both sides had lost good men in the previous months, but both armies were essentially intact and there was, as today's sports commentators say, all to play for. There was literally a kingdom at stake. We have no skaldic poet to help us here, no epic view as at Maldon to lighten the gloom and add to the laconic comments of the *Chronicle*.

The battle was probably fought on the hill of ash trees on 18 October, the day of St Luke, the physician, quite late into the campaigning season. Darkness at that time of year would have fallen at about five o'clock and there is no evidence that this was a two-day fight. The battlefield today is marked by the minster church of St Andrew which Cnut had built to record his victory and which was consecrated in 1020. This presumably was the centre of the battle where the ash grove stood. Almost exactly fifty years later, William of Normandy would build Battle Abbey on the ridge at Senlac, in the centre of what had been Harold Godwinesson's shield wall.

The wind was biting on the sunny February afternoon I visited it, the sharp shadows of Cnut's church lengthening across the Victorian tombstones. There are still hedgerows of ash on the eastern slope, but these are the plantings of the enclosers of the eighteenth century. The ground to the east of the church falls away sharply, as it would have done in 1016 if the ash wood had been embanked as was the Saxon custom. The view is dramatic, the flat Essex marshes stretching away with a visibility of 20 miles on a clear day. Cnut would have had ample time to prepare for Ironside's attack, taking his position on the high ground in the cover of the trees.

We have seen already how armies fought in the eleventh century. The *Anglo-Saxon Chronicle* reports that Ironside had raised the country five times in as many months and this must mean the general fyrd. The fyrd itself is first recorded in the laws of Ine, king of Wessex, in 694. All free men between the ages of fifteen and sixty had to provide military service. By Ironside's time, there appears to have been a more professional force, which modern historians call the select fyrd. Under this system, one man was sent to fight for his king from five hides within each hundred. Since there were twenty-five of these per hundred, each hundred sent 125 men and these served together as later militia and yeomanry would and even the Old Pals Battalions of the First World War. The general fyrd was unreliable, since part-time soldiers were more concerned with the harvest and the weather than defeating an army. As recently as 1016, some of these men had refused to fight unless Aethelred was present in person and the timing of this particular contest probably means that members of the fyrd were home slaughtering their animals when Ironside needed them most. The rank and file were ceorls, commoners who may have been expected to provide a spear and single-edged hacking knife called a *seax* when summoned to the meeting place. There seems to have been something of a pecking order among these men and they traditionally carried spears and axes, the former a symbol of free men and the latter a traditional wood-working tool. In England, axemen did not normally throw their weapons (as they did in Charlemagne's empire) nor swing huge two-handed variants (as Cnut's *huscarls* did later in his reign).

In command of the mass of the ceorls were the thegns, peace and war leaders who were the professionals in the English army. Literally 'one who serves', by Ironside's day, the thegn could own substantial property, by bookland or folkland, whereby they granted lands to favourites whose names were entered into charters (the book), and had his own people. In every respect except the formal winning of spurs ceremony, they were the forerunners of the knights of medieval Europe. Such men were the backbone of Ironside's army in war and his state in peace – except that Aethelred's son would not live to enjoy that. A number of these warriors formed the *hearthwern*, the household troops who represented Ironside's bodyguard. Such men, like Byrhtnoth at Maldon thirty years earlier, would have pursued Cnut on horseback and dismounted to fight on foot at the hill of ash trees.

It is likely that the English advanced on the hill in their *scildburh* formation, a dense block of infantry called a shield-fort, their spears bristling, their shields locked in a looser version of the Roman *testudo* which had not been seen in Essex for seven centuries. Somewhere in the centre and well to the front, marched Ironside himself, on foot like his men, his personal standard carried behind him. We do not know what this was. Cnut was known to fly a black raven on a white field two hundred years before the complex rules of heraldry established such things. Fifty years exactly after Ashingdon, Harold Godwinesson would go down under his own banner, the Fighting Man, carried aloft beside the fish-tailed dragon of Wessex. The Encomiast tells the tale that Cnut's raven was the favourite bird of the god Odin himself and that at Ashingdon, it took on a life of its own, flapping its wings magically to portend victory on a banner that was actually plain white.

Inevitably, in the *Encomium*, Ironside makes a stirring speech to his troops: 'Oh, Englishmen, to-day you will fight or surrender yourselves all together. Therefore, fight for your country, men of understanding.' Shakespeare was busy putting such words into the mouths of other heroes five centuries later.

From the lie of the land today, the English may have had to change their line of approach and come at the Vikings from the north, where the gradient was gentler. At the top of the ridge, Cnut, tall and imposing, stood in the centre of his shield wall, waiting for Ironside to quicken his pace. Tacitus tells us that the Germans of his day advanced on Roman legionaries screaming and chanting wild battle oaths, but by Cnut's time the actual advance was carried out in silence until within spear shot.

As they reached the ridge, a hail of spears hissed through the air, biting into the circular, limewood shields with their leather rims and vicious iron bosses. Men went down, iron in their teeth and dents in their helmets. The shield wall closed to receive the impact of the running English line. We do not know what they shouted as shields collided and swords and axes clashed and scraped. At Hastings in another October, the English line stood immobile, the dead held up by the living, chanting 'Ut! Ut!' (Out! Out!) at the Norman invaders whose heavy warhorses crashed into their lines.

It is impossible to know the maelstrom of a Viking battle. Either the shield wall or the *scildburh* would collapse under pressure as key men fell. Without any means of controlling the outcome or signalling to the flanks, the thegns yelled themselves hoarse in an effort to keep their own units together. If the tactic was to kill the enemy leader, then Cnut's raven must have been a constant target, as must Ironside's standard. There was no room in this steel mêlée for individual duels. It was pitiless hacking in which strength, courage and sheer luck played their part.

The Exeter Book, with its complex riddles, carries one about a shield that took the same punishment as the man carrying it:

> I am solitary, wounded by iron.
> Battered by weapons, tired of battle-play
> Weary of sword-edges. I often witness war,
> Fierce fight, with no hope of help,
> Or any succour, before I,
> Amongst warriors, am totally destroyed.
> Hammered blades, hard-edged and horribly sharp
> Batter me, the handiwork of smiths,
> Biting in the burh.[35]

All we know of the battle of Ashingdon from the *Anglo-Saxon Chronicle* is the actions of Eadric Streona and they are widely open to interpretation: 'Then ealdorman Eadric did as he so often did before, first started with the flight – the Magonsaete and thus betrayed his royal lord and the whole nation.'[36] The Magonsaete or Magesaetan were part of the fyrd raised along the Welsh border in Shropshire and Herefordshire and may well have contained the horswealas (Welsh cavalry) referred to by Ine of Wessex four centuries earlier as messengers. The flight of Streona has a number of explanations. Either he could not control his border levies (such dubious vassals had a reputation of running in the heat of medieval battles) and if not, where were his steadier troops from his own

Mercian heartlands? Or, there could have been an element of a tactical flight here which went wrong, as William of Normandy's nearly did at Hastings. The Encomiast implies this, but he also has Streona saying to his men: 'for I know the hardihood of the Danes'.[37] According to historian Ian Howarth, Streona's forces were 'deliberately kept from supporting either side in battle',[38] implying perhaps that, like Lord Stanley at Bosworth four and a half centuries later, the ealdorman was waiting to see which way the battle went before committing his forces. Whatever the reality, the high moral tone of betrayal in the *Chronicle* fails to take into account the harsh *realpolitik* of the time.

We do not know how long the iron rang, how long the shields buckled and splintered, but by nightfall, surely, it was all over. The Encomiast, so badly informed on the rest of the campaign, waxes lyrical on this battle: 'And if the shining moon had not shown which was the enemy, every man would have cut down his comrade . . . and no man would have survived on either side, unless he had been saved by flight.'[39]

Ironside, perhaps wounded, limped away with his *hearthwern* to the west, to lick his wounds and reform his fyrd. The *Chronicle* lists the dead who lay on the slopes below the ash trees, spattered with blood: '. . . bishop Eadnoth, abbot Wulfsige, ealdorman Aelfric, ealdorman Godwine, Ulfcytel from East Anglia, Aethelweard, son of ealdorman Aethelwine and all the chief men of the nation of the English race'.[40]

It would be a misreading of events and too modern an interpretation to see Ashingdon as a national defeat. Interests were too regional, even parochial for that and the eclipse less total than at Hastings fifty years later. But for all that, it was a disaster and drew a firm line in blood under the unhappy reign of Aethelred. There was a certain poetic justice in the deaths of some of these men. It was Ealdorman Aelfric of Hampshire's convenient and sudden illness back in 1002 that had allowed Cnut's father to destroy Wilton. Ulfcytel was Ulfkell Snilling, the ealdorman of the eastern counties who had provided Forkbeard's Vikings with their 'hard battle-play' in the earlier invasion, and who had engineered the death of Thurkil's brother Henning. The presence of two prominent churchmen – Eadnoth, Bishop of Dorchester and Wulfric, Abbot of Romsey – is a reminder of their role on the battlefield. They would have held services on the slopes of the ash-tree hill. Perhaps Cnut's shield-biting berserkers hacked their way to their tall crosses and cut them down.

> They left behind them corpses for the dark
> Black-coated raven, horny-beaked to enjoy,
> And for the eagle, white-backed and dun-coated,
> The greedy war-hawk, and that grey wild beast,
> The forest wolf.[41]

Possibly Cnut was magnanimous in victory. It was the deepest shame for the Saxons to leave their dead on the battlefield and perhaps the Viking let them carry away their slaughtered leaders for Christian burial elsewhere. Perhaps they became the first occupants of the little graveyard around the later church. Fifty years later when Gyfa, Harold Godwinesson's mother, offered her son's conqueror his weight in gold for his mutilated body, an embarrassed William had it sent to her free of charge to be buried at the Abbey of the Holy Cross at Waltham.

In some ways, after a battle like Ashingdon, the dead were the lucky ones. Research conducted by the York Archaeological Trust on Anglo-Scandinavian bodies in the Jorvik area, found twenty-nine skeletons, all of young men who had clearly died in battle. Their wounds were exactly like those inflicted at Ashingdon. Most of the damage was done to the head, skulls shattered by sword or axe. There were almost twice as many wounds to the left side of the body (the natural situation for right-handed men) and decapitations were common. Injuries to the back may have been inflicted on men lying wounded on the ground, while hacked thigh bones may mean hamstring injuries to incapacitate.

The wounded at Ashingdon, heads split, noses broken under their iron nasals, arms ripped and bodies smashed, would have been patched with herb poultices and bandages of torn linen. Saxon medicine was quite far advanced by the standards of the time, the leechbooks of the tenth century containing sensible, practical cures as well as the more exotic (and useless) 'magic'. Bald's 'Leechbook' deals with battlefield casualties:

> If a bloody wound in a man should turn bad, then take mallow, boil it in water, foment with that . . . If you cannot staunch a bloody wound, take new horse-dung, dry it in the sun or by the fire, rub it to a powder very thoroughly, lay the powder very thick on a linen cloth, bind the wound with that for a night.[42]

The *Lacnunga*, collected perhaps twenty years before Ashingdon, is a list of the wackier ideas, including the Nine Herbs Charm widely used as a back-up to more rational remedies. The best doctors knew Galen and other 'greats' of the classical period, but how many of these accompanied Ironside's or Cnut's armies on campaign is unknown. Garlic, oxgall, onions and copper salts were all used to fight infection; gangrenous limbs were cut off; stomach wounds were stitched with silk. The less educated or more superstitious used a variety of charms – *galdor*, from the verb to sing, a reminder of the importance of incantations – and prayed to God for good measure. No doubt, men were still dying by inches weeks after Ashingdon.

The battle was a resounding victory for Cnut, especially since in the weeks leading up to it, his forces were actually on the run. But the reality of the situation was not as black and white as the *Chronicle* would have us believe: 'and with that [victory, Cnut] won all England'. Cnut's forces moved north-west into Mercia and further into Gloucestershire, 'where he had heard it said that Edmund the king was'.[43] It is not likely that this was a prolonged rout, because that was neither a Viking nor a Saxon tactic. It is possible that Cnut and Ironside fought again in the Forest of Dean, which would explain what they were doing that far west later in the autumn. Ironside probably had an alliance of some kind with the Welsh, since Streona had Welsh troops at Ashingdon. The ever-slippery ealdorman was there again, at Alney, near Deerhurst when the two kings exchanged hostages 'and there affirmed their friendship, both with pledge and with oath'.[44] The fact that Cnut was prepared to strike a deal with Ironside implies that his army had been badly mauled at

Ashingdon – either that, or he had some ulterior plan which time would reveal. The historic meeting took place in the church at Deerhurst, dedicated to St Mary, the mother of Christ. There was a church here in 804, when Aethelric, son of Ealdorman Aethelmund of the Hwicce endowed a priory in the area, and by the time of Cnut, it had undergone a number of rebuilds. A great deal of archaeological and historical research has been undertaken in connection with Deerhurst in the last twenty years.[45] In Cnut's time, the Hwicce church was a monastery built on what was in effect an island in the Severn. The chronicler John of Worcester says that both kings approached it by water in open rowing boats. The current farmhouse was part of the cloister buildings and the very tall church had perhaps four floors inside. Blocked-up doorways high in the walls of the west end of the nave are proof that there was once an ambulatory all the way around. The unique triangular window probably housed the monastery's relics and it is possible that these would have been used in the ceremony that Cnut and Ironside performed. The font with its swirling patterns and the stone wolf heads with their traces of original paint, would have been silent witnesses to the scene. Perhaps this was a significant centre to Ironside in that it was the traditional burial place of kings. Certainly Alney, as an island in 1016, was a neutral place. The Encomiast claims that the kings planned to fight each other in single combat and it was certainly a Viking tradition to use an island – *holm ganga* – for this purpose. Perhaps, too, stories of Uhtred's murder and those of Sigeferth and Morcar encouraged the English king to choose a church. Perhaps here, Cnut would have to leave his sword and his swordsmen outside and walk the chancel with open hands, watched over by the 'angel of Deerhurst' carved into the stone overhead.

The deal that the two men struck at Deerhurst, with their clerks and scribes, their battle-scarred warriors, their horses, their dogs and their hawks, split England into a dual kingdom. And it had a precedent. Sixty years earlier, in the reign of King Edgar, the land had been divided, though there must have been few men in England in 1016 who remembered it. The chronicle of John of Worcester tells us that Ironside had Wessex, East Anglia, Essex and London, and Cnut 'the northern parts'. It is difficult to grasp the subtleties of this.

On the face of it, Ironside had the better of the deal – London, fast replacing Aethelred's Winchester as the most important town in the country (the Encomiast refers to it as the English capital by 1042); Wessex, psychologically the 'heart' of England; East Anglia with its superb farming land. Cnut had the Danelaw, but not all of it, and anyone ruling the far north would have to contend with the irritating and warlike Scots over the border. In the *Saga of Magnus the Good*, Snorri Sturluson wrote of Deerhurst:

> it was agreed that the kings should take the oath of brotherhood and should maintain peace as long as both were on earth; and that if one of them died sonless, the survivor should inherit his realm and all subjects. Twelve men, the most eminent of each kingdom, took the oath with the kings that this agreement should be kept as long as any of them lived.[46]

It may be, of course, that this was merely a holding exercise, a piece of politesse never intended to last, 'Then on St Andrew's Day [30 November] king Edmund passed away and is buried with his paternal ancestor Edgar in Glastonbury . . .'[47]

An infuriating silence descends on all sources concerning Ironside's death. Although no one refers to it in these terms, he died only five weeks after Ashingdon and if he was wounded there, or at a second battle in the Forest of Dean, he may have died of the infection uncountered by the Nine Herbs. On one hand, sudden death, even for a man under thirty, was not uncommon in the eleventh century. On the other hand, Cnut may have had him murdered. The evidence suggests that Ironside was in London when he died. So probably was his stepmother, Emma, the widow of Aethelred, who may, even in late 1016, have come to a separate peace with Cnut. It is likely too that the Danish fleet had the use of London as a port at least and it is not impossible that Cnut was in the town in person. The fact that the *Chronicle* – and other sources – makes no mention of a violent death, nevertheless gives us the option of poisoning as a modus operandi. Hemlock, lords and ladies, white bryony, belladonna, thorn apple, henbane and any number of species of fungi grew widely in what was now Cnut's

England. Despite the relatively advanced state of Anglo-Saxon medicine, symptoms were often misread. An otherwise healthy young man suddenly slipping into a coma would have been placed at the hands of God and His providence. He moved, after all, in mysterious ways. As the Encomiast put it:

> But God, remembering his teaching of olden time, that a kingdom divided against itself cannot long endure, very soon led Edmund's spirit forth from his body, having compassion on the realm of the English, lest if, perchance, both should continue among the living, neither should reign securely and the kingdom be daily annihilated by renewed contention.[48]

Whatever the truth of Edmund Ironside's death, it played perfectly into Cnut's hands. Ashingdon had wiped out many men who might still have rallied to the martyred cause that Ironside might have become. As it was, it was winter, the ground was like iron and men were sick of the slaughters. Ironside's younger brother, Aethelred's Eadwig, got the cold shoulder from everyone. His sons were mere children. 'The dead prince', wrote the Encomiast, 'was buried in a royal tomb [at Glastonbury] and was wept long and sorely by the native people; to him may God grant every joy in the heavenly kingdom.'[49]

Cnut, the Viking thug, the 'destroyer of the chariot of the sea', was king of England.

FIVE

Engla-land

That land is so lovely, endowed
with delights, earth's sweetest scents.
It is an unique, inland island; noble,
unshakeable . . .
The Phoenix, Anon, ninth century

'Here in this year Cnut King succeeded to the whole kingdom of England',[1] says the Worcester manuscript of the *Chronicle* in 1017. What sort of land had the ultimate raider won for himself, by a combination of blood and luck?

He would have been familiar with much of the country's landscape, having tramped over large parts of it at the head of an army. Fifty years after his death, William I's Domesday Book records that 15 per cent of the land area was heavily wooded. Even allowing for the incompleteness of that survey, we would be struck today by the sheer number of trees in Cnut's kingdom. These were unevenly distributed – the fact that Assuendun took its name from an ash grove implies that nearby areas were relatively open; the clump of trees would be visible for miles across flat marshland. The New Forest in Wessex where William Rufus would die a century later, the Forest of Dean where Cnut met Ironside at Deerhurst on the island of Alney – these areas would be thickly forested with oak, elm and ash, maple, hawthorn and hazel. Evergreens were rare, except for the occasional yew. The Saxon word *hurst* means a wood, but other names – holt, scaga, wudu, bearn – presumably refer to the size or nature of an area in a technical terminology we no longer understand. Woodland is mentioned in the charters of a number of Saxon kings before Cnut's time, but we have little information on the clearing of forests for villages or of any conscious replanting. Wistful authors like Peter Vansittart may lament the fact that 'Saxon pick and Viking axe had begun what mines and towns were to complete, the destruction of our forests',[2] but timber was vital for house-building, fortifications and most machinery. The woods were also home to a variety of wildlife – the wolves and the wild boar which would soon be hunted to extinction, the red deer and the red squirrel. Woods were embanked at their edges, but where cattle, sheep or pigs fed nearby, the area often turned to scrubland.

Some of these forests had tribal associations; Wychwood in Oxfordshire was the forest of the Hwicce, early Saxon peoples who still retained their own identity in Cnut's day. The largest single forest area was probably Andredesweald, which, the *Chronicle* for 892 tells us, was 'thirty miles wide and stretching one hundred and twenty miles from east to west'.[3] In today's terms, it covered some 2,500 square miles of the Weald between Kent and Sussex.

There is no doubt that the forest had a magical significance for Cnut's Vikings as it did for Aethelred's English. The Saxon word *trow* means 'true' and 'trustworthy' but it also means 'tree'; and the Vikings already had the notion of the family tree in their word *barnstokker*, literally baby tree trunk. The Christianity that Cnut had embraced by the eleventh century, was doing its best to kill off the magic. 'No one', admonished an early bishop, 'shall go to the trees, or wells or stones . . . or anywhere else except to God's church . . .'[4]

The famous wooden carving in the church at Urnes which gave its name to a whole school of Viking art shows the curling tendrils and branches of Yggdrasil, the World Tree, which lay at the heart of the universe.

Water, too, was everywhere. Cnut's new kingdom had an extensive river network and nearly all of it was navigable to the narrow-hulled Viking dragon-ships. We have seen already the ease with which the raiders sailed up the Thames, the Humber, the Trent and the Orwell in search of plunder. Marshlands were everywhere, like the peatbogs of Cnut's homeland. The church at Deerhurst was on an island in 1016 and most of Cnut's problems in attacking London stemmed from his inability to tame the Thames.

Most of the rivers were already named before the Saxons arrived, because water was sacred to the Celts and Romans alike, but the newcomers readily accepted names that merely meant stream or water – the Don, the Goyt, the Avon are merely dialect terms for these. The Cam, the Groome and the Crummock derive from their winding courses; the Air, the Taw and the Tern were fast-flowing; the Leam, the Lynm and the Lympre were lined with elms; the Derce, the Dart and the Derwent clothed with oak woods. The Trent was a trespasser, liable to encroach over the flat lands that were its flood plain. In the Danelaw to the north, Viking names became the norm after the ninth century. The thirteenth-century Icelander, Snorri Sturluson, was only using a little imagination when he described rivers with names like 'frothing, greedy, strong, way-knowing, sweeping-people-away, slow, broad, cool, battle-defiant, loud-bubbling, forward-rushing, old, spear-teeming'.[5]

If Cnut's armies did not advance inland by water to seize chunks of the kingdom, they had an option in places of travelling by road. Thanks to the Romans, these were more numerous and serviceable than anything in Cnut's Denmark. Ermine Street, Watling Street, the Fosse and Icknield Ways, all of them built or strengthened by the legions seven centuries earlier, were highways of significance, long and straight. Some roads were called *herepaepas*, army roads, but it is not clear whether these were military roads like those of the legions or whether they were merely built by the fyrd. The fact that Harold Godwinesson could march between York and London in ten days or less implies a good road surface by 1066 and no doubt this was true fifty years earlier.

Bridges were vital in a land intersected with broad, deep rivers and soggy with marshes. By the ninth century, most areas had a duty to build and maintain these structures. In eighth-century Mercia, this was one of the *trinoda necessitas* (three essentials), almost feudal obligations which involved *brycggweork* (bridge work), and was probably a national expectation under Aethelred. From charters we know that causeways of rubble (such as the vital one that featured in the battle of Maldon) as well as wooden structures (*bricq* or *ford*) were commonplace. There were major bridges across the Thames at London, the Medway at Rochester and the Thames again at Oxford.

England was Engla-land, a nation bounded in the west by Offa's Dyke to keep out the marauding Weala, the Welsh, and in the north by the crumbling frontier of Hadrian's Wall which no longer deterred the Scots. Everywhere else was bounded by the sea, as much Cnut's kingdom now as was the land. Several references in the *Anglo-Saxon Chronicle* and other sources refer to 'all England' but it had not been a single nation for long and in Cnut's time must have retained strong regional identities.

One of the most infuriating gaps we have in our historical knowledge of any period before our own is how our ancestors would have sounded in everyday speech. In the case of Anglo-Saxon, experts have identified four broad dialects in Cnut's England – Northumbrian, Mercian, Kentish and West Saxon. This is based on surviving texts which indicate sound systems, but the science is clearly inexact. The Northumbrian dialect of the far north, up whose River Humber Cnut sailed with his father in 1013, is estimated from runic inscriptions (themselves Viking, of course), place names and short poems from the early ninth century and 'glosses' of the period that coincide with the resumption of Viking raids. These last are notes or marginalia added to English or Latin texts, often with a dry stylus and only visible under certain light. Their exact purpose is unknown, but they can, in some instances, indicate pronunciation by their syllable stresses. The Mercian dialect can be guessed in the same way from surviving texts such as the tenth-century Rushworth Gospels and the much earlier Vespasian Psalter. Most of the Kentish 'sound' evidence comes from charters, two poems and glosses to a collection of biblical proverbs from the tenth century. Best represented is the Wessex dialect, especially in prose of all kinds from the tenth century, confirming the supremacy of Wessex in the politics of Cnut's reign and providing a rough equivalent for the 'Queen's' or 'BBC' English of our own time. There are more questions than answers for this aspect of Cnut's period. Inevitably the texts were written by scribes, intelligent, educated men. Did they represent their region and if so, what was its extent? Did they represent their social class and if so, in what way was their accent different from, say, that of a thegn or a ceorl? Did each area sound as it did because of the original settlement patterns or did accents develop later, after the Saxon conquest? One thing is very likely – regional variations within each of the four districts were probably very marked; even in the twentieth century such variations could be mystifying.[6]

The flavour of Cnut's England depends on our view of the original Saxon settlements of the fifth and sixth centuries and this is an area of controversy. The Angles, Saxons and Jutes who crossed the Channel and North Sea in the dying years of the Roman Empire were illiterate, and stories of Hengist and Horsa are about as historical as Adam and Eve. The chroniclers Gildas[7] and Bede[8] told tales of fire and sword, but despite the romantic *Götterdämmerung* of Arthur, the process seems to have been much more acclimatization than conquest. Archaeology has more or less complemented Bede's assertions that the Angles settled in the north and the east, the area that would become the Danelaw by the time Cnut arrived; the Jutes occupied the south – Hampshire, Kent and the Isle of Wight. In the sixth century, dialect and dress differences made these groups as disparate as the various Celtic tribes at the time of the Roman invasion. We have no idea, of course, of numbers or of how quickly the invaders were assimilated into Romano-Celtic society. It is likely that Franks, Frisians and pre-Viking Norwegians drifted into the region as well, causing further ethnic confusion for today's historians.

Most of the earliest settlements saw the Germanic people with their fair hair and their florid complexions building villages near rivers where their hoes and light ploughs could cope with the easy soil. Expansion into valley areas was only possible with the adoption of sturdier ploughs, although our view of this settlement pattern is distorted perhaps by the availability today of aerial photography which picks out building foundations more closely in light soil areas. Some of these first settlers continued to farm the furrows of Roman villas. In other cases, they seem to have deliberately struck out elsewhere, often moving a mile or so every few years as the soil became overworked and the crop yield lessened. The Saxon settlement, in other words, was not the direct forerunner of the medieval village with its parish church and manor house. It was not until a generation or two before Cnut's invasion that such nucleic settlements occur and this was probably as much the result of population increase and the centralisation of royal authority as anything else.

We have no idea of the population of Cnut's kingdom. The Domesday Book of 1086–7 is the best guide we have, but this is not a census and there are serious gaps in the record; London and Winchester, the two largest cities in the country are not included, for instance. 'Multipliers' of four or five have been suggested to balance this, which would give us a figure of anything between one and a quarter and four million. Lincolnshire, East Anglia and Kent were the most densely populated then and this was probably true of fifty years earlier. Parts of the south coast, like Southampton, were relatively thickly populated, but the wilder areas of the west – Dartmoor, the Welsh Marches, the area where Ironside and Uhtred ravaged in 1015–16 – probably only had two or three people per square mile. When William's scribes made their entries, they were confronted with deserted villages, many made so by the king's destruction of the north in 1069–70, and marked them with the ominous words 'it is waste'. After the raids of 980–1017, no doubt there would have been similar scenes of devastation.

Wessex was on the rise in Cnut's time, as it had been for many generations. It was the eighth century, according to Bede, before 'West Saxon' became an accepted term. Before that, the inhabitants of the Thames Valley were called the Gewisse and either by conquest or marriage (probably both) extended their control into Hampshire and the Isle of Wight under their king, Caedwalla, in the seventh century. Under his successor, Ine (688–726), the kingdom flourished, Ine's laws being among the most famous in western Europe. Its northern borders, in what today is Berkshire, were constantly being disrupted by the Mercians, a reminder that the heptarchy of seven kingdoms described by Bede (Kent, Sussex, Wessex, Essex, East Anglia, Mercia and Northumbria) was a shifting notion with no fixed demarcation or frontiers. Not only was Wessex rich farming land and the focus for English defence against the Vikings in Alfred the Great's day, it boasted, in Southampton, one of the biggest ports in the country and in Winchester the city that would become the capital of both Aethelred and Cnut. An entire style of art – the

Winchester School – was based there and certain editions of the *Anglo-Saxon Chronicle* written or copied there, probably in the cloisters of the Old Minster. Cnut was already familiar with much of this area. He had almost certainly wintered in the Isle of Wight – perhaps at the Saxon burh on the hill at Carisbrooke – and struck north across Hampshire during the later raids of his father.

The kingdom of Kent was about the size of the county today. Its first 'English' settlers were Jutes, but grave goods from its cemeteries indicate a strong Frankish presence. The Franks were the descendants of the Gauls from what today is France. Originally a migratory tribe from the Lower Rhine, their various subdivisions had become blurred by Bede's day. Trade, coinage and political ties between the rulers of Kent and various Merovingian kings bear witness to a great deal of cross-Channel fertilisation. Kent's wealth in relation to larger kingdoms further north can probably be explained by its proximity to Europe and the steady growth of London as a port and trading centre. At its heart was Canterbury, the most holy site in the country from the Christian point of view, and all the evidence points to an assimilation of new cultures here rather than slaughter under the legendary Hengist and Horsa, which may merely refer to cavalry raids.[9] The kingdom was united in the seventh century under Wihtred, but subsequently, first Mercia then Wessex dominated it and by the time of Cnut's invasion, it had lost nearly all sense of its independence. Again, the new king knew it well. Sandwich had been a Viking watering place for years and it was the obvious approach for an army marching on London as Cnut did twice in the early years of the century.

Mercia in Bede's time meant the border area, which may have referred to the Welsh to the west or the Northumbrians to the north. In the 730s it straddled the river Trent and its land could support an estimated 12,000 families according to existing land records. By the time of Cnut, it was much larger, its north the line of the Humber, its south grating against the Wessex marches and its west standing defiant against the Weala. So large was this area that it contained subdivisions: the Wreocensaetan of North Wales; the Magonsaetan who fought under Eadric Streona in 1016; the Pecsaetan from the Pennines; the Middle Angles; the Middle Saxons and the Hwicce from Gloucestershire. The fact that twenty different 'tribal' groups can be identified among the Middle Angles alone is testimony to the complexity of Saxon settlement and poses questions about how 'English' all these people felt in the event of Viking invasions. Mercia, too, was rich, with perhaps 85,000 hides compared with Kent's 15,000 and Wessex's 100,000. Tribal capitals have survived to become religious centres – Leicester for the Middle Angles, Worcester for the Hwicce and Hereford for the Magonsaetan. By the seventh century, Mercia came to dominate all other kingdoms because of its strong, repressive kings – Penda, Wulfhere and, above all, Offa, whose famous dyke to keep out the Welsh can still be traced along the Marches today. We know little about the careers of these men beyond archaeology, Bede and a few place names (Offchurch in Warwickshire, for instance), but the area was eclipsed by Cnut's time by the Danelaw and the rise of Wessex. Cnut must have crossed the area from east to west. He waited at Gainsborough on the Trent in the Mercian heartlands while his father sent him hostages in 1014–15. He abandoned the people of the Five Boroughs and Lindsey to the pillaging of Ironside and he was possibly still in Mercian-controlled territory when he turned on Ironside at Ashingdon.

Essex had been a far more powerful area in the centuries before the second Viking Age. London was in its control and a bishopric was created there at the church of St Paul in 604. Moving south of the Thames, the East Saxons had clashed with the Cantware of Kent and the West Saxons, and had settled their frontiers at a meeting at Brentford in 705 which must have been similar to that of Cnut and Ironside at Deerhurst. The record of kingship here is confused, with brother ruling with brother and father with son in a series of shared monarchies. By the early eighth century, London had been taken by the Mercians – recent archaeological excavations along the Strand have uncovered their pottery and coinage. By the time Cnut arrived, Essex was merely a subdivision, but whether Mercia or Wessex held the whip hand is debatable.

To the north lay East Anglia, still, in Cnut's time, called Ulfkell's land after the man who had gone down before his spears at Ashingdon. The area had been the stronghold of the Iceni and the

Trinovantes in Roman times, and the North-folk and the South-folk who gave the modern county names were already established by the 680s. Sutton Hoo in Suffolk remains the most striking example of a Saxon burial, although it has Viking influences and was probably the grave of Raedwald, who may have been *bretwalda* (overlord) of an area much bigger than East Anglia. Despite continued pressure from the belligerent Mercia to the west, the kingdom retained its independence and struck its own coinage. By the ninth century, the 'great Danish army' was raiding its coasts with impunity, settling there under their leader Guthrum and carrying on a war of attrition against Alfred of Wessex. It is possible that the epic poem *Beowulf* was written in the area, perhaps at the kingdom's spiritual heart, Bury St Edmunds, with its shrine to the martyred English king.

Northumbria was formed by two earlier kingdoms, Deira and Bernicia. The term *Nordanymbrorum* may have been coined by Bede and it was a single kingdom by the 650s. The extent of it varied with the power and personality of its kings. Edwin (616–33) ruled Anglesey and the Isle of Man; Ecgfrith controlled the Forth, and any one of them had to battle to take Lindsey. The blood feud that Richard Fletcher has written about recently over the murder of Uhtred in Cnut's time was far from unique in these northern hills. Of fourteen eighth-century kings of Northumbria, four were murdered, six overthrown and exiled and two retired to the safety of monasteries. Not that these were impervious to the vicissitudes of life. The abbey of Lindisfarne was famously sacked by the Vikings in 793 when dragons roared among the clouds overhead and the history of Northumbria ever after was one of constant warfare against the raiders.

No region of Cnut's new kingdom is more controversial to modern historians than the Danelaw. The chronicler Symeon of Durham wrote in the twelfth century that it comprised York and fourteen shires. Here, English hundreds were called wapentakes; hides were carucates and place names confirm that the Danelaw had its own superimposed dialect. From 876, Yorkshire fell to the Vikings; East Anglia three years after that. The treaty of 880 between Alfred and Guthrum drew a diagonal line across the country, although the areas to the east and north of this ninth-century 'iron curtain' were by no means wholly under Viking control. Likewise, there appear to have been areas of what is clearly Danish and even Norwegian influence beyond the Danelaw 'line'; up the Severn Valley, for instance, into Worcestershire. Only in certain areas have distinctive Viking place names survived. Eofor-wic (the Northumbrian term for York) became Jorvik; Noro-wordig became Djura-by (Derby). The suffix 'by' indicates a settlement – Dalby was the village in the valley; Kirkby the village with a church and so on. *Thorpe* in place names – Princethorpe in Warwickshire for example – denotes later, generally smaller settlements, and *thveit* – Outhwaite for instance – means a clearing.

One of the points of controversy is who settled where in the area. The 'by' ending is Danish, but other evidence tells us that Norwegians, Swedes, Frisians and even Irish Vikings carved out territory for themselves. We cannot be at all sure of the numbers involved. There seems to have been no mass exodus from Scandinavia, despite the undying image of a bleak, grim homeland. Archaeology is unhelpful. Viking burials are few, although spectacular finds like Sutton Hoo indicate a Viking influence long before the Danelaw became a reality. The range of burials in Denmark and associated graves in England is huge. Cremations, inhumations, ship burials, grave goods for the afterlife – all these can be found side by side in the same cemeteries.[10] In a sense, it matters little what the origin of the invaders is. Historian J.M. Wallace-Hadrill describes them as 'little more than groups of long-haired tourists who occasionally roughed up the natives'. And Simon Keynes comments, 'the Vikings were probably uncouth, certainly unpleasant and decidedly unwelcome'.[11] No doubt much of this is true, but they had the effect of unifying the disparate English kingdoms against them and brought to the fore the doyen of English heroes – Alfred the Great.

Within a generation of the Alfred/Guthrum treaty, there is evidence that most men of the Danelaw regarded the king of 'England', Edward the Elder (899–924), as their overlord and we have several examples of land-holding gentry who are clearly, from their names, Anglo-Danish. There were peculiar survivals of the 'first' Viking culture and even law into and beyond Cnut's time.

Economic growth seems to have been faster in the Danelaw than elsewhere, the *sokemen* or free farmers settling the fenlands of Norfolk and Cambridgeshire. The Church owned less land here than in Wessex and only a few years before Cnut's arrival had it made serious inroads in this context.

The conclusion on the Danelaw is that it should not be seen as a political entity in its own right. Danish law held sway here as the term implies, but regional differences – Northumbrian, Mercian, even that of Lindsey and the Five Boroughs – quickly re-emerged after the original conquest. None of this helps us with the inclinations and attitudes of the inhabitants of the Danelaw in Cnut's time. We have suggested that they welcomed Forkbeard and Cnut in the Humber and Trent because they saw them as compatriots. We have also seen Aethelred's extraordinary pogrom against them on St Brice's Day. But despite these examples of alienation, it is likely that by 1017, the inhabitants of the Danelaw were fully assimilated into an English way of life.

That way of life was agricultural. It was as eternal as the seasons and the weather. In 1017, young men of Cnut's age had never known anything but Viking raids, but older still were the tales their fathers told them of how to till the ground and feed the pigs, shear the sheep and haul the plough. Kings would come and go, but the land went on for ever. The *Julius Work Calendar* made about three years after Cnut took the throne of England, shows the heavy, iron-shod plough slicing through the clay of a heavy English soil. Four oxen, solid, sullen and long-horned, squelch through the frozen mud of January. 'The ploughman feeds us all', the scholar Aelfric had written a century earlier, observing the vital importance of the farming year and the cutting-edge of machinery.

While the seeds that would develop into the summer's harvest waited to be planted, February was the month of pruning. We have seen that vineyards stretched as far north as Ely and the *Calendar* shows young men hacking at the vines with their pruning hooks, tools virtually unchanged to this day.

March saw the spring equinox and the time for sowing; the *Calendar* shows the hard, back-breaking work that this entailed –

digging, mattocking, dragging away the weeds with a rake. And the ceorl walking the ridges that ran between the sunken strips in the open fields, throwing his seed from the basket slung over his shoulders and balanced on his hip is an image as old as time. Because of the need to leave land fallow to replenish its goodness (the vital chemicals unknown to the English or the Vikings) and because of the chance survival of each carelessly thrown seed, only a fraction of the food available each year actually reached human and animal bellies. The great famine of 1005 'such that no man ever remembered one so grim before' as the *Chronicle* said, was not actually a unique experience. Bede records that in Sussex in his own time, 'Frequently forty or fifty emaciated and starving people would go to a cliff or to the edge of the sea, where they would join hands and leap over, to die by the fall or by drowning.'[12] Those who survived ate nettles, acorns, grass and bark to stay alive and prayed to whichever God they thought was listening.

The *Calendar* for May shows a pastoral scene – long-horned, thickly fleeced sheep grazing gentle hills. This was the month of shearing, the shepherds holding the struggling, bleating animals between their knees as they sliced off their wool with broad-bladed knives. Greasy and tangled, its fibres were separated by the women and girls of the village using teasels and spun by hand – spinning wheels would have to wait for three hundred years.

In the June *Calendar* axes are swung into the sturdy trunks, branches lopped off and timber dragged away by ox-cart. The carts themselves, the women's spindles, cups, even plates, were made by a simple pole lathe operated by the feet of experienced carpenters working in villages throughout the country.

The first harvest of the year took place in July – time to cut the grass. Failure could still mean death – the babies, the elderly, the animals. Before the second harvest of corn in August, these weeks could be very lean and may explain various stories of irrational behaviour in rural areas throughout the Middle Ages.

August made everything all right. Ceorls bend and bow in the tall corn on the *Calendar* page for that month, hacking with their sickles, gathering the lifeblood ears in their grateful arms. No children or women are shown, but *everybody* in a local community worked flat out in this month, for as long as there was daylight. The bread that was produced was heavy and coarse by modern standards. It had no yeast and must have been eaten stale more often than not.

September and October were the months of animal slaughter. Each village had its herds of pigs, fed on 'pannage', the roots, acorns and leaves of the forest. These animals were longer in the leg and tougher than their modern counterparts and every bit of the animal was eaten. The corpses were hung in the rafters of smoky huts for slow eating in the leanest months of the darkest winter. By Cnut's time, a pig's intestines were made into tripe, its blood into black pudding, its head into brawn. Its tough hide had the bristles burnt off and cured before being turned into belts, shoes and shield trims. There simply was not enough animal feed to keep all but the strongest animals alive over the winter. The strong spices which would be used to disguise the taste of rancid meat in later centuries – ginger and cinnamon – were not available in anything but tiny quantities; and then were probably used for medicinal purposes. Only salt, as a preservative and flavouring, was widely used and even this was impure and expensive.

November and December saw the villages throughout Cnut's England carrying out essential repairs and maintenance that would keep their harvest and their homes together in the long dark winter. All this year-round toil had a monotony about it, but it was a matter of survival and the laws of England reflected the importance of a rural, agricultural way of life. Ine of Wessex wrote in the eighth century of the importance of meadow and parkland, of the law relating to tree-felling and stray animals. Research over the last generation has abandoned our traditional view of the 'three-field system' of the Saxons and reflects that there was huge regional variation. Significantly, no plough has yet been discovered from the Saxon period. Even the Bayeux Tapestry, stitched *c.* 1070, shows an ard, a simpler, unwheeled form of soil turner. The arable crops well established by Cnut's time were wheat, barley and rye, as well as peas and beans.

Cattle, sheep and pigs were in largest number, although sources say little about them. Occasionally, the *Anglo-Saxon Chronicle* talks of losses of these beasts and Domesday in 1087 talks of plough teams (meaning oxen). From time to time, outbreaks of diseases, something like foot and mouth, wiped out large numbers of animals. The last great outbreak was in the year, ominously, of the millennium. Horses were used for riding – the Church specifically frowned on their being eaten as food. Most of them were between twelve and fourteen hands – a small Arab today in terms of size – and descended from the native breeds like the New Forest ponies. The heavy destriers of William of Normandy's knights at Hastings seem to have been unknown in England. Goats were used for meat and milk; dogs for hunting and herding; cats killed rats and mice; geese and chickens provided eggs, and feathers for pillows.

The ordinary people who populated Cnut's realm were called by Alfred *Angelcynn*, English-kind. In the official records of Cnut's court, they are *Gens Anglorum* and both kings chose to simplify matters by regarding them as members of a single nation. They were tall, fair-haired and blue-eyed, although centuries of inbreeding with the indigenous Romano-British had blurred these racial distinctions. It is difficult to know how long they lived. Men like Forkbeard and Cnut died in their forties or fifties; Ironside in his late twenties. There seemed little rhyme or reason to longevity. Diseases like tuberculosis seem to have increased during the late Saxon period, perhaps because of the growth of relatively large towns. Certainly, scrofula (enlargement of the lymph nodes in the neck) was known by the time of Edward the Confessor (1042–66) and led to the notion of Touching for the King's Evil.[13] The 'new' disease of Saxon times was rheumatoid arthritis and we have no idea why it arose when it did. Many of the outbreaks of epidemic disease are given no natural cause in the records of the time, but they are often associated with famine. Bede and the *Chronicle* both refer to these. Some are probably yellow fever and malaria, in a climate whose summers were much warmer than ours today.

The leechbook belonging to the otherwise unknown man named Bald, probably written a century before Cnut's reign, we have met already and it gives us an insight into how diseases were tackled. Shingles was 'cured' with a mixture of bark from just about every English tree and a rigid diet had to be followed – 'eat neither new cheese, nor fresh goose, nor fresh eel, nor fresh pork . . .' If a man was over-virile, water agrimony diluted in Welsh ale had to be drunk, but only at night. Dog and spider bites were treated with lichen, ferns, pepper and betony, plantain, honey and the white of an egg. Liver diseases were cured by blood-letting (although the symptoms described appear to be appendicitis); headaches were sorted with mustard seed, rue and penny royal rubbed into the temples. Most welcome of all Saxon remedies must have been eating a radish at night while otherwise fasting – it was a sure-fire salvation against a woman's chatter!

Most of these ceorls' lives revolved around their villages, their church and the sheer, grinding slog of survival. The villages burnt so frequently by the armies of Aethelred, Forkbeard, Ironside and Cnut, were clusters of oak-built dwellings, with earth floors, wooden-shuttered windows and thatched roofs. They were dark and damp and smoky with central fires. Repairs on them must have been a constant priority. Their owners ate sitting in circles on the floor, slept on the low straw beds, made love. The women wove on the wooden, upright looms, taught their daughters to do likewise, gave birth. In the winter months, the *Angelcynn* sat cross-legged in their huts playing *taefl*, an early board game not unlike chess. In fine weather, they rode against each other on horseback or raced their dogs. They swam for fun and skated on various degrees of thickness of ice. We know from grave furniture in Cnut's Winchester that their children played with hoops, tops and leather balls. They danced, but possibly in single-sex groups. Women, as we have seen, took part in birth rituals in Denmark – it was perhaps similar in England; although much of their dancing took place in churchyards in connection with the festivities of saints' days. Men may have used dance as part of their ritual training for battle. While none of their music has survived, we know from archaeology that they played simple harp-like instruments and probably sang while working in the fields as well as on their high days and holy days. Metal bells produced a tinkling sound, pipes made from bird bones sounded like shrill whistles. Pipes and flutes were common, examples being found in the Hungate and Coppergate excavations at Jorvik (York). Harps of the English have been found in the extraordinary ship burial at

Sutton Hoo and elsewhere, made from woods of oak, willow and maple. The strings were sheep gut or horsehair.

Bede, writing centuries before Cnut, talks tantalisingly of songs sung and harps played by men who drank with Caedmon on their ale-benches, but we have no idea what they sounded like. They were made from shallow planks with a separate yoke to hold the pegs and with a soundboard nailed across the front. By Cnut's time, the pillar harp, with its peg-arm, soundbox and brightly painted Ringerike monsters, was the most common type, standing perhaps three feet high. Traditionally, the solemn Church disapproved of such frivolous music making, but the author of the poem *The Phoenix* had a different view – music was among 'the joys which God made to gladden man in this sad world',[14] and St Dunstan, who died in the decade before Cnut was born, was, along with his many other talents, a gifted *cithara* player.

Archaeology cannot help us at all in understanding the social structure of Cnut's Engla-land. It is likely that many of the ceorls we have been discussing so far owned slaves. Ten per cent of the population were held in servitude by the time of Domesday and in some regions, the figure was far higher. Most slave men did menial work such as ploughing – the women were dairymaids. In households of high social status, slaves were employed in a variety of tasks. The period of Forkbeard's raids on England and Cnut's subsequent reign probably saw a late and final flowering of the institution as the Vikings transported captives and those not worthy of ransom to slave markets such as that at Rouen in Normandy.

The nuclear family was probably already established. Sons inherited their father's land and daughters had a right to be supported by it. Families helped each other in the communal work on the land, especially at the key times of the farming year – the spring sowing, the harvest, the slaughtering of livestock.

The social structure of the time is difficult to categorise. Like such things in any age, it was subject to subtle fluctuations over time, and in the random evidence of wills and charters, it may be unintentionally distorted. Later generations would base their rank on the ownership of land, but this was not necessarily so in Saxon England. A hierarchy definitely emerges by the seventh century with the slaves, inevitably, at the bottom. A complication exists here, however, because some slaves were merely prisoners of war, but others were slaves by necessity – chronically poor or in debt. The peasants themselves, the ceorls, were freemen with their own land, but there was great variation here, too. One way of sorting out the ceorl tangle is to define the substrata by means of the *wergild* (literally man money) which was paid in compensation to the kin of crime victims. The prices followed a traditional pattern of 1,200-, 600- and 200-shilling people, rather as modern speeding fines vary depending on the motorist's income. The ceorl had land measured in hides (originally meaning household – the amount of land which could physically support a man and his family) and this was roughly 120 acres in tenth-century Mercia for example; elsewhere it was less. Below him in status came the *laet*, whose *wergild* was anything from four-fifths to two-fifths of that of a ceorl. Perhaps a little below the *laet* was the *gebur*, a peasant with a quarter of a hide given to him by the local lord. This level of society was one up from a slave in that *gebwas* seem to have been unable to leave their land without their lord's permission. By Cnut's day there is evidence that freemen had lost many of their rights, giving them away in exchange for protection. That wise and important scholar Archbishop Wulfstan, who helped frame Cnut's laws, wrote: 'Freemen are not allowed to rule themselves, nor to go whither they would, nor to deal with own property as they would.'[15]

By the early eleventh century, there is evidence that the pattern was changing and that the acquisition of land was becoming far more important. The late Saxon kings used a system called bookland. This, before the arrival of the more formal feudal system of the Normans, was one means by which the kings ruled their kingdoms. It was also a means whereby men became great landowners, with all the money and power that that entailed. By Cnut's time, a man had to own at least five hides of land to be 'somebody' in the community. Services to the king or to a lord could be repaid with land – Eadric Streona no doubt hoped to help himself to the confiscated Mercian estates of Morcar and Sigeferth, having had them murdered.

There was no easily identifiable middle class in Cnut's new kingdom. Later centuries would find these groups living in the towns, where commercialism and bustle were the order of the day. We know from the historical and archaeological record that goods were manufactured in English towns and an international trade flourished. The laws of various Saxon kings from the seventh century refer to merchants, how and where they can trade in individual kingdoms and what tolls they had to pay. By the tenth century, the idea of barter, common to all ancient peoples, was already being replaced by coin, although this was intermittent and the direct exchange of goods would take centuries to disappear. The essential exports of England were slaves, metalwork and wool by Cnut's day and although most transactions took place in towns, Domesday records some sixty markets that were held in the countryside, often within the precincts of an abbey or some other religious site. The fairs of medieval England – like Nottingham's Goose Fair and Cambridge's Midsummer – probably had their origins in the eighth and ninth centuries. By Cnut's reign, markets and market towns had spread widely and everyone could purchase commodities there, not merely the rich.

Specialist workers received special status. In a country and a time when precious metals had pride of place, the goldsmith was a seriously rich man. Domesday Book records one of them by name – Theodric – and he held land in three counties. Weapons-makers, blacksmiths, oarsmen, the gleemen who made music and the acrobats who tumbled – all these find mention in various wills and charters of the time, although where they belong in the social hierarchy is difficult to say.

There was no continuity of the urban life that had characterised Roman Britain. It may be that the earliest Saxons were terrified of the very cities they had destroyed because it was not until the seventh century that resettlement began in earnest and then often because such settlements had formed the nucleus of religious centres. Others developed as ports – Wessex had Hamwic (Southampton), Northumbria had Eoforwic (York), Mercia had Lundenwic (London) and so on. Some of these settlements declined or were badly damaged by the arrival of the first Viking Age from the 790s, but had fully revived fifty years later. In the Danelaw in particular, urban growth was rapid. The extraordinary range of finds at Jorvik proves the existence of a manufacturing class with specialised areas for the working of metals – Coppergate for example produced glass, jewellery and cloth.[16] Buildings along the grid-like street plan were in fact shops with storage cellars below ground. Traders were shipping in goods from as far away as the Gulf of Arabia and Samarkand by Cnut's day and neither he nor Forkbeard attacked Jorvik, as though its Viking-influenced culture made it a jewel in their crowns. But York is not unique. Winchester, recently Aethelred's capital and soon to become Cnut's, was also flourishing and must have had its hundreds of merchants and manufacturers. The town was Venta Belgarum to the Romans, the market-place of the Belgae, the tribe whose capital it was. Despite its relative collapse in the fifth century, it is likely that some sort of administrative control continued throughout. In 648, King Cenwalh of Wessex built a church dedicated to St Peter and St Paul, the 'Old Minster' where Cnut was buried. The palace of Aethelred was built nearby and a century before his time, Winchester already had a recognizable street plan, much of it designed by Alfred.

To combat the incursions of the first Viking Age, Alfred of Wessex had initiated a system of burhs or forts to defend stretches of territory. These became the nucleus of towns – the boroughs – in which, increasingly, the Church and men of substance acquired land. Rents and dues from these estates were shared between the local ealdormen and the king. The larger of these properties were *haws*, the name surviving today to mean any domestic building. Domesday Book gives us some seventy boroughs that were not part of Church lands, most prominent among them London, Winchester, York, Chester, Canterbury, Lincoln, Oxford and Gloucester.

Such towns were not yet today's urban centres. Corn mills edged the rivers that meandered through them; gardens and arable plots abounded; open spaces were everywhere; the rolling weald, or the dense forest or the soggy marsh were little more than a spear-shot away.

Inevitably, most information concerning Cnut's England comes from the upper end of the social hierarchy. We have already met the rank of thegn and ealdorman and seen them largely in a military context as war leaders. In practice, thegns were landowners, holding estates by bookland in several areas from the king or by folkland (customary laws of inheritance). These men operated as lords of the manor, overseeing the work of the courts, perhaps as reeves of their shires. They were the most important and powerful social group of Cnut's time. The ceorls were spear-fodder on the battlefield in times of war, yoked to their ploughs on the land in times of peace and so were disposable; we know the names of virtually none of them. The thegns on the other hand were the hirers and firers; before the advent of an ambitious, dangerous, educated middle class, they acted as virtual extensions of royal power into the furthest reaches of a kingdom. Whatever psychological and traditional ploys a man like Cnut could bring to bear as the Lord's Anointed, in essence he was one man and he needed the support and faithful allegiance of his thegns. Slippery ones like the ealdorman Eadric Streona were always trouble.

In the early Saxon period, there were distinctions among this social class, as there were among the ceorls. They were worth up to six times the latter in terms of *wergild* and the most prominent of them became ealdormen often with specific duties at court. Historian Simon Keynes has identified *discòegns*, dish thegns who would have presided over the domestic arrangements of a palace like the one at Winchester, and *burdegns* (in effect butlers) among others who had roles under the king. In return, in a sort of pre-feudal system, the king gave them his protection and favour. 'No one', said a law of Aethelred,[17] 'is to have any jurisdiction over a king's thegn except the king himself.' Archbishop Wulfstan of York defined the status of a thegn half a century before Cnut. Such a man had to have five hides of land, a bell and a fortress gate and a seat in the king's hall.

It was this group with which Cnut would have to work if his reign were to last. He had taken a crown by force and that was never a recipe for lasting success. There was a need for bridge-building, consolidation – and the weeding out of a few problems.

Settling the Kingdom

> The ruler of Jutland let nothing be taken from him when
> he had come to his land. Men were pleased at that.
>
> The *Tøgdrápa* of Sighvat the Skald

The *Anglo-Saxon Chronicle* entry for 1017 establishes very clearly the way Cnut's mind worked:

> Cnut succeeded to the whole kingdom of England and divided it into four: Wessex for himself, and East Anglia for Thurkil and Mercia for Eadric and Northumbria for Eric. And then . . . before 1 August, the king ordered the widow of the former king, Aethelred; Richard's daughter, to be fetched to him as wife.[1]

Almost the only physical description of Cnut comes from the *Knytlinga* Saga of the thirteenth century:

> Knutr was exceptionally tall and strong and the handsomest of men except for his nose, which was thin, high-set and rather hooked. He had a fair complexion and a fine thick head of hair. His eyes were better than those of other men, being both more handsome and keener sighted.[2]

In 1017 he was perhaps twenty-three years old, at the height of his physical strength and he was marrying the widow of his old enemy.

Emma, daughter of Richard of Normandy, may have been ten years Cnut's senior. Portraits of her are unhelpful. Only two are definitely of the twice-queen, both in the conventions of the Winchester School of art with its foliate border and stylised kings, priests and angels. The earlier shows her presenting a gold cross to the New Minster at Winchester in the company of Cnut. She is dressed in the convention of the time, with a many-folded gown lifted by her left hand to show her dark-coloured shoes. She wears jewellery on her wrist and a simple circlet for a crown. Her veil is held aloft by an angel flying overhead and may have religious significance which will be discussed later. The face is plain with a square chin and the merest hint of a smile. The second portrait represents a scene years later and times have changed. The book *Gesta Cnutonis* (The deeds of Cnut), better known as the *Encomium*, is shown being presented to her by the anonymous monk of St Omer who wrote it. He kneels before her, tonsured and humble, offering the work as a labour of love wrapped in a cloth. Her sons, Harthacnut and Edward, hover behind the priest, half hidden by a curtain that is thrown back to reveal the scene. In this picture, Emma is a queen in her own right, sitting on a gilded throne with a jewelled, wide-sleeved robe and a floral crown on her head. Unfortunately, we cannot rely on facial accuracy. The portrait of Cnut in the earlier scene shows a conventional king, with an elaborate cloak, tunic and sword and crown. He has short curly hair and a magnificent beard, but the nose, so prominent in the *Knytlinga*, is small and unremarkable. It is entirely possible that the priestly artists who made these drawings actually saw Emma and Cnut, but realistic interpretations were not the *métier* of the time and the idea of sitting for a portrait lay centuries in the future.

Emma was the daughter of Richard, Count of Rouen, and his Danish wife, Gunnar, and in that sense she and Cnut shared a common ancestry. The Vikings were raiding on the banks of the Seine in the late ninth century and by 911, their leader, Rollo, made a peace treaty with the Frankish king Charles the Simple. In a move which must have seen the great Charlemagne spinning in his grave, the Vikings were given more land as the century wore on – Bayeux in 924, the Cotentin in 933. Such territory was the Frankish equivalent of the Danegeld – land rather than silver – but Normannia, the land of the Northmen, did not survive as an entity for long. Even more than the Danelaw in England, it succumbed to native culture and Christianity very quickly. New settlers in the 940s brought a brief revival of paganism, but Christian burials abound even in that decade. Trade was with Francia and the German territories to the east, rather than with the poorer Scandinavian areas. There was a Norwegian poet in the Norman court in 1025, but to all intents and purposes, the army that crossed the Channel in the September of 1066 with Duke William was French. Their manners, their use of cavalry, even most of their language,[3] had been borrowed from the Franks.

Emma's marriage to Aethelred had been one of pure convenience. The badly advised king was in his mid-thirties and Richard of Normandy's daughter ten or twelve years younger. As Ryan Lavelle says, 'this is hardly to say that Aethelred's new marriage was simply the acquisition of a young trophy second wife as the result of a mid-life crisis'.[4] Normandy was a powerful state in its own right and, harassed as he already was by Forkbeard and his Vikings, Aethelred had need of foreign friends should the going get rough (as indeed it did in 1013). As we have seen, Emma was immediately given the English name Aelfgifu, enormously confusing to us because it was the name of both Aethelred's first wife and Cnut's. The reasons for it are complex; perhaps it reflects a fondness by Aethelred for his first bride or perhaps it was a necessity to stress the fact that the oddly named Emma was, after all, an English queen, thus making it a psychological rechristening.[5] Alistair Campbell, the translator of the *Encomium*, written specifically for the queen after Cnut's death, discusses her name and titles at length. She invariably signed herself Aelfgifu in the various charters, confirming that this was the 'official' name expected of her. Emma was often spelt Ymma and it is possible that the final 'a' was not pronounced.

One of the first 'presents' the young queen received from Aethelred was a grant of land in his capital at Winchester, centring on the still-standing Godbegot House, now a pizzeria and still known in the reign of William the Conqueror as *domus Emmae Reginae* (Queen Emma's house). If Aethelred's wedding to her represents a shift in royal marriages (the previous trend had seen English kings marrying the daughters of thegns), it also marked the beginning of a new power among queens not known in England beforehand. Certainly, Aethelred's mother, the redoubtable Eadgyth, was a prime mover, but she pales in the end beside Emma/Aelfgifu.

The first recorded queen in the Anglo-Saxon period is Bertha, wife of Aethelberht of Kent and, interestingly, she was the daughter of a Frankish king. As a Christian, she was instrumental in 'inclining her husband's mind' to support the mission of Augustine to pagan England. It was highly perceptive of the then pope, Gregory I, to realise that women had this ability to twist their menfolk around their little fingers. Queens were a power in their own right in the early Saxon period, with their own retainers and rights. They were always subject in law, however, to their husbands and their position as widows was highly risky, as Emma discovered in 1016. Some queens seem to have exerted huge influence, but whether through a change in custom or sheer personality is unknown. Cynethryth, the wife of Offa of Mercia, was described as 'dei gratia regina Merciorum' (by the grace of God, queen of the Mercians) and she struck her own coins. In a later generation, Aethelflaed, 'lady of the Mercians', founded schools and was up to her neck in politics. Offa's daughter Eadburh, however, overstepped the mark. Asser, Alfred's biographer, wrote in the 890s that 'she began to behave like a tyrant, to denounce [men] before the king [her husband Bearhtric of Wessex] and this by trickery to deprive them of life or lands, or kill them with poison'.[6]

As the heptarchy developed into a single kingdom by the mid-tenth century, the queen became a solitary figure and infinitely more powerful. It may be that Emma's foreignness prevented her from a greater say in the affairs of Aethelred's reign, but this may have more to do with her mother-in-law's ferocity than any antipathy towards Normandy. Between her marriage to Aethelred in 1002 and his death in 1016 she bore him at least three children. The first was Edward, later king of England and called the Confessor. His veneration and subsequent canonisation was a masterly piece of posthumous propaganda by the monks of Westminster Abbey, the best known of the churches he founded. The atheling Edward was born around 1005. His name Eadward means wealthy guardian and he may have been given it by Aethelred in honour of earlier Wessex kings of the same name. Next came Alfred, born perhaps two years later and destined to die, a murder victim, at the hands of Earl Godwine of Wessex in the tangled political maelstrom that followed

Cnut's death. The girl, Godgifu, or Goda, was born about 1012 and married Drogo, Count of Mantes and the Vexin. On his death, in the same year as Cnut, she married Eustace, Count of Boulogne, badly wounded at Senlac in October 1066. She was dead by 1049. The boys' early years are obscure, but it is at least plausible that some time was spent at their mother's family's court in Rouen. Certainly, in Edward's reign (1042–66), a common criticism of him was his fondness for Norman architecture, Church lands and favourites.

In 1016, both boys ran to the safety of Normandy, realising that their cause, however temporarily, was lost. This decision speaks volumes for the ambiguity of Emma and of her times. The relative ease with which she transferred her loyalty and perhaps even her love to Cnut from Aethelred makes her out as a certain kind of woman. The fact that her own sons fled to their mother's family, where they seem to have been welcomed, tells an entirely different story. Cnut's first biographer, Laurence Larson, refers to her consistently as 'callous Queen Emma'.

We do not know where the ex-queen was in 1017 when she was summoned by Cnut or how much of a surprise this summons was. In the several sieges of London of the previous years, she stubbornly held out against him, anxious to defend her first husband's territory and equally anxious to keep out his pushy son by Aethelred's first marriage, Edmund Ironside. We do not know whether the pair had met before 1017, but it is feasible that they did after the treaty at Deerhurst when it is likely that both of them were in London. Sources are divided over the exact sequence of events. William of Jumièges, writing the *Gesta Normannorum Ducum* in the 1050s, says that Emma was in London throughout and that Cnut effectively bought her out of the siege with her body weight in gold and silver. But he also places the marriage in 1016 and has Ashingdon fought before the death of Aethelred so his chronology is somewhat dubious. The *Encomium* on the other hand, written ten years earlier and at Emma's behest, maintains that she was in Normandy by this time. Modern scholars have doubted this, but it is difficult to see what the twice-widowed queen had to gain by a deliberate lie, unless she was anxious to appear hard to get!

Like the various versions of the *Anglo-Saxon Chronicle*, the *Encomium* is infamous for what it does not say. Clearly, the St Omer monk's brief was to avoid all mention of Aethelred and Emma's previous children. Cnut's wooing of her, therefore, reads like a fairy story: 'Therefore journeys were undertaken through realms and cities and a royal bride was sought.'[7] All she needed was a glass slipper! 'This imperial bride', the Encomiast gushed, 'was . . . found within the bounds of Gaul . . . a lady of the greatest nobility and wealth, but yet the most distinguished of the women of her time for delightful beauty and wisdom, inasmuch as she was a famous queen.'[8]

The wedding probably took place in June or July. There were certainly diplomatic negotiations going on between Cnut and the Norman court in these months, but the Norman chroniclers are suspect in their exact time sequence and it remains debatable whether the marriage had the blessing of Duke Richard or not. It was certainly the custom for widows to wait a year before remarriage, but Cnut had pressing political reasons to push ahead with speed. His alliance with Emma was just that – he maintained her as queen of England with barely a glitch, which was important to some traditionalists, no doubt. And, more importantly, at a stroke he destroyed the succession of Edward and Alfred. Laying aside personal, even sexual considerations, Emma's advantages to Cnut were considerable. Her government of London against his army was impressive – here was a woman with nerve in tough situations. And, as Aethelred's wife and the mother of his children, she probably knew anyone who was anyone in England – vital links for a new, 'foreign' and potentially unwelcome king. The Encomiast raves for nearly two pages on how ecstatic the armies of the English and Vikings were at Cnut's choice, but that hardly makes much sense. As a Norman, Emma was almost as much an interloper as Cnut.

No record survives of the wedding of Cnut and Emma, although it probably took place in the church of St Paul in London. Both had been to altars before, making their vows before God and man; both fully aware of the dynastic contract they were metaphorically signing.

If Emma was willing to give up her sons by Aethelred in favour of her Danish lord and any children she might have with him, what were her motives? We can be sure it was not love at first sight. There was probably nothing of the British queen Victoria and her consort Albert[9] about the match and even if love followed later, this was simply a mutual agreement, the beginning of a symbiotic relationship which would see nearly twenty years of peace and prosperity. A woman like Emma may well have loved power for its own sake. Not for her the obscurity of the veil or the backwater of being the ex-queen of England, gone home to her family in blossomed Normandy. Marriage to Cnut put her back at the hub. She was still probably only in her early thirties – young enough to breed more sons.

But the king of England was married already – to another Aelfgifu, the lady from Northampton, and this raised some ticklish problems of protocol. Divorce was an option, although it is not specifically mentioned in English secular law, for anything other than adultery. The Church recognised it, especially on grounds of impotence. None of this quite fitted the situation. Cnut was clearly not impotent, nor Aelfgifu barren – they had two sons to prove it. Cnut was clearly guilty of bigamy, but this was no furtive fumbling – he had openly married Emma and made her his queen. If there was ever evidence of Cnut's hard grasp of *realpolitik*, it is in his personal relationships. Aelfgifu served her purpose on the Trent when the young heir to Forkbeard needed Northumbrian allies. But that was nearly three years ago. The ealdorman's daughter could not compete with Emma, widow of a king and daughter and sister of dukes. We do not know of course whether the pair actually married. The assumption is that they were living as man and wife at Gainsborough when Forkbeard died and the fleet elected Cnut as his successor. It is likely that both their boys, Swein and Harold, were born by this time. But Cnut clearly had no intention of dismissing his first consort. Her name appears in the *Liber Vitae*, a list of benefactors to Thorney Abbey, and it appears alongside 'Imma Regina' (queen Emma). This may not of course be the same Aelfgifu, the name being common enough in eleventh-century England. But if it is, the implication is that Aelfgifu retained a certain status in her own right, perhaps as the official mistress of Cnut. However much the Church might raise its sanctimonious eyebrows at this situation and whatever kind of hypocrite it made of Cnut, it was not an unusual situation. Royal wives learned to hold their place alongside royal mistresses in the centuries that lay ahead. The king's favourite on the throne was not necessarily his favourite in bed. In any case, Cnut had need of Aelfgifu. She was the mother of Danish princes, still had important Mercian connections and he would have need of her in the years that followed.

Cnut was probably crowned before he married Emma/Aelfgifu and the ceremony is likely to have taken place in London. Ralph of Diceto, writing in the twelfth century as Dean of St Paul's, claims that the event was officiated over by Archbishop Lyfing. Prior to that, Cnut may have gone through an election process at Southampton, presumably by a witan of the local nobility. There is no date for this event and it may have happened before Ashingdon, Southampton having heard of the death of Aethelred and opting for Cnut rather than Ironside as his likely successor.

A coronation was a vitally important event in the life of any heir to a throne, especially one who had recently taken the throne by force. Its importance lay in the legitimising of the king, both in the eyes of men and of God. Cnut's occasionally stormy, paradoxical relationship with the Church we will discuss in a later chapter, but no medieval king could survive for long without its support. The ritual anointing of Christian kings is first recorded in Spain of the Visigoths about 631, and in England Eggfrith of Mercia was 'hallowed to king' in 787. It is possible that Cnut was not anointed at all – neither were his successors, Harold Harefoot and Harthacnut, in their turn. The ceremony may have been purely secular, a repetition of the election at Southampton and nothing more. But if this was the case, why does Ralph of Diceto mention St Paul's and the role of Lyfing? A conqueror as shrewd as Cnut would hardly ruin this chance to win the hearts and minds of his new people, by omitting the Church; they were no doubt looking for some reassurance.

We have no eyewitness accounts of the day, but it would have involved the great and the good of London and as many of the ealdormen, thegns, bishops and abbots as could be crammed into the church on its hill of Ludgate over the Thames, the church that would be destroyed by fire in 1087. Cnut would have made promises, as Aethelred had on his return in 1014, to be a true and faithful lord. Time would tell whether he intended to keep these promises or not. Within months, perhaps weeks, the new king had coins struck, the quatrefoil showing Cnut crowned, with all his power and pomp on display. Aethelred's coins, by contrast, showed him wearing only a diadem, a simple circle of gold. 'In this year also,' says the *Anglo-Saxon Chronicle*, 'ealdorman Eadric [Streona] was killed and Northman, son of ealdorman Leofwine, and Aethelward, son of Aethelmaer the Stout and Beorhtric, son of Aelfheah in Devonshire. And then King Cnut banished the atheling Eadwig and Eadwig king of the ceorls.'[10] What is described here would instantly be recognised by twentieth-century dictators. It is Cnut's version of Josef Stalin's purges and Adolf Hitler's Night of the Long Knives. Streona's duplicity was not likely to go unpunished. Playing the double game as he had been since before Aethelred's escape to self-imposed exile in Normandy, his vacillation at Ashingdon was probably the last straw. According to the *Encomium*, he was killed to encourage the others, 'so that retainers may learn from this example to be faithful, not faithless, to their king'. The *Encomium* records that the man's head was hacked off personally by Earl Yric of Lade, and John of Worcester adds, with what appears to be some delight, that his headless corpse was thrown over London's wall. The Encomiast records Cnut's order to the Viking warlord: '"Pay this man what we owe him." He raised his axe without delay and cut off his head with a mighty blow . . .'[11] In his *Chronicon*, John of Worcester added that Streona was 'a man of low origin, one whom the tongue had brought riches and rank, clever in wit, pleasant in speech, but surpassing all men of the time in envy, perfidy, crime and cruelty'.[12]

This was probably at Christmas time in 1017 and his head was impaled on what is today Tower Hill until it rotted. Revisionists have tried to resurrect the dead ealdorman, stressing his difficulties in the period of Aethelred's decline and Cnut's rise. We need not feel too sorry for him; he was an over-mighty subject himself. Cnut personally ordered his corpse to remain unburied, no doubt so that Londoners who themselves had held out against their new king would learn by experience.

It is possible that others died with Streona. William of Poitiers, writing some sixty years later, claims that Cnut systematically killed all the sons of Aethelred's aristocracy, irrespective of age. But this smacks of a garbled version of Herod and his butchery of the first-born, and the Normans, as we shall see, had no love for Cnut or his memory. The myth of Cnut's savagery dies hard. In 1912, Laurence Larson was still convinced that 'it seems to have been Canute's purpose finally to destroy the house of Alfred [the Great] to the last male descendant'.[13]

The others on Cnut's hit list in the *Chronicle* are more obscure. Northman was the son of Leofwine, 'ealdorman of the provinces of the Hwicce'. The father's name appears on a number of the charters of Aethelred and as a witness to a wedding in 1014. He also figures in the charters of Cnut and seems to have held land in Warwickshire, Hertfordshire and Worcestershire. There is a vague suggestion that Leofwine became ruler of Mercia after Streona's execution, but the evidence is not strong. His sons Eadwine and Leofric ran estates in Mercia too, especially around Evesham and in Worcestershire generally. Leofric became an ealdorman (the Viking term is *jarl*) in the fullness of time and is described by the accounts of Evesham Abbey as 'comes et princeps' (lord and leader) from Worcestershire 'as far as Scotland'. This, if true, seems to be giving the man a vast amount of power; was this Cnut buying the loyalty of a man whose brother he had executed? Did he even regret his actions and are we seeing a sense of guilt in Cnut? The fact that Northman's father and brother continued to serve the new king loyally speaks volumes for the volatile nature of the Anglo-Danish regime. If Northman had been associated with Streona, even his own family might have accepted his death as justified. On the other hand, what was the loss of a rival brother against lands 'as far as Scotland'? And Leofwine had other sons.

Aethelweard was the next to fall foul of Cnut's wrath and his headsman's axe. His father was Aethelmaer, known as the Fat, and it is likely that the son succeeded him about 1016. The problem is that Aethelweard is a common name in Cnut's England and tracing the man is difficult. The reasons for Aethelweard's death are obscure, but they may be linked with another on the list, the enigmatic

Eadwig, 'king of the ceorls'. The last of Cnut's victims listed in the *Chronicle* in the purge of 1017 is Beorhtric, 'son of Aelfheah in Devonshire'. His death at least is easily explained – he was Eadric Streona's brother.

The two others mentioned in the *Chronicle* are the most tantalising of all because we know so little about them. Whereas death was the fate of Streona, Northman, Aethelweard and Beorhtric, exile lay in store for the atheling Eadwig and Eadwig, king of the ceorls. The atheling of course was the son of Aethelred and his continued presence in what had been his father's kingdom and was rightfully his would have caused problems. By 1017, Eadwig was the only son of Aethelred left alive. We have already quoted the will of the eldest boy, Aethelstan, who died on 25 June 1014. Some modern historians claim he died in battle against the Danes, but bearing in mind he had time to ask his father if he might make his will, this seems unlikely. Edgar had died either in 1012 or 1015, as did Edred. Two other sons of Aethelred, Edward and Edric, quite possibly never existed and Egbert had died by 1005.

All versions of the *Chronicle* state that Cnut merely frightened him off – 'put to flight' – except the Abingdon (C) manuscript which adds that he was killed, almost certainly on the orders of Cnut. He was buried in Tavistock Abbey, Devon, but with what ceremony is not recorded. It is entirely possible, as Larson argues, that Eadwig was indeed banished, but his secret return – no doubt to plot to gain a throne he considered rightly his – sealed his fate. Two thegns died with him.

The other Eadwig fascinates because the only mentions of him are in the D and E versions of the *Chronicle*. 'King of the ceorls' implies a peasant leader, a Spartacus, a François Villon, a Che Guevara and perhaps he was a mix of all three. It may not have been his real name – Eadwig, after all, had been a king of England in the 950s, called the 'All-Fair' because of his striking looks. One version of the *Chronicle* has Eadwig's rising – or at least his exile – taking place in 1020 and that is entirely possible (some of the *Chronicle*'s chronology is decidedly shaky). The fact that Aethelweard's death may have occurred then, too, links them rather than Aethelweard and Streona, although why the man should die while his co-

conspirator was merely exiled is unanswerable. It all stems from the various versions of the *Chronicle* and the confusion of names. If Eadwig represents the leadership of a peasant revolt, then it rather puts that of Wat Tyler in 1381 into a certain perspective. With the ongoing raids by both Viking and English armies since 1013, there was a lot for peasants to be angry about – burning buildings, flattened corn, taxation and dead spearmen may have driven Eadwig to desperation. John of Worcester is alone among the chroniclers to record a happy ending for this one – the king of England and the king of the ceorls, he says, were reconciled later.

Edmund Ironside had sons too and Cnut's removal of them reads like a Grimm brothers fairytale. It is possible that the boys were twins, their mother Aldgyth (the murdered Sigeferth's widow) having produced them both by 1016. As such, the babies would present no threat to Cnut, but boys grow. According to John of Worcester, the boys' futures were discussed at the Christmas witan less than a month after their father's death. The articles of the agreement at Deerhurst or an understanding reached afterwards, perhaps put Ironside's family into the care of Cnut in the event of the Englishman's death. After all, the pair had sworn brotherly love and, in theory at least, were running the kingdom in harness until St Andrew's Day and the death of Ironside.

Cnut's decision therefore was to exile them too, presumably with their mother to the 'king of the Slavs' as John of Worcester puts it in *Chronicon*. In fact, his Latin phrase is 'ad regem Suanorum' (to the king of the Swedes) which is probably an eleventh-century 'typo'. John of Worcester hints and Laurence Larson asserts, that the idea was to have the boys killed, rather like babes in the wood, and it was only the tender heart of the 'woodcutter', Cnut's maternal uncle Boleslav Chobri, that saved their lives. Involving a European power, albeit a relative, seems a very protracted way to murder a couple of children. It would be twenty years before the athelings would be of sufficient maturity to stake a claim to the throne and it would be a weak one. Their father had only ruled for a few months and never in practice the whole country. It would be unlikely that any witan would support them, any more than it did William of Normandy in the January of 1066.

The fact that both boys grew up in Hungary must be a result of the alliance between Mieczislav, Boleslav's son and Stephen, king of Hungary, about 1025. Edmund must have lived into his teens, because he had time to marry Hedwig, Stephen's daughter. He was probably dead by twenty and certainly never returned to England. Edward married too; Agatha, the daughter of Bruno, Bishop of Augsburg. By the time he came home to England, Cnut had been dead for over twenty years.

With his immediate enemies dead or in exile, Cnut could now carry out the government of his realm. He took Wessex for himself, probably because of its associations with Aethelred, and this made Winchester his likely home at least in the early part of his reign. Until Elizabeth I all monarchs were peripatetic, the constant moving of the king and his army of retainers the only effective way of keeping an eye on Church and state.

Saxon Winchester was a bustling, vibrant place, boasting not one but two huge minsters side by side. The new church was founded in 901 as part of the town plan of Edward the Elder,[14] himself a tireless defender of England against the Vikings. Edward was buried in the New Minster in 924, having founded the second great religious centre in Winchester, Nunnaminster, later called St Mary's Abbey. Sweeping rebuilding under Edward had led to extension of the monastic lands and in 964 all the clergy of the Minsters were of the Benedictine Order. The Old Minster, where the bones of Cnut lay for sixty years, had as its patron saint Swithun, Bishop of Winchester between 852 and 863. Little is known of the man's life, except that he witnessed a number of charters of King Aethelwulf and may have built a bridge at the town's East Gate. A slightly dubious poem of Cnut's time says that Swithun was chaplain to King Egbert[15] and persuaded Ethelbald to dissolve a marriage with his own stepmother. The legend of the forty days of rain is obscure, but it may be connected with his translation (the exhumation of his body) on 15 July 971. Studious and humble, he had expressed a wish to be buried simply in open ground, but the tomb from which his remains were taken seems to have been a sumptuous one near the Minster's west door. Winchester scholars including Aelfric,

Lantfred and Wufstan all wrote of the miracles wrought at Swithun's shrine and, like Edward the Confessor, he became a cult figure in the late Middle Ages. The Old Minster was enlarged to accommodate Swithun's shrine and a new tower added to the New Minster, perhaps by way of compensation.

Winchester was important to Cnut, not merely as a religious centre, but as the capital of Aethelred. Continuity as well as change was to be vital if the new regime was to win friends. Accordingly, the six mints in the town continued to produce coins bearing the head of the new king. From their designs called quatrefoil, pointed helmet and short cross, they were distributed from many other centres too, but it is unthinkable that Cnut's own headquarters would not have had a certain ascendancy. The dies for coins had probably been cut here since the 970s and Cnut seems to have continued this centralization of coin production as his reign progressed. Kenneth Jonsson records 347 coins of quatrefoil style in Winchester finds, 239 of the helmet variety and 149 of the short-cross pattern.[16] Twenty-nine moneyers worked on the first, nineteen on the second and fourteen on the third. Moneyers at Winchester like Leodmaer and Aegelric were men of status in Cnut's England. Several hundred of their names are recorded in Saxon England and they appear perhaps more important than they actually were because their names are stamped on the coins they made. In Winchester some of them witnessed charters in the reign of Cnut and his son; in York, at least two of them were thegns. Although they probably made the coins themselves, they are the rough equivalent of 'the City' today and in that sense provide the only example of names we know who can be added to the manufacturers and merchants to represent a small but growing middle class.

We know nothing in detail of Cnut's palace or the town's defences at this time. The excavations carried out from the 1960s by Martin Biddle revealed the Saxon street plan and its lack of a link with the earlier Roman site, but the Normans built a castle near the west gate in the 1070s and all the obvious buildings visible today – the cathedral, the gates, the buttercross – are of a later period. It was here nevertheless that Cnut kept his new wife, with her own apartments in Godbegot House, his bodyguard, the *huscarls*, his scribes and his treasury – all the trappings of a successful warrior king on the threshold of greatness. We will discuss them in detail in a later chapter.

Edward the Confessor had a royal prison at Winchester by the 1050s and it may be that Cnut did, too. Oddly, Winchester is missing from the Domesday record, but we know that various priests held houses in the town, as did moneyers, shoemakers, goldsmiths, soap-makers and woodturners. In a fascinating glimpse of everyday life in an age when men often had the same Christian name, their nicknames have survived here – Money-taker, Penny-purse, Clean-hard, Soft-bread and Foul-beard.

It was probably here, about the year 1018, that Emma presented her husband with their firstborn, Hörthaknutr, Harthacnut. The Encomiast, as beholden to this young man as to his mother in 1042, painted a glowing picture of the boy:

> The two parents, happy in the most profound and . . . unparalleled love for this child, sent in fact their other legitimate sons to Normandy to be brought up [!] . . . And so they washed this very dear child, as is the custom of all Christians, in the sacred baptismal font . . . 'Harde' means 'swift' or 'strong', both of which qualities and much more could be recognized in him above all others . . . I cannot enumerate all his excellencies . . .[17]

If Cnut held Wessex as his own preserve, he was happy to give East Anglia to Thurkil the Tall, the redoubtable brother of Strut-Harald the Jomsviking, and this is an example of change in Cnut's kingdom. We have already seen the importance of this man in the years of Forkbeard and the end of Aethelred. He may have come, as Norse legends suggest, to avenge his brother who had previously been killed in England and the *Encomium Emmae* supports this. It was he who presided over, and may have regretted, the murder of Archbishop Aelfheah of Canterbury in April 1012. And it was he who defected speculatively to Aethelred the following year, only to return to Cnut three years later. Whatever sort of reconciliation took place between the two seems to have been genuine in that Cnut was prepared to entrust a valuable area of the Danelaw to him. In the royal charters of 1018 and 1019, Thurkil's name appears first, and there is little doubt that in those years he was regarded by all and sundry as the king's right-hand man. When Cnut was absent in Denmark throughout the winter of 1019–20, he entrusted Thurkil with maintaining law and order throughout the kingdom. It is very likely that, as in Wessex, Thurkil the Viking had underlings who were English and could act as go-betweens to soften the blow of what was, in effect, conquest.

In Northumbria, rule was entrusted to Yric of Lade. Like Thurkil, Yric was a hero long before he set foot on English soil. The son of Hakon Sigurdarson, he had been Thurkil's enemy in the 990s and had helped win the sea battle of Svöld in 999. He and his brother Swein had ruled Norway on behalf of the Danes and he had married Forkbeard's daughter, making him Cnut's brother-in-law. Umpteen dictators from Napoleon to Al Capone have come to realise that family is not always a wise move in employing faithful followers, but Yric seems to have been genuinely loyal and certainly reliable. If the story is true that it was Yric who actually executed Streona, then his loyalty was proven; he suffered flaky fools no more gladly than did Cnut. Yric would rise briefly to be his king's chief adviser in 1022, but from the following year his name disappears from the historical record.

After the execution of Streona, Mercia seems to have divided into smaller areas, probably under the control of various *jarls* appointed by Cnut. Eglaf, for example, was the brother-in-law of Cnut's sister Estrith, and had fought for Forkbeard back in the invasion of 1009. He controlled an area roughly equivalent to today's Gloucestershire, witnessed royal charters up to 1024 and spent much time fighting the Welsh in Dyfed. Ranig held Hertfordshire on Cnut's behalf and appears on charter witness lists between 1018 and 1031. John of Worcester refers to him as 'Hrani [his Viking name] of the Magonsaete' on the rampage in Worcestershire as late as 1041 on the orders of Harthacnut. Worcestershire itself was governed by Hakon, Yric of Lade's son, who had been left behind for a year or so after his father came over to England. The Icelander Snorri Sturluson reported that the boy's hair 'was long and fair like silk'.[18]

We have seen already that Leofwine, whose son, Northman, Cnut executed in 1017, carried out duties in Mercia too, although it is unlikely that he was a straight replacement as ealdorman. Leofric, Leofwine's son, seems to have been altogether more acceptable to Cnut. According to John of Worcester, he 'held him in great esteem',[19] but he seems to have held the job of sheriff in the county. According to the *Anglo-Saxon Chronicle*, 'very wise in divine and temporal matters', he would for ever be associated with founding Coventry Abbey and having a rather odd, exhibitionist wife.[20] There is very little evidence as to how these men governed their territory, but the fragmentation of Mercia was probably a deliberate ploy on Cnut's part. The two men he trusted to govern whole areas – Thurkil and Yric – were his own people, even if one of them had betrayed him earlier. The men we have encountered to replace Streona were likewise Danes, no doubt trusted warriors who had fought with Cnut or his father in the early years. Their appointments were at once their reward for services rendered and a mark of the king's trust in them. It is likely that under each of the four 'rulers' of 1017 – Streona, Thurkil, Yric and Cnut himself – were a whole raft of English thegns and ealdormen who provided continuity and stability in the years ahead. England had need of that. Of Aethelred's leading ealdormen, only two survived Cnut's purge – Aethelweard, who may have clung on until 1020 before being exiled and the dynamic Godwine of Wessex, whose star would rise high under the Viking king. 'And then at Easter,' says the *Chronicle*, 'there was a great assembly in Cirencester . . . and Archbishop Lyfing passed away and in that same year Aethelnoth, a monk and dean at Christchurch [Canterbury], was there ordained as [Arch]bishop.'[21] This was 1020 and in three short years, Cnut had established himself as king, perhaps beyond his wildest expectations. In 1018, the last of the great Danegelds was paid, Cnut's way of paying the army who had stood rock solid on the ridge at Ashingdon. A total of £83,000 was paid, £11,000 of it from London alone, perhaps as a mark of Cnut's displeasure with the town that had held out against him.

'Dane and Englishman came to an agreement at Oxford,' wrote the Chronicler for that year and perhaps the majority of the king's army went home. We have no record of this agreement, but the charters and law codes that followed in the early 1020s were no doubt evidence of Cnut's part of the bargain. The peace of the next seventeen years is evidence of the behaviour of his people. It is possible that throughout this time, Cnut held hostages, perhaps the sons of key players. He had, after all, done this before and slit their noses to remind them of who was master. Perhaps Oxford was the time to let them go.

The Cirencester meeting two years later took place at Easter, on 17 April, and one version of the *Chronicle*[22] says that Aethelweard of Wessex was outlawed, possibly as a result of a decision made by the king and his witan then. Aethelweard is a confusing figure as the name is common – Cnut had already executed another of that name in 1017. This one may have been related to the Aethelnoth elevated to the see of Canterbury in the same year; in which case we once again see the king dividing families, yet receiving support from the branch he did not cut off.

On the anniversary of the battle, the day of St Luke, 18 October, 'the king went to Ashingdon and had built there a minster of stone and lime for the souls of the men who were killed there; and he gave it to his own priest, whose name was Stigand'.[23]

The Hammer and the Cross

On the way, a miracle; water became bone.
The Exeter Book

'When we saw the gift you sent us,' Fulbert, Bishop of Chartres wrote to Cnut, probably in the late 1020s, 'we were amazed at your knowledge as well as your faith . . . since you, whom we had heard to be a pagan prince, we now know to be not only a Christian, but also a most generous donor to churches and God's servants.'[1]

Fulbert of Chartres had hit, no doubt accidentally, on one of the central enigmas of Cnut. The abiding image we have of him is as 'Viking made good' to use Michael Wood's phrase, which essentially means pagan pillager turned to devout Christian. As we shall see, neither of these extremes is strictly true. There is little doubt that Cnut was Christian when he sailed with his father in the dragon-ships bound for the Humber, but his baptism was recent, not from birth, and it is probable that the rank and file of his mixed army of Danes, Norwegians and Swedes in 1016 was still largely pagan.

The Christian Church of the late eighth century feared the Vikings because they attacked monasteries, stole valuables and butchered priests but it feared their gods, too. In Scandinavian mythology, there were two groups of gods, the Aesir and the Vanir, eternally at war with each other a little in the manner of good and bad angels after the Fall in Christian orthodoxy. The Vanir were minor deities, associated with fruitfulness, cupidity, effeminacy and magic. The Aesir were the heroes, with gods like Odin and Thor, Baldur and Loki representing a warrior tradition that almost certainly pre-dates the Viking Age.

Odin was perhaps the first and greatest of the Viking gods. At once all-powerful and sinister, he was in legend the son of Bor, rising to pre-eminence as the raids began against England in the 790s. His one eye represented the brilliance of the sun; the other, floating in the well of Mimir as a gift to the peacemaker, was symbolic of the moon. The Viking warriors loved Odin because he presided over the Einherjar, the glorious dead, in the great hall at Valhalla. It was to him the berserkers prayed as they gyrated on the battlefield, fighting naked and biting their shields. His name means madness. The Viking dead on battlefields from Ashingdon to Byzantium had their souls gathered by the Valkyrie, female demons of death who swooped over the fields on horses of cloud. Like the battle-goddesses of the Celts, they were associated with the raven and the wolf, the *real* scavengers of battlefields, and the souls they raised were taken to Valhalla in the god's home of Asgard. Here, the dead were given drinking horns of mead and bowls of boar stew kept eternally simmering by Andhrimnir the cook in the huge cauldron Eldhrimnir. The walls of Valhalla were hung with shields, helmets, swords and coats of mail, all symbols of a Viking paradise and all in readiness for the last battle of all, Ragnarok, when Odin, his Aesir and his battle-dead would fight the Frost Giants and the loathsome creatures from Hel, the Underworld, the sea monster Jormungand and the terrible wolf Fenrir. The scholar Alcuin of York, who found patronage at Charlemagne's court in the early ninth century, wrote: 'Never before in Britain has such terror appeared as this we have now suffered at the hands of the heathen.'[2] For the Vikings, it was 'an age of lust, of axe and sword, and of crushing shields, of wind and wolf ere the world crumbles', as the skaldic poem the *Voluspá*[3] ran, practice for the final apocalypse. The terror of the last judgement was common to Viking and Christian in the early Middle Ages. The millennium carried fear for Christians, and William the Bastard's survey of 1086–7 was called Domesday because that was what so many of those questioned believed had arrived; they were being called to account.

By the time of Cnut's invasion of 1015, Odin's ascendancy was on the wane and probably the god to whom most of the army prayed on the windy ridge at Ashingdon was Thor, Odin's son. Thor was the thunder god, his mother Fjorgyn, goddess of the earth. If Odin eventually gave his name in English to Wednesday, Thor was the god who was Thursday. Gigantic and fearsome with his mighty hammer and power-giving belt, he could eat a whole ox at one sitting and was drawn across the cold northern skies in a chariot pulled by two goats, Tooth-gnasher and Tooth-grinder. His hammer glowed red-hot, like a thunderbolt, the creation of the dwarf sons of the smith Ivaldi. It was a symbol of luck, rebirth and energy that was at once constructive and destructive. Despite his warlike appearance and behaviour, Thor is associated with the later Viking period – essentially one of settlement – because he represented the colonist and farmer, not the wandering raider. Aelfric of Eynsham, a contemporary of Cnut we shall meet later, wrote that among a company of false gods, their leader 'is among some nations called Thor, one whom the Danish people love most of all'. His only known temple was at Gama Uppsala in Sweden, described by Adam of Bremen late in Cnut's reign as beautiful and gilded. In it were three statues: Thor, who, says the chronicler, controlled the air and the thunder, rain and wind and so the harvest; Odin, the warrior; and Freyr, the god of peace and earthly pleasures (the Vikings called rich cornfields *freyrsakr* after him), who was usually depicted with a huge, erect penis. We can almost hear Adam of Bremen shuddering with horror as he wrote! The Vikings prayed to Odin for victory in the earlier period; to Thor when famine raged; to the playful Freyr for a fruitful dynasty.

Adam's account of the pagan church at Uppsala is important because it was still in use in Cnut's time. Every nine years a massive festival was held, lasting for days, at which each Swedish province had to be represented. Christians as well as pagans had to attend and sacrifices of dogs, horses and even men took place to appease the gods. The quality of Adam's description has the ring of eyewitness authenticity about it and he may well have spoken to people who were there. Certainly, the notion of human sacrifice was common to all Celtic peoples and the curious chemical action of the water-filled peat has given us more 'bog-bodies' in Denmark than anywhere else. By the late Roman period, however, the notion of burying the dead in sacred water had died out and we have no idea what ultimately happened to the victims described by Adam of Bremen.

A bizarre account of a Viking funeral emerges from the time of Cnut's own grandfather and although it took place along the banks of the River Volga, it is likely that most of the elements of it were practised in Scandinavia. Ibn Fadlan was the emissary of the Kalif of Baghdad in 921 and he witnessed the cremation and attending sacrifices of an 'outstanding' man of the Rus, the Scandinavian travellers who later gave their name to Russia. While slave women handmade the garments the dead Viking would be burned in, one of them 'volunteered' to die with him. Vast quantities of an alcoholic drink that the Persian calls *nabid* and may well have been mead were consumed, and while the chieftain's corpse was dressed on the deck of his long-ship which had been dragged ashore and was tended by an old woman called the Angel of Death, the slave girl visited each of the dead man's kinsmen's tents in turn and had sex with them. The ship was then filled with animals for sacrifice – a dog, hacked in half, two horses, two cows, a cockerel and a hen. The girl herself, well doped with *nabid*, was led into the pavilion erected over the body and while the chieftain's retainers banged their shields with sticks to drown out her screams,

> two held her hands and feet; the old woman . . . re-entered and looped a cord around her neck and gave the crossed ends to the two men for them to pull. Then she approached her with a broad-bladed dagger, which she plunged between her ribs repeatedly and the men strangled her . . . until she was dead.

Snorri Sturluson, the Icelandic chronicler writing the *Heimskringla* in the thirteenth century, explained Odin's views on sacrifice:

> He decreed that all the dead should be burned and put on the funeral pyre with all their possessions. He also said that everyone should come into Valhalla with all the property they had on the pyre and he should also enjoy the use of what he himself had buried in the earth, and the ashes should be carried out to sea or buried in the earth and mounds should be raised in memory of men of rank . . . And there should be a sacrifice at the beginning

of winter for a successful year, and at midwinter for regeneration and a third in the summer which was a sacrifice for victory.[4]

But the Vikings who sailed west, south and east in search of plunder and new lands met a new god, not one who revelled in war and demanded sacrifice. He was a just god who had sent his son to earth for the sake of the souls of men more surely than the Valkyrie who came to collect them from the battlefield.

The mark of successful conquerors is a certain tolerance for whatever faith they find locally. The Romans were happy to absorb Celtic deities into their own complex panoply of gods as their empire spread; the Ottoman Turks were able to reach the gates of Vienna in 1683 in part because they left Christianity alone; the wandering Vikings of the eighth and ninth centuries met Christianity wherever they went. Whether into the Frankish kingdom under Rollo or in the service of the Byzantine emperor in the Varangian guard, the symbol of the cross was everywhere and it replaced Thor's hammer as the amulet par excellence. Archaeological finds have frozen this transitional moment in time. A tenth-century silver amulet was clearly made for someone hedging his bets spiritually – a dragon-headed hammer has a cross motif cut into it and a soapstone mould from Trendgården in Jutland in the same century has apertures for making both the hammer and the cross; profit was a very useful by-product of toleration!

No doubt the earliest converts to Christianity embraced the faith only superficially. Helgi Eyvindarson was one of the first Vikings to reach Iceland; though nominally a Christian, calling his farm Kristnes (Christ's Headland), he prayed to Thor before sea journeys. When Alfred the Great forged his treaty with the Viking Guthrum in 892, part of the deal was that the man became a Christian, with Alfred as his godfather. Baptism at sword-point was not likely to produce true converts. Actual conversion was brought about in Denmark by slow, relentless pressure from the Frankish empire of Charlemagne and his successors and the archbishopric of Hamburg-Bremen to the south. More spectacular was the proselytising work of the 'Apostle of the North', Ansgar, a Frankish Benedictine monk from Picardy. He set up a Christian school, perhaps at the Danish border town of Hedeby in the late 820s, and a church there thirty years later. Born in 801, Ansgar was perhaps twenty-five when he began his mission. Surviving hellish sea journeys and a great deal of Danish hostility, he was consecrated Archbishop of Hamburg in 831 and was made papal legate to the people of the North. Narrowly escaping death at the hands of a Viking attack in 845 possibly gave the man the determination to try again, this time at Ribe. Subsequent events proved that Ansgar's mission had no permanent success. The settlement at Ribe was swept away and by 900 the Danes were once again pagan.

The Vikings had an ethical code of their own, with a fierce regard for courage, strength, faithfulness, honesty and hospitality. They are all clearly expressed in the Eddic poem *The High One*, as is the notion of salvation:

> Cattle die, kinsmen die,
> Finally dies oneself;
> But one thing I know that always remains,
> Judgement passed on the dead.[5]

Even so, all this was older and harsher than Christianity. Revenge was a sacred obligation, clashing inexorably with Christ's urgings to forgive. While the biblical Jesus was 'suffering little children', Viking mothers were laying their weak and unwelcome offspring on a bleak hillside to die.

It was Cnut's great-grandfather, Gorm, who found himself faced with the next missionary. Archbishop Unni of Bremen ventured into Denmark in the 930s, but failed to impress the strongholds of Thor. Harald Bluetooth was more receptive, allowing himself to be baptised having been fascinated by the conjuring tricks of the missionary priest Poppo. The man seems to have willingly undergone an ordeal by fire to prove the power of his god. In this, Poppo would have held a red-hot iron in his hand until he could stand the pain no longer and his wounds would have been bound. If they failed to blister (or at least healed sufficiently) within three days, either a felon's innocence was proclaimed or God's kindliness shone through. Within a few years, Bluetooth proudly proclaimed on the royal runestone at Jelling: 'It was this Harald who won for himself all Denmark and Norway and made the Danes Christians', and a crucified Christ is carved alongside, his hair a tangle of Ringerike extravagance.

Exactly how Bluetooth achieved Christianity for his people is not known. The historical record is particularly sparse for the late tenth century in Denmark, but we know that churches were built and bishoprics established at Ribe, Hedeby and Århus. Again, the change was not totally permanent. In the early years of Forkbeard's reign, there seems to have been a partial return to paganism, which probably explains why Cnut was not baptised at birth. Forkbeard's religion seems to have fluctuated with the winds. Laurence Larson says, tongue-in-cheek, that 'Sweyn's religion was of the passive type'.[6] At one point he is known to have sent an English missionary, Godebald, to work in the north-eastern province of Skåne and to become its bishop; on other occasions, he probably wore the hammer of Thor around his neck.

A remarkable amount of hybrid carving has survived from this transitional period. The cross at Gosforth in Northumbria has bas-reliefs from pagan mythology, perhaps Thor killing the terrible dragon Midgardsorm. The Middleton cross in Yorkshire shows a Viking warrior with his conical helmet, his sword, axe and spear as though this is the closest he is allowed to come in a Christian society to taking his grave-goods with him. Even in Cnut's Winchester there were stone carvings in the Old Minster, now in the city museum, which show the hand of God, but they also portray a scene from the *Volsungasaga*, of Sigrid slaying monsters. This was almost certainly commissioned by the king.

As Cnut's biographer M.K. Lawson points out, 'In matters of religion he was largely obliged to play an English game, with English men and by English rules.'[7] His own religious background was mixed and the fact that doubts linger over his piety may be based in part in the now-lost knowledge that Englishmen once had about the date of his baptism. It may have been in his early teens or even later that he was given the baptismal name of Lambert and this suggests the event happening on 17 September, the feast day of St Lambert of

Maastricht. Adam of Bremen records the name and the implication that Lambert was a German saint, so that Cnut may have been baptised by a German churchman. Adémar of Chabennes wrote that Cnut became a Christian after the conquest of England, but although he was a contemporary of Cnut,[8] he lived and wrote in Aquitaine, altogether less in touch with Anglo-Danish events than Adam in the bishopric of Bremen. It may be, then, that the king of Christian England had only been a Christian himself for six years. What a shrewd judge of situations like Cnut cannot have missed, however, is the huge and growing importance of the Church in his kingdom; it was a force and he had to reckon with it.

The original missionary work of Augustine and his followers in bringing Christianity to the 'edge of the world' as the Romans had once called Britain was all but destroyed by successive waves of pagan Saxon incursions, but by the seventh century, the cross had returned in the form of ever larger monasteries and parish priests who were almost the locals' sole source of news and education. These secular priests spoke and wrote English and by the time of Domesday, the parish church, shaped like a cross and made of stone, was a reality all over the country.

People were simple in their needs and aspirations. They accepted fables as the truth and found nothing remotely suspicious about the tall tales of the powers of saints to make the blind see and the crippled walk. In Cnut's own Winchester, the walls of the Old Minster were hung in his day with crutches discarded by those ecstatic born-again walkers who had prayed at the shrine of St Swithun.

Two facts must have quickly borne in on Cnut in 1017: the Church was rich and the Church was political. William the Bastard's Domesday survey gives us the most realistic guide to the former. Canterbury, sacked by Forkbeard and vandalised by Thurkil, had recovered to the extent of an annual revenue of £1,750 by 1085. Cnut's Winchester was valued at over £1,000. The huge monasteries were worth nearly as much, amounting to some 15 per cent of the total land value in the country. Much of this wealth came from rents but it was also received with all humility by a Church only too ready to let men buy their way into heaven. Most of Aethelred's ealdormen had bequeathed land, cash and beautiful objects to monasteries and churches; Cnut and his jarls, even the Viking ones, would do the same.

In the fifty years before Cnut's invasion, there had been a monastic revival, a drive for purity and divinity lacking in the Church in Bede's time three centuries earlier. Men and women gave themselves to the service of God, living in secluded mausolea, growing their own crops and fishing their own ponds. They wrote and prayed in Latin, sang in divine services throughout the day and night and slept in freezing cells on hard wooden boards. This movement, however, had got no further north than Lindsey, and in the old Danelaw, paganism may have lurked on moor and fell long into Cnut's reign and even beyond. *The Law of Northumbrian Priests*, probably written in the 1020s, forbids the worship of idols and frowns at the lingering obsession with weirdly carved stones, trees and wells, symbols of pagan cultism everywhere.

We shall be discussing Cnut as a law-giver in a later chapter, but in the context of the Church, it seems appropriate to discuss these ecclesiastical laws here. As with legislation covering the laity, it is likely that the guiding hand was that of Wulfstan, Archbishop of York, the *éminence grise* to whom the young king often turned. Many of the offences listed were punishable by fines – 20 ores for disregarding a bishop's orders; 12 for ignoring an archdeacon. No priest could carry out communion without wine, or serve it in a wooden chalice. He could not neglect his church, go unshaven or fight another priest. He could not condone or cover up crime in his parish. Although marriage was allowed, adultery was most definitely not – 'let him be anathema'.[9] It was the priest's job to ensure that the papal tax known as Peter's Pence or Rome-pennies was collected. He was not to allow bigamy in his parish and any sleeping with nuns would result in both parties paying *wergild*. 'Blessed be the name of the Lord,' ran the Epilogue in the *Law of Northumbrian Priests*, 'from now and into eternity.' This was one of the few phrases written in Latin.

The political ties of the Church stem largely from the fact that priests, especially those destined for high office, came from those very families whose secular members were ealdormen and thegns. Bishop Eadnoth, who died at Ashingdon, had been a monk at the rich and important abbey of Ramsay and was eventually its abbot. He was presumably there among Ironside's troops at the hill of ash trees in a religious capacity, but he was a political figure too. Dwarfing all such ecclesiastical figures in Cnut's reign is Archbishop Wulfstan of York, whose *Sermon of the Wolf* is one of the surviving masterpieces of medieval writing.

We can catch little today of the visual appearance of Cnut's Church. The minster on the hill at Ashingdon where his men fell has been added to many times over the centuries. That at Deerhurst where he made his peace with Ironside has suffered a thousand years of architectural vandalism. The Minster at Winchester which he would have known is a series of concrete diagrams in the grass and the cathedral's triforium is suspended on arches the Normans built forty years after his death. But this should not detract from the fact that the Church was a powerful visual symbol in Cnut's kingdom. As yet the only buildings to be made entirely from stone, churches were built on east-west axes on high ground – visible to man and close to God – the abbey at Shaftesbury being a prime example.

The most impressive element of Cnut's Church was the multiplicity of monasteries, which Augustine famously called *civitati dei*, cities of God. They usually had a bank and ditch surrounding them – the earliest were often on the sites of Roman camps or Iron Age hill forts; again, Shaftesbury is a case in point. After a certain decline in size and opulence in the ninth century, such sites emerge bigger and bolder in the tenth and eleventh. There were stone cloisters at Glastonbury where Ironside and many of his ancestors lay buried, at St Augustine's Canterbury and at Cnut's own Winchester. Other outbuildings tended to be of oak, thatch, wattle and daub and have not survived.

The life of a churchman, wrote the homilist Aelfic of Eynsham, 'shall not be like that of laymen'.[10] A man of God who refused to stop fornication risked loss of property and burial in unconsecrated ground in the mid-tenth century, as the Northumbrian priests' law says. He must avoid drink, hunting, flashy clothes and tangles with the law – all the things of course which Chaucer's ecclesiastical pilgrims to Canterbury would be busy doing four centuries later.[11] It did not help those who wished to keep Church and state rigidly separate that Archbishop Wulfstan of York was offering a thegn's *wergild* in exchange for chastity, thereby encouraging a taste for the secular life he was probably trying to avoid. We do not have to wait for the Church's Reformation critics to appear; Cnut's contemporaries carped about the laxity of churchmen's morals too and their lack of education.

Unlike his later medieval successors, Cnut did not have a pushy pope keen to organise his church. Not until the 1070s did the pontiff intervene – and Cnut's old friend Stigand lost his post as Archbishop of Canterbury. Instead, the king had to deal with a series of archbishops, bishops and abbots which in a way made his job more complex. The monastic reforms of the previous half-century that saw the foundation of forty monasteries were a real attempt to upgrade the moral fibre of the Church and if we accept that this was genuine, there is no reason to see undue hypocrisy in Cnut's behaviour to God and his Church. There is no actual evidence for this. The *Regularis Concordia*, the rules of the Benedictine Order redrawn under King Edgar, laid down what was expected of monks. This clearly did not apply to kings and Cnut was in no sense 'head' of the Church. Hence his continuing to wage war with or without church approval and even to hang on to the Northamptonshire Aelfgifu despite his marriage to Emma. The fact was that Cnut and his Church shared a symbiotic relationship. He needed it to give his reign legitimacy, hence his Christian coronation officiated at by Archbishop Lyfing and his probable confirmation by Archbishop Aethelnoth; and it needed him to be a bountiful benefactor. Laurence Larson summed it up admirably in 1912:

Canute selected the long-established, the widely-influential shrines and houses and gave his favour chiefly to them. In return he doubtless expected the favour of Saints Cuthbert, Ealfheah, Edmund, Felix and Dunstan and the support of Canterbury, Evesham, Winchester and the other great institutions that he endowed.[12]

Cnut was good at this – so good, perhaps, that it led to the charges of hypocrisy. According to the *Encomium*, with much crying and pounding of his chest, he gave lavish presents to the monastery of St Omer on his pilgrimage to Rome in 1027. According to Symeon of Durham,[13] the king walked barefoot the 5-mile trek to the church of St Cuthbert towering over the loop in the Wear. His most famous gift is the gold cross given to the New Minster. We have described it already in an attempt to picture the king's physical appearance, but the frontispiece to the *Liber Vitae* of Winchester has deep religious significance, too. Historian Jan Gerchow of the Max Planck Institute of Göttingen examines this at length in his essay 'Prayers for King Cnut'.[14] The king and queen stand on either side of the Winchester altar. Above, flanking Christ in Majesty are the New Minster's patron saints, Peter and Mary. In thanks for the cross, Cnut receives a crown from an angel. It appears to have the arched headpiece common to the crowns of Frankish kings. Emma, perhaps standing on the right side of the cross because she was a church benefactress in her own right, receives a veil, even though she is already wearing one. This is, perhaps, symbolic of the *stola secunda*, the cloth that formed part of Christ's dress at the Last Judgement. The 'foreign' crown and the picture of husband and wife smack of Frankish and German examples from the period and it may have been Cnut's intention to identify himself with the emperors of those lands, because he was an emperor, too. Gerchow goes further and contends that the *Liber Vitae* portrait was also made to commemorate Cnut's coronation. The gilded cross itself, of huge proportions if we can trust the drawing's scale, is a plain version of the Lothar cross at Aächen. In fact the Winchester cross was hollow and contained relics. It was melted down in the twelfth century according to William of Malmesbury to provide 30 pounds weight of gold and 500 of silver. A similar cross was given to the monastery at Abingdon, itself rebuilt on the lines of that at Aachen: 'King Cnut and Queen Aelfgifu commanded the making of this reliquary from 230 gold mancuses,[15] refined by fire and two pounds of silver of great weight.'[16] At Wilton, which his father had sacked, he ordered a gold shrine dedicated to St Eadgyth, the former abbess; he may have given the splendid York Gospels to Wulfstan; he certainly bought the right arm of St Cyriacus, the Bishop of Ancona, martyred under Hadrian, for an astonishing 100 marks and had it encased in gold and silver before presenting it to the abbey at Westminster. He gave three manors to the monastery of Saint Benet Hulme; a richly embroidered black chasuble to mark the translation of Abbot Wistan of Evesham, martyred in the ninth century; and individual gifts to churchmen like Bishop Burhwold and Bishop Lyfing of Crediton.

Such gifts were important. First, they established Cnut as a kind benefactor; the eleventh century was not as cynical as we are to see him buying his place at God's right hand. Second, it represented an act of continuity with earlier kings – Aethelred and his predecessors for centuries had done the same. And third, it speaks volumes for the obsession of this and later ages – martyrs, saints and shrines.

As early as the second century, the bodies of those who had died for their faith or led exemplary lives as 'confessors' were held in great veneration. Two hundred years later, those bodies, or parts of them, were for sale on the open market in *scrinia*, reliquary chests, which were usually placed on church altars. The Frankish habit of venerating high churchmen and women led to the creation of cults, their bodies being embalmed and 'translated' to a more religious site, often behind a high altar. The bodies of Swithun at Winchester, Aethelthryth at Ely and Cuthbert at Lindisfarne, all travelled in this way. Contemporary commentators could only write in awe that in each case the corpse was miraculously 'uncorrupted', that is fresh, which was taken as evidence of the deceased's purity. Cnut's shrine to Eadgyth at Wilton was adorned with New Testament scenes of Christ in triumph, perhaps in the Ringerike art style similar to the small panel found at Winchester and now in the triforium of the cathedral there.

Swithun we have discussed already; Eadgyth we will discuss in due course. Cuthbert was the seventh-century missionary and abbot of Lindisfarne for whom the magnificent gospels were written. Churches were dedicated to him from the Trent to the Clyde and his body was transferred from Lindisfarne in 875 to save it from Viking raids. Seventeen years before Cnut became king, it was finally moved to Durham, working daily miracles until the Reformation destroyed the corruption of the Catholic Church and with it, the magic. His tomb nevertheless escaped destruction and when opened in 1826, the skeleton was still intact wrapped in richly embroidered silk.

Aethelthryth was the twice-married, but nevertheless virgin, wife of two kings of East Anglia in the seventh century. She founded the monastery at Ely and lived a life of austerity there before cancer of the neck killed her. She attributed the illness to God's displeasure at her wearing necklaces as a girl. Her shrine was enormously popular and a poem about her was written shortly before Cnut's time in the *Liber Eliensis* by the poet Aelfhelm.

The huge list of martyrs to whom Englishmen prayed exists in fragmented form from the time of Bede. Over two hundred such saints are listed, all of them having provided ample evidence of miracles being performed in their name. The lung of Edward the Martyr was preserved, still breathing, in a glass jar in the abbey at Shaftesbury, where Cnut himself would lie in state in 1035. It is beyond the scope of this book to examine the gullibility of otherwise intelligent men who attested to this nonsense. Some of it was genuine piety, some of it a lack of scientific knowledge; some of it was with the active duplicity of the Church. Ownership of a saint's body or even part of one meant pilgrims and patronage; it was worth mixing a little pig's blood in a phial every now and again for that. Not only monasteries and abbeys, but towns grew rich as a result. The high street of St Albans in the 1970s boasted no less than twenty-six public houses, most or all of them the vestiges of the inns for pilgrims built in the Middle Ages for those visiting the shrine of the Roman soldier who was Britain's first Christian martyr. It was this profiteering – and the loss of income involved in the translation of a saint's bones – that probably led Cnut to have an ostentatiously armed presence of *huscarls* in London in 1023. Canterbury may have been gaining a saint, in the coffin of St Aelfheah, but London was losing one.

The list of relics of Waltham Abbey, contained in a fourteenth-century book but alluding to the eleventh century, gives us an astonishing idea of the number and diversity of objects and body parts associated with saints. The Abbey of the Holy Cross was established by Harold Godwinesson, a boy in Cnut's reign, who would go down fighting in the centre of his shield wall at Hastings, and it probably took 200 years to obtain all 462 of the relics listed. The Abbey itself is linked with Cnut because it was during his reign that a rood (cross) was found buried on a hillside at Montacute in Somerset, on land belonging to Tofig the Proud, one of Cnut's Viking jarls. We know the crucifix was lifesize because Tofig hung his sword around the waist of Christ, itself an act of giving and veneration since a thegn's sword would have been very valuable. Nails could not be driven into the wood of the cross, but when driven into Christ's right arm, drew blood. Tofig had the cross sheathed in silver and Christ given a crown and anklets of gem-encrusted gold.

It may be that the Montacute cross, which casued a huge stir in Cnut's time, was a relic hidden from attack in the first Viking Age in that it had clearly been carefully buried.

Of the other relics at Waltham, several were given by Harold as Earl of Wessex and perhaps during his brief reign as king. Two, we know, came from Cnut's Winchester – a relic of St Swithun and another of St Cecilia. Both the Old Minster and Waltham claimed to have parts of the tomb of Lazarus. Other objects included some of the chains of St Peter and part of his beard, the bones of St Pancras, the hair of Martha and Mary and even a few scraps left over from the miracle of the loaves and fishes, contained, again miraculously, in their original baskets!

Three years before he died, Cnut rode across country to the abbey at Glastonbury to do homage at the tomb of Edmund Ironside. This was Arthur's legendary Isle of Avalon and would still, in Cnut's time, have been surrounded by water on three sides. The abbey of St Mary was probably founded in the reign of Ine in the early eighth century and archaeological investigation has uncovered the existence of a wattle and daub church, later encased in lead, which was certainly standing at the time of Cnut's visit. There was glass-making in the abbey and a huge *vallum* or rampart and ditch around its perimeter. Under Abbot Dunstan, the great churchman who was perhaps the prime mover in the tenth-century monastic revival, considerable new buildings were erected, notably a large cloister. Glastonbury was one of the richest abbeys in the country, owning twelve hides with a number of outlying chapels. On the famous Tor itself, there were tiny monastic cells and a timber church. At nearby Beckery, there were chapels and a cemetery containing forty-six bodies, all but three male, probably the generations of monks who lived there in the seventh to ninth centuries. Of the graves of the Saxon kings Edmund, Edgar and Edmund Ironside there is now no trace. The wrecking influence of the Henrician Reformation was witnessed by a fifteenth-century gothic church which must have dwarfed that of Cnut's time.

On 30 November 1032, the king arrived with his retinue and laid a superb cloak, decorated with peacocks' feathers, on the tomb of Ironside. This was a symbolic gesture par excellence. The peacock was special to both Christian and pagan sensibilities. M.K. Lawson records that it was found on royal trinkets associated with Aethelwulf of Wessex two hundred years earlier; it was also, in the form of birds' bones, found in the hull of a ship buried in ninth-century Gokstad in Norway. What is most intriguing of all is that the exotic bird was a common design on silk robes from Byzantium and one such robe may have been given to Cnut by Emperor Conrad II at the latter's coronation in 1027. It is likely that all through his reign, the suspicion clung that Cnut had had Ironside murdered in the weeks after Deerhurst. The peacock represented resurrection. If the cloak came from Conrad, it may even have represented a dual honour – had Ironside lived, he too would have been present at this coronation. William of Malmesbury records Cnut being very moved by this ceremony. He called Ironside his brother and knew very well that he was honouring an English hero whose sons were still alive.

Edward was another focus of Cnut's piety. The martyr's association with Aethelred gave an immediacy to the Danish king's actions. The boy was eighteen when he was murdered, with or without his mother's complicity, on 18 March 978 in the 'gap of Corfe'. His body was buried hurriedly then at Wareham, but exhumed some months later by Ealdorman Aelfhere, who had it solemnly reinterred at Shaftesbury on its windy ridge. In 1001, the body was translated and the lung that William of Malmesbury saw still breathing 200 years later, placed in a glass bowl. Today, the shrine of Edward is a modern, simple stone sarcophagus placed on the grass where the high altar would have stood. The abbey's museum exhibits a lead casket, 3 feet long and a foot high, which contains the prince's bones; it was found in the excavation of the

North Transept in 1931. Cnut placed a great deal of importance in
Edward, whose 'martyrdom' only became apparent because of the
miracles associated with his shrine. It is possible that the king
endowed Shaftesbury and even that he ordered its rebuilding;
certainly it is no accident that he died here in 1035. The laws he
drafted with the help of Wulfstan celebrate Edward's feast day and
he gave relics of the man to Westminster Abbey. This was not the
magnificent church that stands today and recorded in the Bayeux
Tapestry, nor the building associated with Edward the Confessor,
but a more modest satellite of St Paul's. Dunstan, avid rebuilder that
he was, refounded it in 959 as a Benedictine house. To this abbey
too, Cnut gave the arm of St Cyriacus and the finger of St George.[17]
It may be that in his espousal of Edward the Martyr, Cnut was
making a political statement. The boy should have been king, but
murder had prevented this. All kings of England up to and including
Charles I had to remind their subjects that the king's life was sacred
– take it at your peril.

Aelfheah was performing miracles from beyond the grave by
1023. The archbishop had been beaten to death by Swein
Forkbeard's Vikings in April 1012, probably because of his
arrogance in refusing to be ransomed. Buried first in St Paul's and
translated to his own church at Canterbury, the Worcester
manuscript of the *Anglo-Saxon Chronicle* tells what happened:

In this year [1023] King Cnut in London in St Paul's minster gave
full leave to Archbishop Aethelnoth and Bishop Brihtwine and all
servants of God who were with them that they might take up
from the tomb the archbishop St Aelfheah. And they did so on 8
June and the glorious king and the archbishop and the diocesan
bishops, all the earls and very many ecclesiastical and also lay
people conveyed his holy body by ship over the Thames to
Southwark and there entrusted the holy martyr to the archbishop
and his company, and they then with a distinguished crowd and
pleasant joy took him to Rochester. Then on the third day Emma
the lady came with her kingly child HathaCnut and they then all
with great pomp and joy and songs of praise conveyed the holy
archbishop to Canterbury and thus brought him worthily into

Christ Church on 11 June. Afterwards, on the eighth day, on 15 June, Archbishop Aethelnoth and Bishop Aelfsige and Bishop Brihtwine and all who were with them placed St Aelfheah's holy body on the north side of Christ's altar, to the praise of God and the honour of the holy archbishop, and to the eternal salvation of all those who daily seek his holy body there with devoted hearts and with all humility. May God Almighty have mercy through the holy merits of St Aelfheah.[18]

There are relatively few entries in the *Chronicle* as a whole for the reign of Cnut and this is by far the most detailed account of Aelfheah's translation available. Such pomp and circumstance must have attended all the king's visits to shrines however; an army of clerics, footsoldiers, thegns, scribes and hangers-on traipsing the countryside to be gawped at by ceorls in their furrows.

Osbern, the eleventh-century precentor of Christ Church, adds a gloss which throws a rather different light on the ceremony. Cnut had something of a love–hate relationship with London. It had held out against him and his father before 1017 and he exacted a separate and very heavy Danegeld from its inhabitants. There may have been ongoing tensions into the 1020s. According to Osbern, Cnut's *huscarls* were there in numbers at the time of Aelfheah's translation. Was this mere protocol or did the king expect trouble? If Aelfheah was a martyr at all, he was a martyr in English eyes and it was Cnut's father's men who had killed him.

St Edmund may also have served a political purpose. East Anglia had been particularly badly hit by the Viking raids from the 880s. From Maldon to Ashingdon, the great and good of the area had gone down before the axes of the Northmen and there were bridges to be rebuilt. It is difficult to construct a detailed chronology of Cnut's reign, but it is likely that he went to work on the East Anglian saint's shrine in the same year that he built the church at Ashingdon, 1020. It cannot be chance that Cnut had St Edmund's new church consecrated on St Luke's Day. Killed, probably by defeat in battle, by a Viking force in 869, Edmund's remains were taken to the burial place of an earlier king, Sigeberht, at Bedricesweord, renamed the fortress of Edmund in his honour. Secular priests tended the shrine until 1020 when Cnut stepped in to replace them with Benedictine monks and to build a new rotunda to house the saint/king's shrine. The story told by John of Worcester, that Swein Forkbeard died, not of natural causes, but by being skewered by a supernatural spear from the ghostly Edmund, may have been widely believed at the time and if so, here was Cnut carrying out a particularly magnanimous gesture.

The dead saint was exacting revenge, allegedly, not only for his own death, but for the bad treatment of the monks tending his shrine in 1013–14. A trench was dug around the perimeter of St Edmund's chapel on Cnut's orders beyond which no tax was to be paid. Legend says that Queen Emma gave an annual gift of four thousand eels from her estate at Lakenheath nearby. In a very real sense, Cnut actually founded one of the most important shrines of medieval England.

Cnut's relationship with the Church was not always so benign. Although the monks of Ely composed Cnut's Song[19] for the arrival of the royal ships, their abbot may well have clashed with the king – Cnut had, after all, attacked the place in 1016. At Ramsay in Lincolnshire, there must have been little love for the man – their abbot, Wulfsige, had gone down fighting at Ashingdon. But an incident occurred here according to the Peterborough chronicler Hugh Candidas which led Cnut to demand the monastery be torn down and its monks kicked out. The king was apparently furious at whatever crime some of the Ramsay men had committed, but Aelfsige and the queen intervened and persuaded Cnut to change his mind. On the positive side, he may well have laid charters on the altar of Christ Church Canterbury, as the shadowy *scriptorium princeps* (chief scribe) known as Eadui Basan suggests.

All English kings since Edgar had patronised the Church and for the same reason – churchmen were impressed by generosity (what Cnut's skaldic poets called 'destroying treasure'; in other words, spending madly) and they in turn would pray for the king's soul. Sometimes, no doubt, Cnut promoted churchmen because they came from families who were important to him in a political sense – Brihtheah became Bishop of Worcester probably because he was related to Cnut's right-hand churchman, Wulfstan of York. At other times, men seem to have been promoted internally, either with a bishopric or an abbey. Aethelnoth was given the see of Canterbury in 1020 perhaps because his father was Aethelmaer, ealdorman of Wessex and the brother of the Aethelweard beheaded on Cnut's orders in the purge of 1017. Duduc was a royal appointee, made Bishop of Wells in 1024; Aelfwine got the job at Cnut's own Winchester the previous year.

Occasionally, he clashed openly with his Church, not in the systematic way that Henry II did two centuries later, but now and again, as a result of what may have been Viking temper. According to the chronicler Goscelin who came from the great monastery of St Omer in France many years after Cnut's death, the king was full of veneration for the shrine of St Eadgyth, to which he gave a gold cross. William of Malmesbury, however, says that Cnut's visit led him to berate the dead woman by saying that a lecher like Edgar could never be the father of a saint. Outraged, Archbishop Aethelnoth argued with him and Cnut ordered the tomb torn open then and there to see if the body was corrupted or not. It clearly was not, says Malmesbury, because the corpse was in such good condition that it leapt to its feet and attacked Cnut, knocking him out! Such stories are the stuff of superstitious churchmen as terrified of the supernatural as the peasants who were their flocks, but they occasionally have a smattering of truth. Perhaps Cnut did insist that the tomb be opened to prove the saint's veracity before spending money on her shrine. What happened next belongs to William of Malmesbury's gullibility and imagination.

What we are left with in examining Cnut's links with his Church is, in the end, an enigma. There is little doubt that he saw the need to work with the Church, as a powerful institution within his new kingdom. He may have been a genuine convert, as his late baptism with the name Lambert suggests. And there is no hard evidence that he was any more cynical than any other medieval ruler, on either side of the Channel, who gave gifts to his Church and so to his God. At a time when other Viking leaders, like Olaf the Stout, were insisting on a rigidly Christian line in all that they did, Cnut, however, was happy to let his poets link him with the old Norse gods: 'The prince, the battle-bold reddener of the mail shirt of the breast, alone rules England and Denmark; peace becomes easier. The Freya of the warrior has also cast under him Norway; the battle-server diminishes the hunger of the valkyries' hawks.'[20] Perhaps, even to the end, Cnut was spiritually hedging his bets.

EIGHT

The Lawspeaker

> Many men understand the mysterious saying
> of the red gold and, as the ring said,
> wisely entrust their salvation to God.
>
> The Exeter Book

Among the institutions that mark a civilised society is the
existence of the rule of law. It was also a vital means by which
rulers stamped their wishes on their people and by which invaders
controlled their subjects.

For Cnut to win battles was one thing; but unless a system of law
could be created, he was destined to live in a state of perpetual
warfare – in other words, permanent anarchy. One man could not
hope to overawe a population of anything up to four million,
especially when that population was scattered, resentful and hostile,
and that man was a foreign interloper.

In seeking to establish just such a system, Cnut drew upon his
own Danish expertise as well as, wisely, adopting English law as it
had evolved over time. It is not until Cnut's reign or shortly before it
that we can discern what Viking law was all about. Some of it was
common to all Scandinavian countries and, indeed, to northern
Europe in general; some of it was specific to Denmark. All of it, no
doubt, like any law at any time, was at the relative mercy of those
who executed it; there were few absolutes.

Iceland in the Middle Ages has the best documented legal system,
but it is likely that very similar ideas prevailed in the Denmark of
Swein Forkbeard or Harald Bluetooth. The states of both kings were
divided into districts called *heruð* in Old Norse. The law was kept
here by the *Thing*, a council of freemen similar to the English witan
and composed of men of similar status – warriors and landowners.

Nowhere was the law comprehensively written down, but it was handed down orally among the *Thing*, generation upon generation, the *Thing* itself serving as keeper of the nation's memories as much as acting as a decision-making body.

The military duties of the *heruð* perhaps took first place. The word derives from the Old Norse for army and each district had to furnish warriors and ships for warfare and raids. By Cnut's time, several *Things* met together at one of three centres. Called the *landþing* at this level, they met at Lund in Skåne, Ringsted in Zealand and Visorg in Jutland. All three of these were major towns by the late tenth century, Lund in particular, in its archaeology, giving a vivid picture of Viking life with its rich, organic soil, heather-made roads and even a toddler's high chair. At such gatherings, crucial decisions were made by the men who mattered – the election of a king, the choice of war or peace, the question of right.

Justice was worked out on a careful scale of penalties vaguely reminiscent of the Old Testament, the code of an eye for an eye and a tooth for a tooth. Murder, the most serious of crimes, was dealt with by *mannboetr*, literally, man money. The maximum amount, payable in silver, was given for a life or for serious mutilation; the loss of an eye earned half that amount; of an ear, a quarter and so on. All members of the *Thing* acted as judges in these matters, but the execution of revenge under this system had to be made by the victim himself, or failing that, his nearest kin. There were times, therefore, when justice was not only not seen to be done, but not done at all.

The Vikings used the system of ordeal shared by the Christian communities to the south. The *járnburdr* was the ordeal by fire, the carrying of a red-hot iron bar for a specified number of paces. If the blisters healed without infection after three days, the gods were smiling on the accused and had judged him innocent. The fact that the Vikings used this ordeal makes the antics of the missionary Poppo in converting Harald Bluetooth to Christianity all the more remarkable. Unknown to the English, but practised by the Danish Vikings and their Norman cousins, was the *hólmganga*, the ordeal by battle, in which two men involved in a dispute, perhaps over territory or plunder, would hack at each other with axe or sword.

This appealed to a people toughened by a harsh life and bred to war. It is most clearly seen in Swedish law from the same period, but it probably existed all over the Viking lands. The battle ordeal probably often degenerated into private duels fought over trifles, but honour was far from a trifle to the Vikings and may go far to explain their heroic stands in battles from Clontarf to Byzantium. Strangely enough, the most common crime, theft, was met with death by hanging. The Vikings, in common with most early medieval peoples, had no prisons in the modern sense. Keeping prisoners was difficult and expensive and concepts such as rehabilitation were probably alien to the Northmen. Hanging was a quick and cheap solution, carried out on the strictly practical grounds that poor men committed thefts because of necessity; such men could not afford the *mannboetr*, so their lives must be forfeit instead. For a Viking, the worst punishment was not death – for that meant at least some promise of an afterlife – but exile. This was the punishment doled out by the higher court of the *landþing* in the event of a culprit refusing to accept the verdict of the *Thing*. It was a court of last resort.

The English had laws of their own. Virtually the first of these of which we have any extensive knowledge are those of Aethelberht of Kent, from the days of the heptarchy. Tellingly, he was the first Saxon king to embrace Christianity, at some time between 560 and 590. Since he may have held *bretwalda* (overlord) status, it is possible that his laws extended beyond his south-eastern kingdom as far north as the Humber. His law code was drawn up in Old English, probably with the help of the missionary Augustine about 602. What is fascinating about this is its establishment of Christian values and precepts and the fact that it favoured Augustine's new Church so strongly, protecting its lands and valuables. All laws that followed into the days of Cnut and far beyond, adopted the same pattern.

By the seventh century, there was a discernible growth of royal justice and evidence of what today could be called due process was kicking in. Wihtred of Kent drew up his law codes in 695 and the influence of the Church was huge. There were rules on keeping the Sabbath, maintaining fidelity in marriage and remembering to fast during Lent.

Ine of Wessex produced his laws in concert with his father Cenred in the closing years of the seventh century. Again, the Christian ethic was paramount, with strictures on baptism and the payment of tithes to the Church. They were altogether harder than the Kentish efforts and implied that if the laws were broken, it was the king himself with whom men would have to deal. It is from Ine that we learn for the first time of the administration of the law via ealdormen and shires.

It is not until Alfred that we have detailed written evidence of the law, although clearly it was in operation in various forms in the late heptarchy, with varying help from strong kings and self-serving churchmen. Alfred's code was based, according to the king himself, on earlier edicts of Ine (from whom he was descended) and Offa of Mercia, of whose laws we know virtually nothing. Alfred's law, however, extended the power of the king of Wessex and ultimately of all England; for the first time we have laws concerning treason (the most damning crime in the centuries that lay ahead) and loyalty to the king. As with Wihtred, we have the notion of the people as God's folk, enjoined by his laws as much as by man's.

The establishment of the Danelaw from Alfred's time provided a complication, but as we have seen, local customs surfaced quickly on a regional level, so the laws of Northumbria and Mercia probably co-existed with the Viking system outlined above. With the notable exception of the battle-ordeal, they were broadly similar anyway and as the Vikings were relatively happy to embrace Christianity, there is no need to assume undue difficulties in the working of the law. It was Cnut's own lawspeaker, Wulfstan, who effectively framed the laws in Cnut's time. The lawspeaker (*lögsögumadr*) was a Viking office held by the member of the *Thing* most learned in the law. In that respect, he conforms to the Lord Chancellor created in Norman England. And no one was more learned in the law than Wulfstan. Little is known of the man before 996 when he was appointed Bishop of London, but the fact that he was buried at Ely perhaps implies that he came from there or the surrounding fenlands. An outstanding prose-writer, he used the pen-name Lupus – the wolf (a pun on his name) – extensively on either side of the millennium. So distinctive was his writing style, with its

clever wordplay, alliteration and double-stressed phrases, that it is
identifiable in works everywhere, both for Church and secular
purposes. Such was the power of the Church by Cnut's reign that
distinctions between the regular and secular were becoming
increasingly blurred, many of Wulfstan's homilies being translated in
effect into the laws of Cnut.

The king in his turn was happy to give Wulfstan his head. The
man had been preaching to kings and making laws when the Viking
was still a boy. In 1002 Aethelred made Wulfstan Bishop of
Worcester and Archbishop of York, a mark, no doubt, of his respect
for him. Although he may have resigned the former, he held York for
twenty-one years until his death and his grasp of politics as well as
dogma made him indispensable to Cnut. It is noticeable that Cnut's
laws date largely from the early 1020s when he was still feeling his
way as king; 1023 was also the year of Wulfstan's death.

The Wolf was at his most brilliant in the blistering attack he
delivered, probably in 1013, to Aethelred and his court. The hapless
king had just returned from Normandy, promising a new dawn and
ready to mix it with Swein Forkbeard. The country was
demoralised, torn apart by years of ravaging and slaughter.
Treachery, feud, uncertainty were everywhere. It was time for *Sermo
Lupi*, the Sermon of the Wolf:

> Understand . . . completely that the devil has deceived this people
> too much and there has been little faith among men, though they
> speak fair words and too many crimes have gone unchecked in the
> land . . . there has been warfare and famine, burning and
> bloodshed in every district time and again, and theft and murder,
> plague and pestilence, murrain[1] and disease, malice and hate and
> plundering of robbers have harmed us very severely.

In full flow, Wulfstan raged at the criminality of the times:

> And it is shameful to speak of that which happens too widely and
> it is terrible to know what too many do often who commit that
> crime, who contribute together and buy a woman as a common
> purchase and with that one woman practise abomination, one

after the other and each after another, most like dogs that have no regard for filth.

England was rife with 'murder and evil deeds', 'avarice and greed', 'stealing and robbery'. Betrayal was the order of the day, fornication, incest and pagan abuses:

Here too many in the land, as it may appear, are grievously stained by the stains of sin. Here are murderers and slayers of kin and killers of priests and persecutors of monasteries; and here are perjurers and contrivers of murder; and here are harlots and child murderers and many foul adulterous whoremongers; and here are wizards and witches; and here are plunderers and robbers and thieves and . . . a countless number of all crimes and foul deeds.

How did the man who railed in the Sermon against disloyalty to Aethelred and slammed the Vikings for their cruelty become the lawspeaker in all but name to the Viking king, Cnut? The answer probably lies in the kind of man Wulfstan was. The recurring theme in his twenty-one surviving sermons is the chaos of the times and the lack of reverence to God. In his *Institutes of Policy* he wrote:

'Oratores' are prayer-men, who must serve God and earnestly intercede both day and night for the entire nation. 'Laboratores' are workmen who must supply that by which the entire nation shall live. 'Bellatores' are soldiers, who must defend the land by fighting with weapons. Every throne in a Christian nation must stand aright on these three pillars.[2]

He realised that it was easier to control the man on the throne than correct the vices of the two million-odd English who were rapidly going to the devil. A strong king, imbued with the Christian ethic and willing to put his shoulder to the moral wheel, could work wonders. And in comparison with the 'unraed' Aethelred, Cnut was a positive breath of fresh air.

If there is one word entirely missing from the Sermon of the Wolf, but present in virtually every other homily delivered at the time, it is the word 'peace'. What it meant was, in effect, the rule of law, which had been absent for so long in England. The common enjoinder by all members of the Church to fellow travellers was 'pax vobiscum' (peace be with you) and this applied as much to man's peace as to God's. It was a familiar wish across Europe, the nearest thing we have to a pacifist movement in the early medieval period. Bishop Guy of le Puy in the Frankish kingdom famously said in a sermon of 994 that without peace, no one could hope to see the Lord. In 1008, when Aethelred, in a moment of uncharacteristic energy, was building a fleet to oppose Forkbeard's forces, a great council was held at Pentecost at Enham, in Hampshire. The time and the place were both significant and the symbol carried by Wulfstan and Aelfheah, still then Archbishop of Canterbury, was the *agnus dei*, the lamb of God, representing peace. Pentecost fell that year on 16 May, in the lambing season, and Enham means the lamb's birthplace. In this idyllic setting, the Archbishop and the king drew up laws which were agreed by the witan. Three texts have survived from the council – two in Old English, one in Latin – and it is clear that the churchmen called the meeting, not Aethelred. The bishops seem to have thrashed matters out before presenting the council's decision, almost as a fait accompli to the secular witan. Certainly, the king produced a 'pacifist' penny, either in 1008 or 1009, showing the lamb of God and the dove of peace in place of the crowned head. It is not likely that Aethelred's order to raise a fleet came out of the churchmen's deliberations, but Wulfstan and Aelfheah both had an excellent grasp of *realpolitik* and neither flinched from war as long as God sanctioned it.

Ten years after Enham, Wulfstan was working his magic on Cnut. The all-important meeting of the witan at Oxford in 1018 set the seal on Cnut's relationship with his people and on the relationships between Englishman and Viking. A manuscript, now in the Parker collection at Corpus Christi College, Cambridge, is the resulting text of that meeting and it is likely, from the style, that Wulfstan wrote it. By modern standards it is rather vague, exhorting the people, as the Sermon of the Wolf did, to do their duty by God and man.

I Cnut, as it is styled today, is the first of the legal documents, dealing specifically with the ecclesiastical situation. Canon law related to the Church and first surfaced as a set of rules ratified by the earliest known Church council at Niccea in Greece in 325. These laws referred almost entirely to Church matters, but through Wulfstan there is in *I Cnut* an overlay of civil law, too: 'This is the ordinance which King Cnut, king of all England and king of the Danes and of the Norwegians[3] and his councillors decreed, for the praise of God and for his own royal dignity and benefit; let one resolve whichever one will.' The prologue tells us that the laws were written 'at the holy Christmas season at Winchester' and the year was probably 1021 or 1022. It states: 'First, merely, that above all other things they [Cnut's churchmen] would ever love and honour one God and steadfastly hold one Christian faith, and love King Cnut with due loyalty.' We see here a continuance of Wihtred's notion that the king was special. At one with God. It was in many ways the beginning of the concept of divine right. Much of *I Cnut* was borrowed from earlier practice and earlier laws. There were sections on criminous clerks, churchmen's behaviour and the rights of sanctuary from Aethelred's day (which Wulfstan would have known well); extracts from Edgar on the observance of Church festivals and the all-important payment of Church dues.

It is in *II Cnut* that our interest really lies, because this was Cnut's secular law and as such both affected more people than *I Cnut* and, partly at least, still continues as the law of the land. We cannot know, after all these centuries, whether there is any special significance in the order of the king's laws, but it is reasonable to assume that Cnut, Wulfstan and his court at Winchester would have had some sort of hierarchical structure in mind. Clause 5.1 warns:

> It is heathen practice if one worships idols, namely . . . heathen gods and the sun or the moon, fire or flood, wells or stones or any kind of forest trees, or if one practises witchcraft or encompasses . . . death by any means, either by sacrifice or divination, or takes part in such delusions.

The laws of the Northumbrian priests, as we have seen, used similar language and there is little doubt that the threat against idolatry and witchcraft was aimed at the still partially pagan Danelaw.

Christianity had not quite taken a firm hold here – outside the monasteries and abbeys of centres like York, Durham and Lincoln there were probably equally potent centres of what folklorists today like to call Middle Earth, a twilight never-never world of mystery and magic. Various *Lacnunga* and leechbooks from Cnut's time or shortly before it, discuss goblins and elves as if they were as real – and as annoying – as snake bite or nettle rash. Bald's *Leechbook*, written in Cnut's Winchester a century before his time, states:

Make thus a salve against the race of elves, goblins and those women with whom the devil copulates; take the female hop plant, wormwood, betony, lupin, vervain, henbane, dittander, viper's bugloss, bilberry plants, cropleek, garlic, madder grains, corn cockle, fennel. Put those plants into a vat; place under an altar; sing nine masses over it; boil it in butter and in sheep's grease; add much holy salt strain through a cloth; throw the herbs into running water. If any temptation come to a man, or elf or goblin, anoint his face with this salve, and put it on his eyes and where his body is sore, and cense him and frequently sign him with the cross; his condition will soon be better.[4]

If elves and goblins were real, so were witches, 'those women with whom the Devil copulates'. Female shamanism was probably still a commonplace in the more remote reaches of Cnut's Danelaw, surviving for centuries until the advent of education and science in the form of the village 'cunning women' who delivered babies, cured piles and laid out the dead. Aelfric of Eynsham, the most learned scholar of his day, wrote when Cnut was a boy, 'Still witches resort to heathen burial sites with their evil rites, and call upon the devil, and he arrives in the form of the person who lies buried there as if he had arisen from death.' Divination, to which Cnut refers, is associated with wizards, renowned for their powers of prophecy. Odin, the god of his childhood, was lord of the wizards and there is a great irony here, that the man who now rejected the old Norse gods with their concept of sacrifice, was now perfectly happy to accept the equally false idol, Jesus Christ.

In all lists of medieval laws, there is a homiletic element – almost an insucking of breath – wholly missing from today's legislation.

How much of this holier-than-thou attitude was Cnut and how much Wulfstan in impossible to say, but many of the clauses of *II Cnut* smack of the latter.

'Homicides and perjurers, injurers of the clergy and adulterers', 'hypocrites and liars, robbers and plunderers' were listed among the most serious – and serial – wrongdoers of Cnut's England. 'And he', said Clause 7.1, 'who wishes to purify the country rightly and to put down wrongdoing and to love righteousness must then diligently restrain and shun such things.' There was actually a world of difference between 'restraining' and 'shunning' – the proactive peacekeeper we call a police officer today and those non-Samaritans who walk by on the other side of the road. It would be fascinating to know if Cnut's laws had any hierarchical significance, because Clause 8 deals with coinage. Although it is lifted from Aethelred's legislation, the fact that it occurs so early in the text might imply Cnut's sound economic sense and the need to circulate his likeness and his name among his people for political and psychological, as well as economic reasons.

Clauses 12 to 15 established what in effect was Cnut's royal prerogative:

> Those are the rights which the king possesses over all men in Wessex, namely mundbryce and hamsocn, forstal and [the fine for] the harbouring of fugitives, and the fine for neglecting military service . . . And if anyone commits a deed punishable by outlawry, the king [alone] is to have power to grant his peace.

Mundbryce was the right to fine for any breach of the peace; *hamsocn* the authority to levy fines for housebreaking; *forstal*, the prerogative of fining for highway robbery, and although those rights of Cnut were specified as pertaining to Wessex, they actually applied in Mercia and the Danelaw, too.

Many of the clauses of *II Cnut* deal with the vital importance of the oath and the use of ordeals as a means of judging a man's honesty in the eyes of God and man. We shall examine them later in this chapter. Obligations, too, were important in a state with nothing approximating to a police force and men were expected to look out for their communities' and families' actions, a little reminiscent of the modern Neighbourhood Watch.

One of the problems in a semi-literate society was how to disseminate the law. The Romans placed theirs on public view in the forum; today, the assumption is made (ludicrously) that we know it and ignorance is no defence. In Cnut's time, the pulpit was the most effective news sheet there was. Much of *II Cnut* deals with the Church's role in society, but some of it concerns the frequency of court meetings and crimes committed in Wessex. Edgar's laws are recognisable here, but some of the material appears to be new and may come from Cnut's own government. The best example of this is the frequent commutation of the death penalty to one of mutilation. We know that Cnut used permanent disfigurement as a means of punishment, but the idea was probably Wulfstan's; hanging harms the soul as well as the spinal column and entry to Heaven was not possible in this state. The merely mutilated would meet St Peter.

A first offender was to pay a twofold compensation to his accuser and *wergild* to his lord. The second offence would result in the loss of hands or feet or both 'in proportion to the deed'. How such a cripple could go on to commit 'still further crimes' is a fascinating question, but if he did, 'his eyes are to be put out and his nose and ears and upper lip cut off, or his scalp removed'.

The law served as important a function in Cnut's England as it does today. It was the essential framework by which he governed, a line in the sand that no man could cross with safety. And it introduces us to an interesting figure; Clause 8 talks of *bonda*, the ordinary householder, any law-abiding member of society who was used as a yardstick of good and bad behaviour, right and wrong. He was what the Victorians called 'the man on the Clapham omnibus'; today's Joe Public. The law was also a source of money to a king constantly in need of funds. Later generations would pass the fiscal power to parliament, but kings like Cnut had absolute control over money. Confiscation of land, swingeing fines and climbing taxation improved Cnut's cash flow and made his gifts to the Church all the more lavish and his army and navy ever more impressive. Nowhere is this more apparent than in the arrangements made by Cnut for the *Heriot*. The word in Old English was *heregeatu* – war gear – and it symbolised the military relationship between lord and man seventy years before the Normans formalised it with their feudal system. The *Heriot* itself was a death duty, payable at three levels:

> An earl's as belongs thereto, namely eight horses, four saddled and four unsaddled, and four helmets and four coats of mail and eight spears and as many shields and four swords and 200 mancuses of gold. And next, the king's thegns, who are closest to him; four horses, two saddled and two unsaddled, and two swords and four spears and as many shields and a helmet and coat of mail and 50 mancuses of gold.

Lesser thegns' *heriots* were 'a horse and trappings and weapons, along with four pounds of silver or gold. And he who is of lower position; two pounds.'

It is difficult to know how much, if any, of Cnut's laws were actually Cnut's. As M.K. Lawson warns: 'Cnut's laws, which initially look such promising sources, are in reality something of a quicksand in which their compiler and his motives can never be forgotten.'[5] But the compiler was Wulfstan, hence the dilemma.

Several of the clauses of *II Cnut* deal with the legal status of women. A widow was to remain unmarried for twelve months, but it was very likely that Cnut had married Aethelred's Emma within this proscribed time. A man marrying within the twelve months had to pay his *wergeld* to the king or 'to him who has granted it'. The widow herself would lose her 'morning gift' and all her former possessions. Women were to be protected against rape, assault and marriage by force, and Clause 73.3 urges 'a widow is never to be consecrated [as a nun] too hastily'.

We know little of family law in Cnut's time, but the nine clauses relating to betrothal almost certainly date from the 1020s. 'Concerning the betrothal of a woman' states that a man's intentions must be honourable, 'that he will maintain her according to God's law as a man should maintain his wife' and he needed friends to 'stand surety for it'. This involved a financial commitment, a public statement of what was on offer rather like the somewhat unsavoury 'pre-nup' of modern America. In the normal run of things, the bride could expect half her husband's goods and all of it if they had a child. Only when all this was agreed could the betrothal go ahead and the phrase for that agreement was the Danish 'sammaele beon'.

Clause 77 of *II Cnut* appears to be the king's himself, however, promising death and loss of estates to a deserter: 'And the man, who in his cowardice deserts his lord or his comrades, whether it is on an expedition by sea or on one on land, is to forfeit all that he owns and his own life . . .' Cnut could not forget that he came to be a king and lawmaker by force and the bonds forged on the battlefield were not to be easily broken. And in the infamous clause of 54.1 *II Cnut*, that of keeping a mistress, we know that Cnut himself was guilty as sin.

And if anyone has a lawful wife and also a concubine, no priest is to do for him any of the offices which must be done for a Christian man, until he desists and atones for it as deeply as the bishop directs him and desists from such for ever.

Perhaps, like kings before him and since, the Viking saw himself in some senses above the law.

Much of our knowledge of the law in Cnut's reign actually comes from Domesday Book, concerned as it is with the complexities of land tenure. It frequently uses the initials 't.r.e' (*tempus rex edwardii*) – 'in the time of King Edward [the Confessor]' – but it is highly likely that much of the Confessor's law was Cnutian in origin, as Edward himself was not only Cnut's son-in-law, but is not particularly remembered as a lawgiver. The compilers of Domesday write of the law of Wessex, of Mercia and of the Danelaw and it may well be that local customs still overruled anything that might be seen as a national law. Edgar, the first king of all England, had said: 'Moreover it is my will that among the Danes such good laws should be valid as they best appoint; and I always conceded this to them and will concede it as long as my life lasts . . .'[6] It lasted until 975 and in the slow-moving world of the early Middle Ages, no doubt pertained until well into the eleventh century. We have already commented on the 'separateness' of the Danelaw, albeit tempered with regional variations; it is no accident that the North held out far longest not against Cnut, but against William the

Bastard who became their second conqueror in fifty years. *II Cnut*, in fact, dealt specifically with the regions, which has an odd, modern, devolutionary ring to it. The *Norðleoda Laga* was the law of the North people, the Danelaw. Virtually all the clauses here refer to monetary value; the *wergild* of an archbishop and an atheling was 15,000 thrymsas; that of a bishop and ealdorman 8,000; mass and secular priests were worth 2,000; ceorls only 266. Status was described in this section and may again have been written by Wulfstan. There is a certain irony in the fact that, in the Danelaw at least, a man could not rise above his station: 'And even if he prospers so that he possesses a helmet and a coat of mail and a gold-plated sword, if he has not the land, he is a ceorl all the same.'

The *Mircna Laga* was the Mercian law and, again, its clauses merely recite the various values of the *wergild* and stress the importance of the *Að*, the oath: 'The oath of a mass-priest and of a secular thegn is in the law of the English reckoned equally valuable'. In the sacred oaths taken by priests, not merely in Mercia, but everywhere, '. . . there are seven steps of the ecclesiastical degrees and holy orders, and seven times a day should the servants of God praise Him in church and intercede zealously for all Christian people'.

Copies of Cnut's laws would have been sent out to ealdormen and probably thegns in the regions and to bishops and abbots who would have the responsibility of disseminating them still further. Is it just coincidence that not a single original copy of the 'secular' version has survived or did Wulfstan's Church have a vested interest in keeping their copies carefully?

The judicial structure in Cnut's England had been developing for over three centuries. At the top was the king himself, acting with the wisdom of Solomon in matters great and small, although, one suspects, mostly great. Below Cnut came the ealdormen, like Thurkil, Godwine of Wessex, Yric of Lade and, while he lasted, Eadric Streona. At the next level came the shire reeve, a new office created when Cnut was still a boy. Cnut's laws, like those of Alfred and Edgar before him, carried warnings about corrupt officials at all levels: 'And he is always to forfeit his thegnly status unless he redeem it from the king'.

The hundred, created in the mid-tenth century, had its own court that met every month; the higher shire court convened twice a year. Cnut's laws make it clear that appeals could be made to the higher court if a supplicant failed to get justice. In reality there was a great deal of overlapping of function. Courts met at well-known landmarks and in the countryside rather than towns – Spellow in Norfolk, for instance, means the meeting hill. In the towns, the burh court met three times a year and all these gatherings were an excellent opportunity for the king to disseminate his views and issue decrees.

Such courts were formal in their procedure, but bore little resemblance to anything we know today. The plaintiff summoned the accused and if he failed to appear, he lost his suit by default. Such a man became a 'wolf's head', an outlaw, with a price on his head and no friends in the world. His only chance was to obtain a pardon from Cnut himself. If the accused appealed, he swore his innocence on oath – 'By the Lord, I am guiltless both of deed and instigation of the crime . . .'[7] – and his oath-helpers were on hand to support his claim. Oaths were taken very seriously by Saxon and Viking alike. Certainly from Ine's time, the system of compurgation or oath-helping had operated in English courts. A number of men of good character, in practice usually the friends of the accused, would swear on oath as to the accused's blameless reputation. They did not provide an alibi, as modern witnesses might, but a sense of disbelief that wrongdoing was likely in this particular man. Oath-helpers were men of property. A king's companion (*comes*) counted for sixty hides of land, a ceorl a mere five, but the crucial point was a property qualification. Alfred's laws had stipulated that 'we teach, as is most necessary, that each man keep his oath and pledge'.[8] One of the most famous of Cnut's laws is that every male over twelve years of age was eligible to take an oath, and further, that that oath in itself was a promise to keep the peace: 'And it is our will that every man over twelve years of age is to give an oath that he will not be a thief or accessory to a theft.' By his time, the oath to the king was paramount over that to a lord, and royal charters issued by Cnut and several of his predecessors imply loss of land for disloyalty – the forerunner of the *escheat* system whereby the crown acquired the lands of the dispossessed. Sigeferth and Morcar in the reign of Aethelred were prime examples.

The accused had thirty days in which to find his oath-helpers and if he failed or was otherwise deemed dubious in the eyes of the court, he had to submit to the ordeal. For three days he fasted, then took part in a solemn Mass as the priest stood before him at the altar and intoned in English so that there should be no doubt:

> I charge you by the Father and the Son and by the Holy Ghost, and by your Christianity which you have received, and by the holy cross on which God suffered and by the holy gospel and the relics which are in this church, that you should not dare to partake of this sacrament nor to go to the altar if you did this of which you are accused, or know who did it.[9]

It was the creation of the Danelaw and the accession of Cnut that effectively created the outlaw. The word itself is Viking and fear of the punishment greatest among the Northmen. The sense of alienation and abandonment detested in Scandinavia became a commonplace in England and throws a new light on the earliest viciousness of Robin Hood.[10]

Richard Fletcher says, rightly, that Cnut's laws 'were the most comprehensive and sophisticated piece of legislation issued by any early medieval English king'.[11] And the philosopher David Hume, writing eight centuries later and with no love for his subject, found himself obliged to write: '[Cnut] made no distinction between Danes and English in the distribution of justice: And he took care, by a strict execution of law, to protect the lives and properties of all his people.'[12]

NINE

Court, Carls, Coinage and Celts

Thus was the lay sung,
the song of the poet. The hall echoed with joy,
waves of noise broke out along the beaches . . .
And the spokesman Unferth sat at the feet
of a Danish lord.

Beowulf

At the height of his power, about 1030, Cnut's Winchester was not only the capital of England, but of the whole of his northern empire. Given the slowness of communication in the eleventh century, the reality of this situation was somewhat dubious. Cnut had no choice but to rule via viceroys in his absence from Denmark – and, by 1030, Norway and part of Sweden – but Winchester, to countless merchants, warriors, churchmen, skalds and a whole host of 'wannabes', must have represented the gates of heaven. Other races and faiths would see Mecca or Amritsar in a similar light and not until Mayor Richard Whittington's day in the fourteenth century would Englishmen see the streets of another city – London – paved with gold.

Long before archaeologist Martin Biddle uncovered something of the reality of Winchester in Cnut's time, Laurence Larson pictured it as a cosmopolitan, bustling centre, on a grander scale than anything else in Europe perhaps, except the Holy Roman Emperor's city of Berlin and the eternal city of Rome. Cnut's court cannot have been English in the sense that it had been under Aethelred. Its complex series of buildings, large halls of oak clothed in wattle and thatch, lie under what is today St Thomas and Symonds Streets and are almost entirely a closed book in terms of eyewitness accounts or archaeology. It is likely that the eastern end was linked to the Old

Minster, thus providing a view for Cnut down the aisle of his principal church. From its eastern windows, the view would have been the double towers of the Old and New Minsters, the latter's tower perhaps six storeys high, decorated with giant biblical figures in bas-relief and bright paint, a constant reminder to the king of the need to court the favour of the medieval Church he had inherited from Aethelred.

Archaeologist Martin Biddle, twenty years ago, conjectured that the New Minster served 'as the principal church of the refounded city, while Old Minster as the see church looked out to the diocese at large'.[1] '"It was remembered"', he quotes, '"that the singing of the brethren . . . in one choir fought with the voices of those singing in the other, while the ringing of the bells made confusion worse confounded."' The churches were so close that a man could barely walk between them.

In the cloisters, monks painted the bright biblical and political scenes of the Winchester School. Sculptors carved in ivory, bone, gold and silver. The great organ of the New Minster with its twenty-six bellows, seventy blowers, forty slides, four hundred apertures and four hundred pipes could be heard across the city and to water meadows to the south.

The language of Cnut's court is uncertain. Increasingly, the official phraseology, especially in Church documents, was Latin, but this would not become standard until after the Norman Conquest. In daily conversation, Old English and Old Norse must have been heard in a cacophony of noise in the main halls. The *huscarls* who were Cnut's bodyguard were mostly Scandinavian, Vikings of the old school. They may have been bilingual to an extent, but among themselves (and they seem to have been an elite group) they would have spoken Norse with its thick, lilting sounds and its widely differing dialects. About half the thegns who signed Cnut's charters were, from their names at least, Scandinavian and the fact that some names occur regularly indicate that the court was a regular home for some of them. The skaldic poets who sang Cnut's praises were, by definition, Scandinavian; the three most prominent from Iceland. The bishops sent by Cnut to establish churches in Denmark have largely Flemish names; Guillaume, possibly a scribe or chancellor to

1. 'Thus far shalt thou go and no further.' Cnut and the waves – the popular image of the king as seen through the eyes of a Victorian engraver. *(Bettmann/Corbis)*

2. 'Where a priest and Aelfgifu . . .', a scene from the Bayeux Tapestry. Is this Cnut's first wife, the lady from Northampton? *(By permission of the Centre Guillaume le Conquérant)*

3. Ashingdon Church in Essex, built by Cnut in 1020 on the site of his victory over Edmund Ironside. *(Carol Trow)*

4. All that remains of Cnut, Emma and Harthacnut, jumbled in the mortuary chest at Winchester Cathedral. *(John Crook)*

5. The beaker that once held the heart of a king, now in the Triforium of Winchester Cathedral. *(John Crook)*

QVI IACET HIC
REGNI SCEPTRVM TVLIT
HARDICANVTVS,
EMMÆ CNVTONIS
GNATVS & IPSE FVIT.
OBIIT A.D. JO42.

6. The tomb of Harthacnut in Fox's presbytery screen, Winchester Cathedral, showing a relief of a ship, early sixteenth century. *(John Crook)*

7. Short-cross coin of Cnut, one of nineteen in existence from the mint at Ely, *c.* 1030. *(Author's collection)*

8. Religion in transition – the Hammer of Thor and the Cross of Jesus in a single amulet, Scandinavian, tenth century. *(Werner Forman/ Corbis)*

9. The priest of Ashingdon who became an Archbishop. Stigand from the Bayeux Tapestry. *(By permission of the Centre Guillaume le Conquérant)*

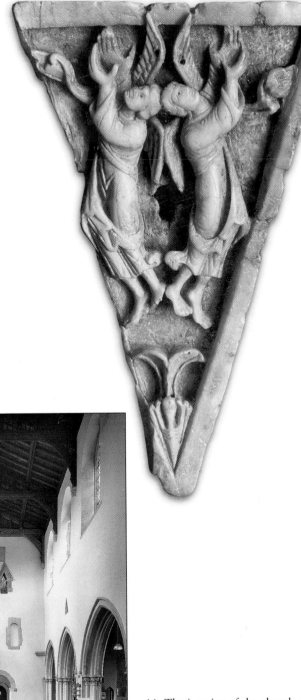

10. Walrus ivory carving of angels from the New Minster, Winchester, *c.* 1000. *(Winchester Museum Service)*

11. The interior of the church at Deerhurst in the Isle of Olney, where Cnut and Ironside agreed to divide England. *(John Crook)*

12. Part of the fourteenth-century retrochoir screen in Winchester Cathedral, with the two niches for Cnut and Harthacnut. Today the niches are occupied by brightly coloured icons. (*John Crook*)

13. The resting-place of kings. Tituli of Cnut and Harthacnut. (*John Crook*)

the king, became Bishop of Roskilde. Paid though he was to do it, the skald Sighvat probably meant what he said when he wrote, 'Knutr was under Heaven the most glorious King'.[2] And the Icelander Snorri Sturluson, writing of a man whom he actually disliked, had to agree that Cnut's court at Wintanceaster possessed 'greater magnificence than in any other place, both as to the number in daily attendance and as to the furnishings and equipment of the palaces that he owned and occupied'.[3]

Larson was probably right to believe there was a Slavic element in Cnut's court, too. His mother, after all, was a Pole and this dimension adds fascinating questions as to the king's upbringing and personality. One of his sisters had the Slavic name Santslaue; we know she lived at least for a time in Winchester, because her name is among the benefactors to the Minsters in the *Liber Vitae*. Another sister married, according to John of Worcester, Wyrtgeorn, a Slav prince who may be the Wrytsleof who signed a charter of Cnut in 1026. Prominent among the king's *huscarls* was Godescalc, like Cnut the product of a Slavic–Danish marriage. After the king's death, Godescalc went home to bring Christianity to the Wends, inhabitants of today's north-west Germany and Estonia.

It is in the existence of the *huscarls* that we see Cnut's unique military contribution. Various authors today contend that as a military unit they were raised by Swein Forkbeard, perhaps even specifically for his invasion of England. The archaeologists of sixty years ago were tempted to see the giant circular fortresses in Denmark as their holding camps. Even if Forkbeard did create them, it was Cnut who developed them into a permanent institution; the father 'reigned' for a few months – the son for nearly twenty years. Today, the *huscarls* have a romantic image as the defenders of an old way of life. On their ridge at Senlac in the misty October of 1066, they died in huge numbers behind their shield wall, the dead held up by the living, around the mutilated body of the last king of the English. Laurence Larson makes a great deal of the elite separateness of the *huscarls*, not unlike the brotherhood of the Jomsvikings who were their contemporaries. Groups like this have an appeal – the all powerful Praetorians of Rome, the sinister head-worshipping Templars of the Middle Ages – but the actual evidence for such elitism in the reign of Cnut is slight. According to the Danish chronicler Sveno,[4] the king only accepted into this cult warriors whose swords were inlaid with gold and that there was an unseemly rush among the wealthier warriors to the smiths to decorate their weapons in order to meet the criterion. Saxo Grammaticus[5] paints a picture of a rigid protocol and hierarchy among the *huscarls*. As bodyguards to the king, their major role was to protect Cnut's life and in this respect they went wherever he did, especially early in the reign when much of the country must have been hostile to him. The average ceorl, however oppressed by taxation and Viking raids, would think twice before taking on a *huscarl*, a professional fighter with his mail shirt, helmet, sword, axe and shield. At the king's hall, says Saxo, each man sat according to his valour, length of service or aristocratic birth – removal to a lower table was the ultimate disgrace. The *huscarls'* loyalty was to Cnut and they were paid handsomely, a monthly salary according to Larson. The unwritten contract was that Cnut could dispense with a man's service only on New Year's Day. Quarrels between *huscarls* were to be resolved by a *Thing* in the king's presence. Offenders were ignored by the others, sat at the lowest place at table and could be pelted with discarded bones. Treason was punishable by death and loss of property. These rules were developed in Denmark by the early twelfth century but we have no way of knowing whether any of them actually operated in Cnut's time. The chronicler Langebeck[6] tells us that the king himself appeared before the *Thing* having killed a *huscarl* in a flash of temper. As Cnut effectively presided over the *Thing*, as a commanding officer would in much later military courts martial, he was in effect sentencing himself. The usual fine was forty marks but Cnut paid a voluntary 369 to be divided among the dead man's family, the *huscarl* fraternity and the poor. In that Cnut probably did attempt to expiate his crimes by giving to the Church and that he was a genuinely generous man, the story has its possibilities. But altogether it smacks too much of homiletic neatness and is almost certainly a fabrication.

Nicholas Hooper[7] argues that the *huscarls* were no different from the plethora of other household troops all over Europe and that they certainly did not constitute a standing army. We hear of them only twice in the period. In 1023, they formed a strong presence in London should the townspeople take matters into their own hands at the removal of 'their' saint, the murdered archbishop Aelfheah, to his new shrine at Canterbury. After Cnut's death, they were employed as tax collectors by his unpopular son Harthacnut in what was probably a spontaneous revolt in Worcester in 1041. John of Worcester records: 'In this year Harthacnut . . . sent his *huscarls* through all the provinces of his kingdom to collect the tax which he had imposed. Two of them, namely Feader and Thurston, were killed . . . by the people of Worcester . . .'[8] Furious, Harthacnut sent an avenging force led by five of his leading earls, 'and almost all his *huscarls*, with a great army . . . ordering them to kill . . . and plunder and burn . . .' We can infer from this that *huscarls* were used, at least occasionally, in the role of 'aiding the civil power' which the regular British army was still called on to do, on increasingly limited occasions, well into the twentieth century. What we cannot know is whether this was a regular use of them, or whether Worcester was somehow an exception. Perhaps Harthacnut was expecting trouble there and sent Feader and Thurston as men he thought could handle it.

Other evidence that some *huscarls* at least acted in a political, as opposed to purely military, sphere comes from Cnut's charters. The first actual grant of land to one, Bovi, dates from 1033, but Urk the *huscarl* received land as early as 1024. Both men were referred to by the Latin term *minister*, which merely means servant in its original form and perhaps has some of the connotations of its modern use as a civilian politician.

We have no idea of the numbers of *huscarls* on Cnut's payroll, but the likelihood is that they never exceeded more than two thousand men. Laurence Larson expressed the view that although they probably had horses, they were in no sense a cavalry force and other historians have criticised Cnut for not developing this arm of his forces. This is a silly argument based on hindsight. William the Bastard's cavalry were hailed as a revolutionary force on the battlefield at Senlac, but they only *just* won the day and the majority of the impossibly spectacular English victories of the Hundred Years War (1337–1453) were won by knights, billmen and archers standing firmly on their own two legs.[9]

The other vexed question about the *huscarls* is, where were they? Saxo Grammaticus had no doubt that they were scattered as garrisons throughout England, especially in the more obvious strategic centres. A runic slab in Uppsala, Sweden, was raised by the sons of a man who 'sat out west in Thinglith'.[10] 'West' probably does mean England, but the Viking word lið is fraught with problems. It meant, as we have seen, a force, but of what size? When, in other words, does a raiding party become an army? The Valleberfa stone bears the inscription 'Swein and Thurgot raised this monument in memory of Manna and Swein. God help their souls well. But they lie buried in London.'[11] There is actually no proof at all that these men were *huscarls*.

If the *huscarls* did form the nucleus at least of garrisons rather than merely acting as Cnut's bodyguards, the chances are they would be based on the marches of Wales and Scotland. We shall look at the king's relations with Strathclyde and the northern kingdom in a later chapter, but what of Wales? We know that both Aethelred and Edmund Ironside employed Welsh cavalry in their armies and that it was likely to have been part of the remit of various ealdormen and earls of Mercia that they watch their backs along the Welsh borders. It is likely that when Thietmar of Merseburg wrote of the 'Britannis'[12] fighting with Ironside at Sherston, he meant the Welsh. Likewise, the skaldic poem *Liðsmannaflokker*, written about 1017, talks of the swords ringing on *brezkum* mail shirts and this again would seem to mean the Welsh. As we have seen, one reason why Cnut met Ironside in the Isle of Alney at Deerhurst may have been that it was close to the Welsh border and that Ironside had allies there.

Laurence Larson was right to say that no contemporary source talks of Cnut's plans to invade Wales, but there is some circumstantial evidence and it would be a little strange, given his aggrandisement, if he did not at least toy with the idea. We know that Eadric Streona led a punitive raid on St David's in Pembrokeshire in 1012. According to the *Annales Cambriae* of Williams ap Ithel, Cnut's earl, Egluf, unleashed troops (who may have had *huscarls* with them) in what is today's Dyfed in 1022. The fact that Cnut himself was in Denmark then implies that this was not invasion, but merely a raid, perhaps punitive. A twelfth-century charter in the bishopric of Llandaff claims that Rhydderch ap Iestyn, a native prince of Wales, promoted Joseph to the bishopric with letters of support from Cnut. We know no more than that and the charter itself is forged (i.e. copied) so we cannot be sure of its authenticity. Was it merely an assumption on the copyist's part that the king of England also ruled some, at least, of Wales and so did he add Cnut accordingly? The Annals of Ulster tell us that Rhydderch's son, Caradog, was killed by the English in the year of Cnut's death, but again, infuriatingly, we have no more details than that. In none of the intermittent warfare and extension of territory on Cnut's borders do we see anything of his *huscarls*.

Of a different organisational type were Cnut's liðsmen. As we have seen, the lið in Forkbeard's time seems to have been a large raiding party, but more specifically, and already by 1016, they were in far greater numbers than the *huscarls* and nearer in some ways to the concept of a standing army. The first specific mention we have of them comes from the year after Cnut's death. The complexity of that period will be dealt with later, but the Abingdon (C) text of the *Anglo-Saxon Chronicle* records that among those who elected Harold Harefoot as regent in England were 'the men of the fleet' (liðsmen). This was not the first time the fleet had elected a king. On the death of Forkbeard, Cnut himself was chosen by his shipmen at Gainsborough in 1014. The implication then is that there were sufficient Danish nobles aboard the dragon-ships to constitute a *Thing* and so make the election legal. We do not know if this still pertained in the London of 1036 and so we have no way of knowing what sort of men these were.

In many ways, Cnut's navy is a curiously blank page. As a Viking, the sea was in his blood. He came as a raider and conqueror by ship, probably lived on board ship in his days on the Humber and the Trent, by definition travelled to his other kingdoms and to Rome by ship, yet we have surprisingly little information about all this. The most famous Viking long-ships are those discovered in burial mounds at Oseberg and Gokstad, but these are probably not warships and they date from a century and a half before Cnut. Sources that postdate Cnut are equally unhelpful. Snorri Sturluson describes Cnut's ships and those of Olaf Haraldsson as being high-turreted, which sounds suspiciously like the squat warships of his own time, with their embrasured forecastles and aft-castles. The Bayeux Tapestry, made within twenty years of Cnut's death, has such appalling notions of scale that we have no idea of the size of the ships that brought William's Norman army to England. Even so, the method of shipbuilding remained remarkably unchanged. The Norman craftsmen at work on planks with their axes and their planes were following a craft that was at least three centuries old. Hulls were made of clinker-laid planks, overlapping each other and fastened to the keel, prow and stern by wooden pegs. Animal hair was tarred and rammed as caulking between the planks which were hammered flat with iron nails and washers. The single mast was slotted into a keelson, a solid block of wood amidships designed to take its colossal weight.

We have seen that the Encomiast wrote dramatically about the Viking armadas, with such style that it seems likely he actually saw them himself; and as we shall see, various Scandinavian chroniclers, especially the saga writer Snorri Sturluson, describe Cnut's dragon-ships, but the best account of the men who manned them comes from John of Worcester's rendering of the peace-offering/bribe offered to Harthacnut by Earl Godwine. There were eighty warriors

> of whom each one had on each arm a golden arm-ring weighing sixteen ounces, a triple corselet [mail shirt]; on the head, a helmet in part overlaid with gold; each was girded with a sword that was golden-hilted and bore a Danish axe inlaid with silver and gold hanging from the left shoulder, the left hand held the shield with gilded boss and rivets; in the right hand lay the spear that the English call the aetgar.[13]

Larson assumed that these men were *huscarls*, but the likelihood is that they were liðsmen and, in the quality of their arms at least, not typical. A man like Godwine of Wessex knew the value of bribery and he needed Harthacnut on his side, so expense was no object. Larson's confusion comes from the fact that there was little or no distinction between *huscarls* and liðsmen in their appearance and weaponry. Naval battles were simply land encounters that happened on water; in no sense were the liðsmen the forerunners of the British navy, but merely floating soldiers.[14]

The huge difference between *huscarls* and liðsmen in Cnut's reign is that the latter owed no particular allegiance to him and seem to have operated as mercenary fleets. Liðsmen were very well paid, perhaps because as sailors and navigators they possessed skills not expected or found among the *huscarls*. Unlike the *huscarls*, who were given land as a sort of 'retirement lump sum', the liðsmen never received land.

If the existence of two professional forces of fighters is the hallmark of a powerful king, the charters of Cnut put another complexion on his reign. In a grant of land in Landrake and Tinnel to Burhold, Bishop of Cornwall, in 1018, Cnut's scribe wrote, 'I, Cnut, monarch of the whole of Britain, have strengthened the gift of my liberality with the miraculous sign of the Holy Cross.' It was important that the 'whole of Britain' was mentioned; Cornwall, like Wales, was still an alien Celtic never-never land in which English laws and English ways had made relatively limited inroads.

Many of Cnut's charters are quite poetic. The grant of lands to Archbishop Lyfing of Canterbury in 1018 begins:

> All things which are seen by human eyes in this present world quickly disappear, but the things which are located on the mountains above flourish in continued amenity, remaining fixed in eternity under the rule of the great thunderer; and therefore it is for us children of a dying age to devote ourselves, so that by good works we may earn enjoyment of the good things of heaven, to live forever with the holy angels.[15]

Whatever else these are, they are not the words of Cnut. We cannot see here the personal handiwork or even viewpoint of later rulers – Henry VII checking with his spidery handwriting the accounts of his household; Napoleon lying in his bath dictating simultaneously four different letters of state. Preambles like this, often written in Latin, were stock beginnings to charters, written by scribes who did this kind of thing for a living. The rest of the charter, added later in

English, is the boundary clause, which specifies in an age before maps, exactly what land the charter is referring to: 'These are the forest boundaries of Hazelhurst. Firstly along the stream of the fern-clearing to the boundary of Rowley, from the Rowley boundary along the Holbeanwood boundary . . .'[16] and so on. Charters are useful records of the legal translations of the times. Written on parchment, they record the generosity of the king, the lists of privileges of the receivers of land and even the sketchy careers of the great and good in early eleventh-century England. But there is a downside. Only thirty-six charters still exist for the reign of Cnut and several of these are forgeries. Just as the *Anglo-Saxon Chronicle* gives us little information, especially for the closing years of the reign, so there are fewer charters of Cnut than any king between Aethelstan and Edward the Confessor. It is impossible now to decide who wrote these. Referred to by number and prefixed by the letter S for Professor Peter Sayer who remains the most famous editor of these documents, they are the work of various hands throughout the reign. Some are original, others (often careless) copies; still others are forged. The most likely authors (and forgers, for the same reason) are the monks from the monasteries, abbeys and individuals who received the grants in the first place. The Charters seem to have been kept in the relevant abbey church and occasionally copied into psalters by later generations anxious to prove ownership. Unfortunately, many of the charter writers seem to have been concerned to produce beautiful, symmetrical works of art, so the witnesses are arranged in neat rows of equal numbers with a rank hierarchy, Cnut inevitably at the top. This is not likely to give an accurate list of who was present at the witans, councils and other meetings where these decisions were made. So, too, the regular occurrence of names does not necessarily indicate the same man, therefore charting the size of Cnut's court and who were its constituent members is hugely difficult.

What we cannot say is that the king possessed a secretariat at Winchester, a group of clerks with ink and parchment, who accompanied him on his various progresses and campaigns. We know that Aethelred had a scribe and the likelihood is that Cnut did, too. He may have been the writer of S956, a grant of land at

Drayton, Hampshire, to the New Minster, Winchester, which seems to be an original manuscript.

But if there was nothing approaching a secretariat at Wintanceaster, there was certainly a mint. We have seen clearly the importance of moneyers in Cnut's kingdom. Some of them had the rank of thegn and they were all important enough to strike their names on the reverse of the king's coins. The system of coinage Cnut clearly inherited from Aethelred, but the redeless king had allowed mint rights to drift from him (if he had ever had them at all) so that a number of churchmen in particular were producing their own currency. By Cnut's reign we have a coinage system without equal anywhere in Europe. Even the lands of the Holy Roman Emperors did not produce so many or of such quality. Moneyers in this period were not technically royal servants, but they held a licence from Cnut and probably paid handsomely for the privilege. The king controlled the flow of money with reasonable effectiveness by holding a monopoly on the iron dies used to stamp the soft silver. In July 1990 just such a die was found under the old Thames Exchange building near the spot where the Walbrook stream ran into the river. The bulldozer driver who first found it picked it up and smashed it against his machine, to quote Michael O'Hara,[17] 'with the immortal words "'ere, there's a coin stuck on the end of this"'. The die was still coated with resin of pine and other woods used throughout the Middle Ages to preserve metal from corrosion. The die bears the name of the moneyer and his mint – *Drvlf O Nord* – and the obverse would have had a bust of Cnut with the legend *Cnvt Rex A*.

Since the reform of the coinage in the 970s, all coins had followed a certain range of patterns. In Cnut's reign in England, there were three types. The first, chronologically, is the Quatrefoil, which shows a left-facing head of the king with a quatrefoil and on the reverse a long-armed, voided cross. This type was in circulation from 1017 to about 1024 when it was replaced with the second, the Pointed Helmet design. Numismatist Kenneth Jonsson conjectures that new issues were made at the feast of Michaelmas in September, which conforms to a sort of 'beginning of the financial year' for Saxon and Viking alike. The king appears dressed for war in a conical helmet which is contemporary and he seems to be holding a baubled sceptre.

The last design, the Short Cross, appeared somewhere around 1030. The sceptred king is curiously bareheaded in this one, which may have some link with the various stories of him hanging his crown on the altar at Winchester, and the reverse has a short-armed cross with an amulet. In none of these depictions can we see a realistic likeness of Cnut. The coins of Aethelred and Harthacnut are remarkably similar. It is not until the eighteenth century that we see a passable resemblance to the monarch depicted on his coins.

To the historian, as opposed to the numismatist, the importance of the existence of coinage is that it is *the* symbol of a settled, ordered state. About 20,000 coins survive from the early eleventh century,[18] but only 1,300 of them come from England. Kenneth Jonsson[19] has made estimates of the hoards that have been found: the highest number was in Sweden (9,500); then Denmark (2,300); the West Slav (Witland) region (2,200). The fewest were found in the Wendlands (750) in what is today Estonia. In England the largest single hoard (839 coins) was found at Halton Moor in Yorkshire. The reason for so few in England is that coinage was exchanged when it was renewed (more or less as it is today with old style £5 notes handed in for new ones) so hoarding was unnecessary. In Scandinavia, this did not happen and money was valued by weight (hence the *pounds* of silver given in Danegeld). It was once assumed that Cnut's coins found in Denmark and Sweden were the result of crafty Vikings burying their share of the Danegeld or *Heregeld* for a rainy day, but today, the profits of regular trade seem more likely to have accrued an amount worth burying.

D.M. Metcalf,[20] extrapolating from the various amounts of Danegeld paid in Aethelred's reign, estimates that some 83 million coins were struck during the years of Cnut's reign, the Quatrefoil type (at 47 million) clearly leading the field of all coins struck between 973 (the reign of Edgar) and 1062 (Edward the Confessor).

The existence of an Empire of the North by 1030 did not imply a common 'single currency' any more than it implied a common set of laws, customs or language. In Denmark, Cnut's English coins were widely used and far outnumbered native examples struck at the king's mints of Roskilde, Idense, Hedeberg and Lund. No coins were struck by Cnut in Norway or the Wendlands.

In terms of Cnut's economic policy, his acceptance by the witan in September 1016 and his subsequent coronation, if he had one, meant that he became the lord of one of the richest countries in Europe, a far cry from the relatively impoverished Denmark. The organization of the country under Aethelred, with its shires, its hundreds and its wapentakes, meant that tax collection could and did happen; and although its collection caused grim hardship from the 980s onwards, the fact that it was collected at all speaks volumes for the social status of England and its serious wealth. In 991, the Danegeld stood, according to the *Anglo-Saxon Chronicle*, at 10,000 pounds of silver. By 1012, when Swein Forkbeard was on the rampage, the amount had rocketed to £48,000. Cnut, seeking perhaps to draw a financial line under the hideously expensive process, collected £72,000 to pay his liðsmen and others in 1018 (perhaps 30 tonnes in weight) with an extra £10,500 from what may already have been the richest city in the country, London.

But taxation occurred in other forms than the hated Danegeld and when Aelfgifu of Northampton, acting as regent for her son Swein, tried to impose taxes in Norway, there was virtually open rebellion. Every hearth in the land had to give to the court a measure of malt, the leg of an adult ox and 'as much unspun flax as could be held between the thumb and middle finger'.[21] A number of Cnut's laws reflect economic issues. Before 1023, he enacted:

and about the improvement of the coinage in such a way that one coinage is to be current throughout all this nation without anything false, and no man is to refuse it. And he who after this coins false money is to forfeit the hand with which he coined the false money.[22]

Since the bulk of crimes in Cnut's England were punished by swingeing fines, these must have represented a sizeable income for the king throughout his reign. In a sense, Domesday Book is our best testimony of Cnut's economic grasp. It was written fifty years after his death, but unless the Confessor and Conqueror had managed the nation worse than we know they did, the manors, the demesnes, the mills, the cattle, the sheep and the value of the land must have been much the same as in Cnut's day.

One group of men who made the king's court what it was were his skalds, his poets.

> One will settle beside his harp
> at his lord's feet, be handed treasures,
> and always quickly pluck the strings
> with a plectrum – with that hard, hopping thing
> he creates harmonies. Harpist, heart's desire![23]

Larson picks out three who were perhaps Cnut's favourites: Thorarin Praisetongue, Ottar the Black and Sighvat Thortharson. All three were Icelanders, and all three visited England, presumably writing and performing for Cnut at Winchester. Ottar refers to Cnut's victory, if that was what it was, at the Holy River in 1026. Praisetongue records his conquest of Norway in 1028 in his poem 'Stretch Song'. One legend attributed to Cnut is that he heard that Praisetongue had written a long poem about himself and threatened him with hanging the next day, unless he composed something comparable glorifying Cnut. 'Knutr guards the land,' the flatterer entoned the following morning, 'as the lord of the kingdom of Heaven.' Cnut was pleased; Praisetongue did not swing and the poem came to be known as 'Head Ransom'. When Ottar the Black declaimed Cnut's greatness, the king filled his Russian cap with silver and gave it to the poet. Many of these stories came from the fertile pen of Snorri Sturluson, writing the *Olafsaga* many years later, but there is no doubt that Cnut liked flattery and was exceedingly generous to his own people. In this respect, there must have been times when Winchester resembled the mythic halls of Vikings, with wolfhounds dozing before roaring fires as the poets sang the praises of their Cnut, the 'greatest king under Heaven', and the mead flowed freely.

In her fascinating analysis of Cnut's skalds, Roberta Flack[24] makes the pertinent point that only Scandinavian audiences could have understood and appreciated the poetry declaimed to them. England became the centre of verse production in the king's reign, but always the theme was that Cnut was the ruler of *Denmark*; he was always portrayed as defender of the *Jutes*. The total number of poems about

Cnut is small: Thoror Kolbiensson's *Eiríksdrapa*; the three *Knútsdrápa* of Sighvat Thortharson, Ottar the Black and Hallvarðr Háreksblesi; the *Tøgdrápa* of Thorarin Praisetongue; and the anonymous *Liðsmannaflokkr*. The problem with gleaning any actual *history* from these is that some are incomplete, the verses in an uncertain order and, to the modern ear, the phraseology is impossibly convoluted and euphemistic. For example, ships are referred to as horses and reindeer; the 'girdle of all lands' is the ocean; 'Lord of Monks' is God; a 'circle-land' is a shield and so on. We have seen already that Cnut was perfectly happy, unlike other Vikings-turned-Christians such as Olaf the Stout, to hear his name sung in pagan praises and archaic phraseology and the reason for this tells us more about the consummate politician he was. Likewise, he was happy to commission a stone bas-relief of the pagan legend of Sigurd the dragon slayer for inclusion in the Old or New Minster, alongside scenes from the Old and New Testaments. His Christian English subjects loved him for his generous gifts to churches; thegn and ceorl alike appreciated and admired his laws. But his Vikings needed to believe that secretly he was still a warrior, like them, bred to the sword and the axe. His campaigns in Denmark, Norway, Sweden and perhaps Scotland gave them the actual chance of slaughter and pillage; his poets reminded them that he was still, after all the piety, one of them.

Sighvat traced Cnut's ancestry, a little spuriously, to the Scyldings, the 'shield men' who had first invaded England two hundred years earlier. He is constantly referred to as 'shield', 'shield-strengthener', and 'defender' throughout the poems written for him. His warships, state-of-the-art weapons as they must have been, are referred to frequently; they are 'slender sea-animals', 'long-planked warships', 'long dragons'. Roberta Flack compares them with the Dreadnoughts of the early twentieth century in terms of cost, prestige and power. Cnut 'was ahead in the first great arms race of the eleventh century'.[25]

The skalds were perfectly happy to promote Cnut's Christianity, too. Sighvat refers to him as 'under Heaven the foremost great Lord'; Praisetongue: 'Knutr protects the land as the guardian of Byzantium [God] [does] Heaven'; Háreksblesi: 'Knutr protects the land as the lord of all [does] the splendid hall of the mountains [heaven]'. As was common, the poetry is written in the third person, but it was certainly delivered to Cnut and in front of an audience. Háreksblesi in particular was concerned to link the great king with his mythological Viking past:

> Knutr, you let the hard-byrnied[26] ships resound forward to Fljót; the famous guardian of the lightnings of battle [swords] sailed, battle-bold, over the sea. Noble strengthener of the sea-horse [ship] of Ullr [shield] you bound your fleet to Aella's[27] family inheritance [England] and rejoiced the seagull of the valkyrie [raven].

There must have been music at the court of King Cnut, although its precise sound is the subject of furious debate among historians. In Saxon England, the professional musician was the *scop*, a lyricist and music maker, poet and probably performer. We do not know whether they sang to an accompanist as today or merely declaimed, probably as the skaldic poets did. The *gleemen* were travelling minstrels long before the wandering troubadours of the high Middle Ages. The anonymous writer of the poem *Widsith* wrote: 'So the people's gleemen go wandering fatedly through many lands . . . Always, whether south to north, they will meet someone discerning of songs and unniggardly of gifts.'[28] Many of these performers were the forerunners of the music hall and the variety theatre; they were dancers, acrobats and jugglers, employed, no doubt, to brighten a dull Hampshire evening.

But if this was the public face that Cnut wanted to show to the world, there must have been a private man behind it all. Somewhere in the labyrinth of rooms at Winchester were his private quarters where he spent time with his family. Of his queen, Emma Aelfgifu, we hear nothing in skaldic poetry. 'Perhaps', suggests Roberta Flack, tongue-in-cheek, 'dominant dowagers did not go over big with the housecarls.'[29] She has two portraits (to Cnut's one) in the outpourings of the Winchester School artwork; she stands with Cnut endowing the Old Minster with the gold cross and she sits to receive the *Encomium* from the monk of St Omer. We know that she had her own apartments at Godbegot House and that she outlived two kings, dying at the age of about seventy in 1052.

Cnut's own siblings were numerous. His elder brother Harald had succeeded his father, Swein Forkbeard, as king of Denmark soon after 3 February 1014. We have seen that Harald's death in 1018 or 1019 precipitated Cnut's taking the Danish throne. His younger sister Gytha married, as we know, Yric of Lade, the Jarl of Hlathir, who ruled Northumbria in 1013. Their son Hákon became the Earl of Worcester and married Gunhilda, the daughter of Wytgeorn of the Wends. It is unlikely that in the extended family that was Cnut's, Gytha spent much time, if any, at Winchester. Saintslaue was the next sister, but since she was born and died in Denmark and we have no dates for either, it may be that she never came to England. Thyra may have been born in 993 in Denmark, which would actually make her the oldest of Forkbeard's children. Earl Godwine of Wessex, who would become the most prominent nobleman in England by the time of Cnut's death, did the thing that all earnest risers do and married 'the boss's' daughter; this was Thyra. The union produced children, but we have no details of them. Most sources agree that she died in 1018, which may have represented something of a blow to the ambitious Godwine, suddenly bereft of a close family relationship with his king. There was probably another daughter of Forkbeard and his first wife Gunhilda, but her name is unknown.

Swein Forkbeard's second marriage to Sigrid the Haughty, shortly before the millennium, may have produced five daughters, who were Cnut's half-sisters The only one of note was Estrith, whom the Normans called Margaret. She married either Richard of Normandy or his son Robert (the records are unclear). Her links to Normandy strengthened Cnut's relationship with the Duchy via Emma but were short-lived. Robert may have divorced her and her second husband was Ulf Thorgilson, the brother of Gytha.

Cnut's first 'marriage' was perhaps already a fact by 1013 but there is no record of it and Aelfgifu of Northampton may well have been relegated to her home county on the advent of the Norman Emma four years later. It would be fascinating to know if these two powerful women ever shared the king's attention at Winchester or whether the 'lady of Northampton' was ever an awkward guest at

Godbegot House. Their two sons were Swein Knutsson, who would go on to rule Norway briefly, with his mother, in the hated 'Aelfgifu's time'; and Harold Harefoot, who would become king of England. Contemporaries openly doubted whether these two were actually the sons of Cnut, although why is not clear. Neither lived long after their father and were both dead by their mid-twenties.

The king's second marriage to Emma produced Harthacnut. He was probably born about 1018 and is specifically mentioned in the ceremony, five years later, of transferring the bones of St Aelfheah from London to Canterbury. As Cnut's only truly legitimate heir, he was probably the child of whom the king was most fond, but no anecdotes have survived of their relationship. Cnut's second child by Emma was Gunhilda, sometimes referred to as Aethelfrida. She was born about 1020 and was betrothed, as an important piece of empire-building, to Henry, the Holy Roman Emperor, whom she married in June 1036, eight months after the death of her father. Ironically, she never actually became Empress because she died in July 1038 on the Adriatic coast before her husband was crowned. Another daughter was born to Cnut and Emma, whose name we do not know. She lived to be eight and was buried in Bosham church in Sussex. In 1865, excavations were carried out in the church from which, eight hundred years earlier, Harold Godwinesson had set out on his fateful journey to Normandy. A stone coffin was found to contain the bones of a child, perhaps confirming the local tradition that the little princess fell into the mill race behind the church and drowned. Certainly, Cnut had a house there and the story may be based on actual events. Laurence Larson makes a passing mention, and without sources, to a mistress 'whom Canute loved above all others' and it would be odd perhaps if the king did not have at least one mistress and possibly several. He cannot have been with Emma constantly and probably saw little of Aelfgifu, so a boudoir companion would have had its attractions.

To rule in Winchester was one thing, but that would only have made Cnut king of England. We need to know what was happening in his other dominions to understand why he was called Emperor of the North.

TEN

Denmark's Crown

A curious, fair creature came floating on the waves,
shouting out to the distant shores . . .
her laughter was terrible.

The Exeter Book

The only entry in the Abingdon and Peterborough manuscripts of
the *Anglo-Saxon Chronicle* for the year 1019 reads: 'In this year
King Cnut turned to Denmark and dwelt there all winter.' The
Worcester edition adds some domestic news: 'And here passed away
Archbishop Aelfstan, who was named Lyfing and he was a man firm
in counsel, both before God and before the world.'[1] Aelfstan was the
other Lyfing in Cnut's reign, not the man from Crediton who became
Bishop of Tavistock, but the Archbishop of Canterbury who
probably crowned the Viking three years earlier. He was one of the
few churchmen who received from Cnut a personal land grant of
property in Sussex in 1018. When he returned from his visit to Rome
to receive his pallium from Pope Benedict VIII, he brought letters
from the pontiff, pressing upon Cnut the need to 'everywhere exalt
God's praise and suppress wrong'. Lyfing died on 12 June 1019.

In a sense, 1019–20 is something of a watershed in Cnut's reign.
He had won the kingdom and settled it, and although no one could
have predicted it after six years of warfare, it was the beginning of a
period of domestic peace.

We must look elsewhere to see what the king was doing and what
led him to winter in Denmark. And therein lies the problem. The
Chronicle is often infuriatingly terse. In 1024, 1025 and 1027 there
is no entry at all in the Abingdon, Worcester or Peterborough
manuscripts, making a chronological account of Cnut's reign
impossible. The *Encomium* was written for specific political

purposes and is openly biased. The poems of Cnut's skalds are not only 'over the top' in terms of description and allegory, but they were performed to the man's face and paid for by the man's money; they can at best be seen as propaganda. And if we consult the thin and contradictory Danish sources, we are left with a confusing and chaotic narrative. All we can do is to look at the evidence we have and try to make some sense of it.

One possibility is that Cnut returned to Denmark in 1019 to take the throne on the death of his brother Harald – and here the problems begin. The *Encomium* maintains consistently that Cnut was the elder brother, the eldest surviving son of Swein Forkbeard, although, as we have seen, there may have been an earlier Harald who died in infancy. Certainly it was a Danish tradition to use a grandfather's name for a newborn and this would follow the pattern. It is more likely, however, that Harald was the elder, which explains why Forkbeard left him in Denmark (a country that was, after all, already his) and took Cnut to England (a country he had yet to win). This may also have happened because of the different personalities of the boys. We know nothing about Harald Sweynsson, but perhaps he was the more dependable, a diplomat rather than a headstrong warrior. Whatever the birth order, the *Encomium* implies a close working relationship between the brothers in which Cnut asked Harald to join him in the 'enterprise of England' and, once it was conquered, they should decide who would rule which. The Encomiast went so far as to put dialogue into the brothers' mouths: "It is my part to rule [said Harald] the heritage which our father gave me with your approval; as for you, if you have lost a greater one, I regret it, but, though prepared to help you, I will not endure that my kingdom be divided."[2] This actually makes little sense. Harald had not won England, Forkbeard and Cnut had, so in no sense was his kingdom becoming divided by Cnut's offer. Harald evidently refused this, but rather than the brothers quarrelling, they both travelled east to bring their exiled mother back from Poland before Cnut returned to England in 1015 to begin his battles with Ironside. Only the *Encomium* carries this version of events and modern scholars, wary of the work's bias, tend to doubt it. We are returning to Larson, the evidence of the sagas and the numismatic spread of Cnut's currency, in contending that the Wendlands – in effect, western Poland – were important to the king.

Thietmar of Merseburg, however, has Harald with Cnut and his army laying siege to London in 1016 and there are numismatists today who claim that the coins probably struck in Lincoln in 1015 already carried the legend *Cnut Rex Daenor* (Cnut, king of the Danes) as though the younger brother had the throne four years before he was actually crowned. Does this imply some sort of joint kingship? Will we one day find a coin in Denmark that reads *Harald Rex Anglor* (Harald, King of the English)?

A bizarre twist which lends some credence to Cnut as king of Denmark in 1015 comes from the *Annales Ryenses*, written by a Cistercian monk in the monastery of Ryd near Flensborg about 1250. According to this, the *Thing* deposed Harald because of his effeminacy and replaced him with Cnut, only to reverse the situation because of Cnut's later prolonged absences in England. Certainly the Vikings hated effeminacy of any sort, and the 'Handbook of Penance', written by Theodore, the Greek-born Archbishop of Canterbury, about 690 puts the Christian gloss on it: 'A male who commits fornication with a male shall do penance for ten years' and 'Sodomites shall do penance for seven years and the effeminate man is an adulteress'. Historian Alistair Campbell dismisses the *Annales* as 'absurd', but the short reign of Harald and our almost total lack of knowledge of him, leaves the door open to all kinds of speculation.

Whatever the situation, there is no evidence other than that Cnut and Harald got on with each other. A surviving document has Harald entering into a confraternity with Christ Church, Canterbury, which is exactly the sort of thing that Cnut would spend the rest of his life doing. It does not prove of course that Harald was ever actually *in* England, merely that Cnut added his name as a benefactor. Historian Niels Lund has shown, however, that Cnut only visited Denmark four times during his reign in England and only ever for the winter. The fact that he was prepared to leave his newly won kingdom after only three years implies that there were problems in Denmark that needed his urgent attention. And winter was the time of bitter winds and impassable roads, when rebellion in England was least likely.

According to the Worcester version of the *Chronicle*, he took only nine ships with him, which implies less than an army. Even if those vessels were the largest sea-serpent type, he would have a force of less than a thousand men, but perhaps he could reckon on his presence or his cash to be enough to cope with whatever problems existed. It was from Denmark in the winter of 1019 that he wrote the first of the two letters to his people he was to produce during his reign. It is likely that this was actually sent to Wulfstan of York, who almost certainly (from the tone of the text and the subject matter) added his own ideas to it. There is no equivalent today to Cnut's letters; perhaps the nearest we come to it is a manifesto or a party political broadcast. It was written by a scribe of course (we have no actual evidence that Cnut could write) and of the twenty paragraphs, nine (Wulfstan's?) refer to the Church.

From the tone, Cnut was clearly concerned for the maintenance of law and order, and it was probably on his return to England that he and Wulfstan framed the laws discussed in Chapter Seven. He had put his trust in his earls, and particularly the omnipotent Thurkil the Tall, in that he refers to him specifically in his opening: 'King Cnut greets in friendship his archbishop and his diocesan bishops and Earl Thurkil and all his earls, whether men of a twelve hundred wergild or a two hundred, ecclesiastic and lay, in England.'[3] He clearly echoed the promises made by the *unraed* Aethelred in 1013: 'And I inform you that I will be a gracious lord and a faithful observer of God's rights and just secular law.' He exhorted his ealdormen to help the bishops in the maintenance of 'furthering God's rights and my royal dignity and the benefit of the people'. And his threat was not an idle one:

> If anyone, ecclesiastic or layman, Dane or Englishman, is so presumptuous as to defy God's law and my royal authority or the secular laws, and he will not make amends and desist according to the direction of my bishops, I then pray, and also command, Earl Thurkil, if he can, to cause the evil-doer to do right. And if he cannot, then it is my will that with the power of us both he shall destroy him in the land or drive him out of the land, whether he be of high or low rank.

And he reminded his people via Wulfstan, of the need for continuity and the rule of law: 'And it is my will that all the nation, ecclesiastical and lay, shall steadfastly observe Edgar's laws, which all men have chosen and sworn at Oxford.' This meeting of course had taken place in the previous year and clearly was the political starting point for the rest of Cnut's reign. Paragraphs 14–20 clearly bear the stamp of Wulfstan, with strict reminders of the need to be wary of murderers, perjurers, wizards, sorcerers, adulterers and 'incestuous deeds'. The observance of Sunday was to last from midday on Saturday until dawn on Monday and all trade and other business was banned during that time.

It is with the veiled references to what we might term foreign policy that we are most concerned here. 'Since I did not spare my money,' Cnut wrote in paragraph 4, 'as long as hostility was threatening you, I have now with God's help put an end to it with my money.' Some of those hearing the bishop's delivery of this letter throughout England would no doubt have been furious with Cnut's hypocrisy. The money he refers to was almost certainly his private cut of the vast Danegeld paid the previous year and as such it represented the hard-paid-for taxation with which the English had been saddled for thirty years. The letter is at once condescending and infuriatingly vague, in that we have no idea as to what it referred. Thietmar of Merseburg in his *Chronicon* refers to a naval victory under Cnut in 1018. We know that some of the chronicler's chronology is suspect and no other source backs it up, but a perfectly feasible scenario is that this battle, if it happened, represented the destruction of an invasion fleet. Thietmar tells us there were thirty ships, but gives no details. If he is right, who were the invaders? Ironically, they may have been the very liðsmen who fought for Cnut in 1015–17. We know that many of this force were mercenaries, fighting not for the Viking king but for plunder and loot. This is what the Danegeld of 1018 was all about; but what if some of the army were unhappy with the amount they received? Pillaging along the coast of England and even far inland was a Viking way of life; the mere fact that the king of England was now a Viking would have made little difference.

Viking naval battles were fought as much like land battles as possible. It would be many centuries before gunpowder would make a difference to tactics at sea. Ships were roped together to give a mutual support platform, driven at top speed towards the enemy by the oarsmen, while the decks bristled with the weapons of mail-coated, helmeted men. Most of these battles were fought near the coast, but the lack of confirmation by the *Anglo-Saxon Chronicle* possibly means that it was fought off the coast of Denmark. If the *Chronicle* is right that Cnut sailed with only nine ships, then he was either heavily outnumbered in this engagement, or obtained reinforcements from Denmark. Either way, he was victorious and the defeated crews were hacked down and thrown overboard.

Snorri Sturluson's account of the battle of Svoldr, fought when Cnut was a boy, is a graphic description of what Cnut may have gone through. King Olaf Trygvasson's ship, the *Long Serpent*, was cut off by several of his enemies' vessels, in particular Yric Hakonsson of Lade's *Iron Beard*:

> Earl Yric was in the forehold of his ship, where a shield wall had been set up. Having heavy weapons – the sword and axe – and thrusting spears alike were being used in the fighting and everything that could be used as a missile was being thrown. In fact, so many weapons rained down on the *Serpent*, so thickly flew the spears and arrows that the shields could scarcely withstand them . . .[4]

Sturluson continues with this merciless hand-to-hand slaughter until, in a poetic moment that surely never happened, an archer's bow snaps with a thunderous noise: "'What was that, that broke with such a noise?" called king Olaf. "Norway, King," cried Einar [Tambarskelve], "from your grip."

> Desperate was the defence of the *Serpent* . . . Now the fighting became really intense on all sides . . . the battle was raging even in the forehold, but there were by now so many of the Earl's men on board the *Serpent* as could find room and his ships lay all around her. There were nowhere near enough defenders left to repel so great a number and before long most of the *Serpent*'s men had been killed, brave and stout though they were.

Olaf Tryggvason leapt overboard rather than be taken alive. He 'threw his shield above his head and sank beneath the surface'. The runic carvings on the great stone at Aarhus are in memory of one 'who died on the sea to the eastward when the kings were fighting'.[5]

Cnut's letter, however, refers to money not open warfare and the subsequent paragraphs are no clearer:

> Then I was informed that greater danger was approaching us than we liked at all; and then I went myself with the men who accompanied me to Denmark, from where the greatest injury had come to you, and with God's help I have taken measures so that never henceforth shall hostility reach you from there as long as you support me rightly and my life lasts. Now I thank Almighty God for his help and his mercy, that I have settled the great dangers which were approaching us that we need fear no danger to us from there; but [we may reckon] on full help and deliverance, if we need it.

Harald of Denmark was dead and the danger to which Cnut referred, coming specifically from Denmark, could only mean a resurgence of the Viking raids by lawless jarls revelling in the lack of royal control. Cnut's reference to going himself with the men who accompanied him may seem a truism, but it is likely to refer to a meeting he probably called early in 1019 to establish the same kind of *métier* he had achieved at Oxford with his English subjects. The men who went with him were probably his Danish earls, men like Eglaf, Hrani, Hakon, Halfdan, his brother-in-law Ulf and perhaps even Thrym, although any one of these may have stayed behind to hold England under Thurkil. It is also possible that Cnut took hostages with him, the sons of his earls, both Viking and English, to ensure loyalty. His 1019 letter has all the hallmarks of a man worried that all may not be well in his absence and we know that some sort of rebellion occurred under Eadwig, the 'king of the ceorls', despite Thurkil's strong-arm tactics. Laurence Larson has an interesting take on the rising, assuming that because Cnut's Easter witan met at Cirencester, somewhat off the beaten track, Eadwig's rebellion had happened somewhere along the Severn.

In his letter Cnut sounds fairly confident of the fact that the Danish threat was averted. Was this simply accomplished by cash, the recipient of the Danegeld paying Danegeld himself? Very possibly, but there was more. Although there are no records of it, Cnut must have been crowned king of Denmark in the winter of 1019 to fill the void created by Harald's death. The fact that the dead man had no heirs (the result of his effeminacy?) meant that Cnut's accession was not complicated. But how was the threat of a renewed Danish onslaught to be averted once the king had sailed back to England, as he had by Easter 1020? A quarter of a century ago, historian C.A. Christensen argued that this may have been achieved by the Danish bishops. He contended that Cnut gave his new bishops, some of them Englishmen with English monastic training, the right of the *navigium*, the almost feudal obligation to raise ships for his navy and therefore endowed them with secular authority by which they ruled through him. Certainly, the letter of 1019 hints at this practice in England – 'and also I charge all my ealdormen that they help the bishops' – as though bishops had the greater power and seniority. We must remember, however, that this is England, not Denmark, and that Cnut's letter was tinkered with by the churchman, Wulfstan.

As Neils Lund maintains, the Christian Church was still too new in Denmark for this sort of organizational authority to exist; it did by the fourteenth century, but hardly at all in the eleventh. Much more likely is that one or more of the Danish earls referred to above was left behind as regent in Denmark, much as Thurkil had been in England, and this may be guessed from the relatively few charters they witness in Cnut's reign. It may even explain why some of them disappear altogether from the English record; they were not dead, but carrying on the king's government in his homeland. Certainly, this would be Thurkil's role in 1023.

We have already seen what happened on Cnut's return to England. All texts of the *Anglo-Saxon Chronicle* agree that there was a great council at Cirencester where Aethelweard was outlawed. This was the year of the consecration of the church at Ashingdon and the monk Aethelnoth was consecrated as Archbishop of Canterbury.

It is the events of the next two years that are confusing. In 1021 'at Martinmas [11 November] King Cnut outlawed Earl Thurkil'. This is part of the love–hate relationship these two had for each other. We have seen already that Thurkil was a renowned warrior, older than Cnut by several years, with his own following amounting to several thousand men. We have seen, too, that he could be treacherous, throwing in his lot with Aethelred before returning to Cnut in 1015. The fact that he was regent in the king's absence four years later speaks volumes for his re-found trustworthiness – he is the only earl whom Cnut mentions by name in the 1019 letter; and once again, the father–son relationship of the Jomsviking and his protégé would explain it. No information is given by any source as to why Cnut should expel the man in 1021, especially as he effectively gave him the regency of Denmark two years later. We know how the king dealt with slippery self-servers – Eadric Streona is the prime example, his decapitated body left to rot under London's walls. Yet he kept taking Thurkil back. Why? The only satisfactory explanation is that Cnut had planned this all along. Thurkil had helped him win the kingdom back in 1016; he governed it for him in 1019. But by 1021 he had outlived his usefulness and he could be a threat. A spirit as powerful and competent as Thurkil may well be a rival to Cnut in the years ahead, yet he had done the king a great service – so exile, rather than death, was the answer. There is a vague idea that Thurkil's expulsion had to do with the king's anger over whatever happened at the abbey at Ely, but this may simply have been an excuse. John of Worcester says that the great jarl took his wife with him into exile.

The *Chronicle*'s entry for 1022 takes us back into the 'scenarioland' forced upon us by the many gaps in the reign of Cnut. Most texts of the *Chronicle* tell us: 'In this year King Cnut went out with his ships to Wiht'. We know that the Isle of Wight played a special part in the history of Anglo-Viking relationships. Several times, the raiders had used the island as a winter camp and a springboard for attacks along the south coast. Aethelred had fled there in the uncertain months of 1015. What is not clear at all is why Cnut should take the fleet (a possible eighty ships) and, on a technical note, where they would have anchored.[6]

Two scenarios suggest themselves here. The first and more obvious, is an invasion threat from the newly exiled Thurkil. Our hindsight knowledge that he was reconciled with Cnut again in the following year should not blind us to the fact that he was a dangerous man, with his own ships and troops. His brother commanded the Jomsvikings, legendary warriors whom Cnut would have known. By basing his fleet in battle readiness in the Wight, Cnut could have struck quickly to meet an invasion threat anywhere in the south, especially if, in reality, his ships were not based at the island, but were patrolling the waters of the Solent.

A second possibility involves the Normans. Cnut's relationship with his wife's people was rather ambivalent. We are perhaps overawed by hindsight. Aware of 1066 and all that that entailed, we see Normandy as some all-powerful force waiting in the wings, a kind of inevitability that would destroy Anglo-Scandinavian England for ever. The fact, of course, is that Duke Richard's duchy was far inferior to Cnut's England in every sense. Some historians have argued that were it not for Harold Godwinesson having to march north to defeat Harald Hardrada's army at Stamford Bridge, near York, he would have routed William at Senlac with a fresh, undamaged force. And in 1022 the future Conqueror was not yet born. Richard of Normandy seems to have been keeping his options open. The fact that his sister, Emma, was married to Cnut implies at least cordiality – their sons, the possible future kings of England, were the Norman duke's nephews. A charter of Cnut's, known as S949, deals with the king's grant to the abbey at Fécamp, which we know was one of Richard's favourites. On the other hand, the athelings, the sons of Aethelred by Emma, were at the Norman court and they posed an ongoing threat to Cnut he could never quite afford to ignore. Even so, there is no evidence of a deterioration in the relationship between Cnut and Richard which would have necessitated maintaining a fleet to repel invasion.

A third scenario entirely for the events of 1022 comes from the Worcester manuscript of the *Anglo-Saxon Chronicle*: 'In this year King Cnut went out with his ships to Wihtland and Archbishop Aethelnoth went to Rome . . .' The other texts mention Aethelnoth's travels, too, but Wiht*land* may imply a journey altogether further than four miles off England's south coast. The fact that the Abingdon manuscript tells us that Cnut returned to England in 1023 implies an altogether longer commitment than sailing around the treacherous rocks that would become the Needles. The historian J. Steenstrup identifies Wihtland with an area along the Vistula in Poland and given that Cnut's mother may have come from this area, it is at least possible. The king would have sailed through the Skaggerat, via Denmark and on to the Baltic, although what this campaign was all about is unknown. Was it perhaps an all-out clash with the disgruntled Thurkil, raising troops in eastern Scandinavia? Such frantic and dangerous activity concertinaed into a few months seems unlikely, but it does give some credence to the fact that Cnut and Thurkil were reconciled early in 1023, somewhere other than England.

The whole area was in fact well known to Viking travellers, and even to Englishmen. A wanderer called Wulfstan (no connection to the bishop!) visited shortly after the reign of Alfred the Great. He left the Danish port of Hedeby and reached Truso in seven days and nights by sail with Wendland on his starboard and Largeland, Lacland and Skane on his port *'and all these lands pay tribute to Denmark'*[7] [my italics]. According to Wulfstan: 'This new Vistula is a very great river and it divides Witland and Wend-land and this Witland belongs to the Estonians.' Estonia itself, Wulfstan tells us,[8] had many kings, one per city, who drank mare's milk where the ceorls drank mead. Internecine strife was a way of life: 'And among the Estonians there is a tribe which knows how to embalm in ice . . .'

Laurence Larson in 1912 had no problem identifying Wihtland with the coastal area to the east of the Vistula in what would centuries later become Prussia. He further implies that the expedition three years later to bring back his mother was somehow linked to a further extension of Cnut's power. This would explain what otherwise can only have been manoeuvres, hardly a reason for the *Anglo-Saxon Chronicle* to mention them at all.

The Danish historian Steenstrup a century ago established that the Slavic tribes west of the Vistula had no organised state in the eleventh century, which left the area wide open to encroachment by both Germans and Danes. As early as the reign of Charlemagne (800–814), Cnut's forebears had settled in a city called Reric. They traded cattle, fish, mead, timber, spices and horses with the native Wends and seem to have lived in peace with them along the lines of the Danelaw in England. Modern archaeology has established that most of the settlements in the East were actually Swedish – Danish and Norwegian Vikings concentrating largely in the West. What links Cnut to the area is the town of Wolin in today's Poland at the mouth of the Oder, for this was Jomsberg, the fortress home of the Jomsvikings of Strut-Haraldsson where the boy who would be king was perhaps raised. It was the centre of a Slavic religious cult, but what dominated was the Viking stronghold overlooking the harbour that could once, according to legend, accommodate a fleet of 300 dragon-ships. Adam of Bremen knew it well:

> It is verily the greatest city in Europe. It is inhabited by Slavs and other peoples, Greeks and barbarians . . . all the inhabitants are still chained to the errors of heathen idolatry. In other respects, especially as to manners and hospitality, a more obliging and honourable people cannot be found.[9]

Larson speculates that Cnut's second reconciliation with Thurkil took place in the fortress they both knew so well.

The *Anglo-Saxon Chronicle*'s texts are full with the details of the translation ceremony of Archbishop Aelfheah's bones in 1023, at which we know little Harthacnut, perhaps five years old, was present. The swapping of the sons of Cnut and Thurkil probably refers to an earlier child by Aelfgifu of Northampton, but whether this was a token hostage situation in which Thurkil promised to behave himself or whether it is an example of the already established practice of boys being brought up in another's great house, is unclear. We do not know what happened to Thurkil. He disappears from the record entirely after 1023. Was he ever actually regent of Denmark, especially as Ulf held that position three years later? Did he simply die? Or was he finally murdered on the orders of Cnut, the king being unable to trust his wayward vassal and sometime mentor any longer?

The Abingdon and Worcester texts of the *Anglo-Saxon Chronicle* have no entries at all for 1024 and 1025. Two of the greatest figures of Cnut's age, Wulfstan, Archbishop of York and Thurkil the Tall, warlord and perhaps regent in Denmark, were probably both dead and the king had to make his way without them. The Peterborough manuscript has a Latin entry for 1024, which records the death of Richard of Normandy and the succession of his son Robert, but this was probably a later addition inserted after 1066. The same text for 1025 reads:

> Here King Cnut went to Denmark in ships to the battle place [*holme*, meaning an island], at the Holy River and Ulf and Eilaf came against him and a very great raiding-army, both a land and a ship-army from the Swedish nation, and there many men perished on King Cnut's side, both Danishmen and of English; the Swedes had possession of the place of slaughter.[10]

Sweden is 1,000 miles long. The northern part was called Norrland, a bleak, inhospitable place within the Arctic Circle, covered in thick forests of dark pine and fir, elsewhere with grey slabs of bare rock. The country's soil is poor in the north, better in the warmer south and it was here, in the centuries before Cnut, that two regions co-existed, the Svear (from which the modern nation's name is derived) and the Götar. The Svear to the east was dominated by the people of Uppland and the kings of Sweden had their palace at Uppsala, north of Lake Mälar. The Götar peoples lived further west around lakes Väner and Vätter in the respective provinces of Västergötland and Östergötland. The boundaries of these regions were blurred, the southernmost point, Skåne, belonging to Denmark (and thus to Cnut) and some of the areas in modern Finland and the Baltic to Sweden. The population was sparse, as it still is, and settlement was confined to the more fertile areas of the south, centring on Västergötland, Östergötland and the island of Gohl, where there is ample archaeological evidence of early trade. The northern reaches of the Baltic along the Gulf of Bothnia, are frozen over for part of the year and even in the warmer eleventh century, this was likely to have been the case.

One of Sweden's most thriving towns shortly before Cnut's day was Birka on the island of Björkö in Lake Mälar. There is a modern cross there dedicated to the Christian missionary Anskar, on the high ground where the fort used to stand. In the reign of Harald Bluetooth, the town had perhaps a thousand inhabitants and its own *Thing*, although a falling off of trade and the rising land level made it a rapidly declining site in Cnut's time. By 1070, when Adam of Bremen wrote of it, it had gone altogether. The area today is known as Black Earth because of the high concentration of industrial debris charcoal just below the surface. It had its own iron forges, its bronze workshops and its bone-carving centres. A large number of weighing scales is testimony to the importance of Birka as a port, with markets all year round. In the winter, trappers from the north would bring their furs on sledges across the frozen sea into the inlets of the Cargo Boat Harbour and the Cross Harbour. Arabic coins have been found within the 30-acre site and the huge Hemlanden cemetery housed almost 1,200 bodies, buried still in the pagan tradition with glass, pottery, wine, rune-inscribed swords and Byzantine silks.

Very little is known about Sweden in the Viking Age. In the years shortly before Cnut's birth, the only king about whom we have any knowledge is Olaf Skötkonung, a Christian who founded the first bishopric at Skara in Östergötland. Even so, the conversion to Christianity was only partial and when Cnut faced invasion from here, he was probably confronted by a largely pagan force.

Most experts today place Cnut's battle of the Holy River in 1026, not 1025 as the *Chronicle* does, and for the next two years he would be committed to sporadic fighting in defence of what was, in effect, a Northern Empire. No Viking had ever before held such territory and this fact alone must have made him enemies. Ranged against him now were Norwegians, Swedes and his own regent and brother-in-law, Ulf. This war is complicated because the sources contradict each other with a vengeance.

The first problem comes in trying to identify Ulf and Eglaf. These two were probably brothers, Ulf the husband of Cnut's sister, Estrith. Eglaf was an earl in England and he witnessed a charter – S961, granting lands to the monastery of Abbotsbury in Dorset – in 1024. The Swedish chronicler Saxo Grammaticus, among others, contends that Eglaf was at the Holy River, too. There is a certain amount of doubt about whose side the pair were on. According to Snorri Sturluson in the *Olafsaga*, they were the sons of Thorgils Sprakaleg and Ulf, as a senior jarl, acting as regent of Denmark by 1026, was spearheading a plot to place the boy Harthacnut on the throne. There is no other evidence of this, but it is not beyond the bounds of possibility and, if correct, would certainly be a motive for Cnut's confrontation with him at the Holy River.

The leaders of the opposition to Cnut were certainly Olaf Haraldsson (the Stout), king of Norway, and Anund Jakob of Sweden. Haraldsson first emerges in English history in the Viking attacks on London in 1009. Like Cnut and Yric of Lade, the mercenary-turned-Christian would have his exploits commemorated in skaldic poetry. He became a convert in Normandy in 1013 and returned to Norway the following year to seize the throne and continue the Christianization begun by Olaf Tryggvason. Snorri Sturluson's *Heimskringla* is the best known of these epics and may reflect earlier verses from the eleventh century.

Anund Jakob was the son of Olaf of Sweden, a stepson of Swein Forkbeard. Olaf died about 1022 and Jakob continued the hostility shown by his father towards the Danes in general and Cnut in particular. There is a sense that with Forkbeard's death and the prolonged absence of Cnut, the Danish grip on Norway and southern Sweden was being lost. Certainly, Jakob lost little time in joining with Haraldsson and the shifting Ulf in concentrating his ships and his army.

Using Sturluson and Saxo's *Gesta Danorum* as his source material, Laurence Larson painted a plausible picture of events in this campaign. Haraldsson was on the coast of Zealand when Cnut's fleet was sighted and his scouts at first reported that they were merchantmen. Haraldsson's reply was that they were merchantmen who had come to buy Denmark with iron. Larson speculates that Cnut sailed from Lime Firth to the Sound, effectively cutting off Haraldsson's retreat. According to Saxo, he found and destroyed part of the Swedish fleet at Strangeberg before Jakob could join forces with Haraldsson. What was left of Jakob's force reached Haraldsson in Skåne and while the Swedes formed up in battle order aboard ship in the mouth of the Holy River, Haraldsson worked inland to build a dam which would act as a trap for the Anglo-Danish fleet. Sturluson's account tells that Cnut was caught off guard:

At dawn the next morning, a large part of Knutr's forces was found to have landed; some were conversing, others seeking amusement. Then, without the least warning, the waters came down in torrents, dashing the floating trees against the ships. The ships were damaged and the waters overflowed the river banks, drowning the men who had gone on land and also many who were still on the ships. Those who were able to do so cut the ropes and allowed their ships to drift, each in its own direction. The great dragon that Knutr himself commanded was among these; it was not easily managed by the oars alone and drifted out toward the hostile fleet. When all the allies [Haraldsson and Jakob] recognised the ship, they immediately surrounded it; but it was not easily attacked, for the ship was high like a castle and had a number of men on board, who were carefully chosen, thoroughly armed and very reliable. It was not long before Jarl Ulfr came up alongside with his ships and the battle was now joined in earnest. Knutr's forces now came up from all sides. Then the kings Olaf and Anund realised that they had won as much as fate had allowed them for this time, so they ordered a retreat, withdrew from Knutr's fleet and separated from the fight.[11]

There is nowhere in Scandinavia today called the Holy River. The *Knútsdrápa* written by the skald Sighvat about 1040 has Haraldsson's Norwegians moving south along the River Nid near Lade to Zealand, but is vague as to where the armies met. He also says that Jakob was moving with a Swedish force, perhaps to catch Cnut in a pincer movement. A breakaway force, possibly an advance guard under an anonymous leader referred to as 'destroyer of the Danes', attacked Skåne, which was probably already under Cnut's control. The Sighvat poem makes no mention of a battle at all and Ottar the Black's version describes Cnut as 'withstander' as though he only stopped the joint onslaught, but did not wipe it out. The *Anglo-Saxon Chronicle*'s version – that 'the Swedes had the power of the place of slaughter' – is so at odds with this that various commentators have claimed that this means 'possessed the field with their dead', which seems a tortuous interpretation.

The battle may have been an amphibious one, or at least one fought on the river bank, not unlike the epic clash at Maldon on the causeway to Northsey Island. It was probably shield wall to shield wall, a slogging infantry fight of axes, swords and spears. And the result was probably inconclusive, hence the claims to victory by both sides. It would not have been unlike Napoleon's battle of Borodino in the Russian campaign of 1812 – the army of Khutuzov gave him a bloody nose, but did not stop him marching on to Moscow and the Russians were too weak to try again. According to Sturluson, who is likely to have been better informed on the movements of his hero, Haraldsson, than his enemy, Cnut, Jakob had only 120 ships out of the 420 he started with at the beginning of the summer. Even with Haraldsson's sixty Norwegian dragon-ships, Cnut's navy still outnumbered them. We need not take these numbers too literally, but the ratio was probably right. Jakob proposed they go home, lick their wounds and try again in the next campaigning season. Cnut's losses, in ships and men, may well have been heavy and all he could do, according to Sturluson's sagas, was to block the Sound of Zealand in an attempt to catch Haraldsson on his way home. In the event, the wily old Viking-turned-fanatic-Christian abandoned most of his fleet and went home overland.

So, in his second letter to the English, in 1027, Cnut refers to himself as king of England, Denmark, the Norwegians and some of the Swedes – *rex partis Suanorum*. This may of course be hyperbole, a reassuring piece of propaganda sent back to England exactly as Napoleon misreported the Russian disaster with his famous 'the Emperor is in excellent health'. However, the existence of a coin of the king's with the legend *Cnut Rex Swein*, struck at Sigtuna in central Sweden, seems to clinch the fact. Similar coins of Olaf Skotkonung and Anund Jakob, however, carry the legend *Rex A[nglorum]* – king of the English – and neither of these men ever was. In other words, the dies of various coins were copied slavishly without regard to what they actually said.

Numismatist Kenneth Jonsson comes to a sensible compromise on all this contradiction.[12] If Cnut had really fought and won a decisive victory in central Sweden, then surely he would have claimed to be *Rex Suanorum*, king of *all* the Swedes, not merely of a part. Jonsson remarks that the Holy River battle was probably fought at Helgeå, the river that reaches the sea at Kristianstad. There are tantalising clues from elsewhere. Historian Bo Gräslund[13] has an area near Stockholm as the likely battle site and there are runestones in Västergötland covered with the English title thegn, echoed by the place name Thegnaby near Oslo.

Sturluson's *Olafsaga* takes the story beyond the Holy River, however. It was September 1026 and on the day before Michaelmas, Cnut went to Roskilde. In a bizarre situation not explained in the sagas, Ulf hosted a celebration for the king. The only possible explanation of this, if it happened at all, is that it was a reconciliation. We know that Cnut effected such things, genuine or otherwise, as part of his *métier*. If Ulf was actually an earl in England and the king's brother-in-law, he had risked all by defecting to Haraldsson. There were bridges to be built and perhaps that was what Michaelmas at Roskilde was all about. It did not work.

According to Sturluson, the pair were playing chess and Cnut made a wrong move allowing Ulf to take one of his knights. Cnut promptly disallowed the move and the earl threw over the board and made for the door.

'Are you running away now, timid wolf?' said the king.
The Earl turned in the doorway and replied, 'Further you would run at Holy River, if you had been able. You did not then call Ulfr timid, when I rushed up to help you, when the Swedes were thrashing you and your men like dogs.'[14]

Sturluson's version of events is suspect. The notion that Ulf was on Cnut's side in the battle at Skåne, or perhaps that he defected during it, does not accord at all with the English version of events. What it does is set the scene for what followed. Ulf, realising that he may have pushed the short-fused Cnut too far, spent the night in the sanctuary of the Church of the Holy Trinity in the town. Cnut was still seething in the morning and sent a servant to kill the troublesome jarl. The man refused, on the grounds that Ulf was in a holy place. Ivor White, one of Cnut's *huscarls*, had no such qualms, and soon returned to the king with his sword red with Ulf's blood.

'A life had been taken in God's own house,' wrote Laurence Larson dramatically, 'blood had been shed before the very altar.' We know that Cnut eliminated his enemies by murder, battle and exile. As much as the Viking who would invade England unsuccessfully in the autumn of 1066, his name might have been *Hardrada*, the hard ruler. Such men did not take prisoners, or if they did, they mutilated them!

If Ulf was murdered, as the *Olafsaga* contends, and if Cnut was responsible, is this why he gave large grants of land to the church at Roskilde? Is this why he gave similar endowments to his widowed sister, Estrith? And is this why she, unable to trust her volatile brother, sent her own eight-year-old son Swein to Sweden to be out of Cnut's reach?

The evidence for what happened in Cnut's other dominions in this period is infuriatingly vague, but in essence there can be little doubt that by 1028 at the latest, Cnut had re-established the powerbase once held by his father, Swein Forkbeard, in Scandinavia. The fact that he also held England made him, in effect, an emperor. Legend has it that when he came home to Winchester, he came as a conqueror for a second time and hung his old English crown, with its gold flowers, on the altar of the Old Minster before sailing north and west to claim a new one.

ELEVEN

Emperor of the North

> The most famous princes in the North from the midst of Fife
> have brought their heads to Knutr; that was to buy peace.
>
> Sighvat the skald

'King Cnut went to Rome,' the Chronicle tells us for 1027, 'and as soon as he came home then he went to Scotland.' As we have seen, the chronology of Cnut's reign is vastly difficult to establish. Not only are there four versions of the *Anglo-Saxon Chronicle*, written by different men in different places, but they include later additions, inserted with hindsight, and they often disagree with each other and certainly with Scandinavian sources, especially on exact dates. So Cnut's visit to Rome could have taken place at any time between 1026 and 1031. It is even possible that he went twice and that both visits have become garbled into one. We know that he was in the eternal city in March 1027 but when he had set out and how long it took him to get there are unknown.

There is no precedent for such a visit by a Danish king, although archbishops carried out the trip by definition to receive their pallium, the Y-shaped white woollen stole which was a badge of their office, from the Pope. For instance, the Worcester manuscript of the *Chronicle* for 1022 records that:

> Bishop Aethelnoth went to Rome and was there received with much honour by Benedict, the reverend pope and he placed the pallium on him with his own hands and consecrated and blessed him with great reverence on 7 October. And the archbishop immediately sang Mass on the same day and soon thereafter dined in state with the pope himself. And also he himself took the

pallium from St Peter's altar, and then afterwards journeyed happily home to his own country.[1]

Kings of England had also made the pilgrimage. The saintly Aethelwulf, unhappy that war and politics were forced on him, went to Rome in 855 and spent a year there, leaving the country in the hands of his son, Aethelbald. With him travelled the young Alfred, later called the Great, on the second of two visits before he was seven. Burgred, king of Mercia in the days of the heptarchy, fled the Vikings in 873 to spend his remaining years in Rome. Nearly two centuries earlier, Caedwalla of Wessex seems to have had a particular down on the people of the Isle of Wight and attacked, intending to exterminate them and repopulate the island with his own Christians. Wounded in the attempt, he left England in the summer of 688, endowing a church at Samer near Calais and another in Lombardy, south of the Alps, before arriving in Rome by Easter 689. Frank Stenton believes he was a dying man and that the visit to Rome merely confirms this. If so, he took his time. If he knew he was dying, presumably from blood poisoning from an infected wound, his dawdling of eight months seems to have been chancing his arm. The Pope gave Caedwalla the baptismal name of Peter and the king died ten days later, still wearing his white robes. And Ine of Wessex, prefiguring Burgred's policy, 'commended his kingdom to younger men', according to Bede and died in Rome in 726.

Three centuries later, Cnut followed the same path, although he had no intention of giving up his kingdom or dying in Rome. In his letter of 1027, he wrote that he had undertaken the pilgrimage 'because I heard from wise men that St Peter the Apostle has received from the Lord a great power of binding and loosing, and bears the keys of the kingdom of Heaven; and therefore I deemed it useful in no ordinary degree to seek his patronage before God'.[2] Cnut was buying his place in heaven and he did not care who knew it. There is always, even in his most mystical dealings, an air of practical, hard-edged realism about Cnut very much echoed in the papacy itself. It may be that he needed to wash his hands in public for the murder of Ulf; more likely he wanted some sort of papal backing, if not absolution, for opposing King Olaf Haraldsson, whose muscular Christianity Cnut may have appeared to be challenging at the Holy River. This is Laurence Larson's argument and it is not a strong one, but it hinges on what the papacy knew or did not know about Cnut's own religiosity. And the journey itself was a carefully rehearsed piece of theatre.

Whether he returned to England to leave his old crown, symbolically and actually, behind, he probably did come back, if only to show his face in his kingdom after, no doubt, rumours of his defeat had found their way back home. An accomplished warrior and politician like Cnut would not have left the Holy River war unfinished, so he was happy enough with the outcome, whatever it actually was, to travel east. Confusion abounds on Cnut's pilgrimage to Rome because the various *Anglo-Saxon Chronicle* dates differ. The chronicler Goscelin, writing a history of St Augustine's, Canterbury, implies that the bones of St Mildred were translated there from Thanet on condition that her prayers would give him safe passage across the sea. This however was probably Whit Sunday, 30 May 1030, so may refer to a second visit by Cnut to Rome.

Although Cnut's 1027 letter implies that he sailed from Denmark, it is just as likely that his point of embarkation was Sandwich. The *Encomium* tells us that Cnut's first visit on European soil was to the monastery of St Omer, the home of its author, in Flanders. What better way for Cnut, the Emperor of the North, to impress with his money and his piety, than to lavish the area's foremost monastery with precious gifts? It was a moment of pure theatre, handing out coins to the poor with his own hands, crying and beating his breast. The Encomiast was there:

> When he had entered the monasteries [of St Omer and St Bertin] and had been received with great honour, he advanced humbly, and with complete concentration prayed for the intercession of the saints in a manner wonderfully reverent, fixing his eyes upon the ground, and freely pouring forth, so to speak, rivers of tears. But when the time came when he desired to heap the holy altars with royal offerings, how often did he first, with tears, press kisses on the pavement, how often did self-inflicted blows punish that

revered breast; what signs he gave, how often did he pray that the heavenly mercy might not be displeased with him![3]

How much was it faith and how much propaganda? If indeed he gave further gifts to the cathedral at Chartres, then he was travelling overland through the great Frankish kingdom, presumably with an entourage of earls, thegns, churchmen and *huscarls* that marked all his royal processions. We do not know if he sailed from Marseilles or crossed the treacherous Alps – the Encomiast is rather vague about his itinerary – but the Viking in him would surely have chosen the former. The Viking saga *Fagrskinna* recorded: 'he took [the pilgrim's] staff, as did all the men who travelled with him and journeyed southward to Rome; and the Emperor himself came out to meet him and he accompanied him all the way to the Roman city'.[4]

Rome in 1027 was home to a papacy in crisis. Ever since Peter, Christ's apostle, had been crucified, according to legend upside down as he claimed he was unworthy to die the same death as his lord, a succession of spiritual leaders of hugely variable character and talent had held the Holy See and attempted to be the guiding spiritual light of Christendom. Peter had been a hard act to follow – 'Thou art Peter,' Matthew's Gospel claims Christ said, 'and upon this rock I will build my church and I will give you the keys of the kingdom of heaven,'[5] – and the first figure accorded the title of Pope was St Linus, who died some time around AD 80. The 153rd in line of succession after him was John XIX, Romanus of Tusculum, who had been chosen by the cardinals on 19 April 1024 after offering a huge bribe. So fast had been his elevation to the holy throne that he woke up a layman in the morning and was wearing the papal crown by the time he went to bed. Peter must have turned in his grave.

For a while, at the millennium, there had been a ray of hope for the papacy. Forty years earlier, the German Emperor Otto I restored Charlemagne's tradition of having his son crowned the Holy Roman Emperor by Pope John XIII; it was to mark a long period in which the Germans dominated the papacy and re-created an office which would last until, obsolete and exhausted, it would be destroyed by Napoleon in the nineteenth century.[6] In 1000, the bizarre relationship between the 'two halves of God' was represented by

Otto III and Sylvester II. Both men were newly enthroned and they shared a ceremony in that year in which they pledged to resurrect the Christian empire which had been weakened by schism and secular politics. Sylvester was the first French pope, Gerbert d'Aurillac, a scholar with such wide-ranging interests – astronomy, philosophy, music, mathematics and theology – that his detractors accused him of having signed a pact with Satan. Clearly, no one expected the Pope to be intelligent! Otto, still only twenty, had been his pupil and, despite his position as German Emperor, had a love for Rome and a sense of the mystically theatrical that made him highly unusual. He dressed sumptuously in gold, always ate alone and visitors to his palace on the Aventine Hill had to lie face-down before him. He was deeply and probably genuinely devout and spent much time with three hermits: Romauld, who had travelled the world; Adalbert, the Bishop of Prague, who would be murdered by the Prussians; and Nilus, who lived until the age of ninety-six in a hut outside the city walls. 'I ask you only one thing,' Sylvester said to Otto, 'to think of the salvation of your soul.'[7] Tears poured down the Emperor's face as he placed his gold crown in the old man's hands. All three hermits would be saints within twenty years. Otto built a church on the site of the ancient temple of Aesculapius, the god of healing; a carving of the Emperor has survived in a well inside the church of St Bartolomeo dell'Isola. He died in 1002 and Sylvester followed him a year later.

Yet even in this brief, golden age of the papacy, when the partnership of pope and emperor promised so much, discord and trouble dogged their footsteps. A rival of Sylvester from the pushy and powerful Crescenti family, had risen against the duo. Otto had Crescentius and the twelve leaders of the rising decapitated and their mutilated bodies hung up by their feet on a hill near Rome, now Monte Mariso, but originally, ever since that event, Mons Malus, the hill of evil. What followed was a sordid power struggle between the Crescenti and Sylvester's own family, the Counts of Tusculum, so the papacy in Cnut's day was firmly in the pockets of the German emperors who supported the latter.

In fact the papacy was even more vulnerable than the position of many European kings. Between 963 and 1003, two popes had been murdered and seven exiled from Rome, almost always as a result of the fact that warring families saw the occupancy of the Holy See as their right and that even the humblest people in Rome still saw themselves as inhabitants of the most powerful city on earth, with some sort of preordained right to take to the streets in defiance of or opposition to great men. As historian Eamon Duffy says, '. . . the reality was that the popes [of the tenth and eleventh centuries] were harassed Italian prince-bishops, desperately struggling to preserve the territory of St Peter . . .'[8]

None of Sylvester's successors lasted long. John Sicco became John XVII in May 1003, but he was gone by November. John Fasonus lasted six years as John XVIII while Swein Forkbeard was ravaging England. Pietro Buscaporca (Pig's Snout) ascended the Holy Throne in July 1009 and left it three years later. His successor Gregory VI lasted only eight months and as the young Cnut was making his mark along the Humber, Theophylact of Tusculum became Benedict VIII. Not until 1046 would a pope be a non-Italian, so in Cnut's time, the papacy had a distinctly local, even parochial flavour. In the century between 955 and 1057, of the twenty-five popes, just over half were appointed by local lords; the others by German emperors.

And this last explains Cnut's visit to Rome in 1027. It was a marvellous piece of propaganda, not merely to show his piety in kissing the ring of the Lord's Anointed, God's vicar on earth, but to stand shoulder to shoulder on the same pedestal as the most powerful ruler in Europe. March 1027 saw the coronation of Conrad II.

Conrad was of an age with Cnut and in Rome they treated each other, according to various sources, like brothers. Both men came hot foot from battle – Cnut from his war in Denmark, Conrad from putting down a rebellion in Italy. Both men were enjoying a leisurely royal progress – Cnut endowing Frankish churches with gifts, Conrad being crowned at Milan before arriving in Rome. Both men, too, may have had unfinished business – Cnut returned to Denmark the following year to expel Olaf Haraldsson and Conrad would face four more rebellions in the next three years.

We know nothing of Cnut's relationship with Conrad's predecessor, Henry II, whose finely carved stone effigy in Bamberg

Cathedral shows a handsome, bearded, curly-haired king in a magnificent floral crown. He lies beside his wife, Cunegund, and the pair were crowned together in St Peter's, Rome, the models of Christian piety. The German lands to the south of Denmark were vital to Cnut in that they lay on the southern border of that part of his empire. The existence of the Danevirke and the probing over 200 years by Christian missionaries from Hamburg-Bremen are reminders of the potential aggrandisement of the German princes long before it became associated with Prussian militarism and the blood and iron of Bismarck's day.[9] Henry, however, seems to have had no designs on Cnut's territory and while Swein Forkbeard and his son were conquering England, the Emperor was fighting campaigns in Italy and Lotharingia,[10] far to the south and west. Even so, his enemy in Poland was Boleslav, the brother of Cnut's mother, and perhaps it was only the removal of that generation (Henry dying in 1024, Boleslav a year later) that cleared the air between Cnut and Conrad.

The chronicler Adam of Bremen says that the royal pair made a treaty through the intercession of the Archbishop of Hamburg-Bremen, but there is no surviving record of this. A complicated series of negotiations involving the betrothal of Cnut's daughter Gunhilda to Conrad's son, Henry, may have begun while both men were in Rome, but the reality is that they probably began later. Certainly the actual marriage did not happen until 1036, after Cnut's death, the Viking Empress dying, perhaps of plague, two years later.

The ceremony of Conrad's magnificent coronation in Rome was carried out with all the piety and symbolism of the occasion as can be seen in a surviving liturgical hymn scroll in the Vatican library, which shows the coronation of Otto II on Christmas Day 967. The Pope is not shown, merely the imposing figure of the Emperor carrying two flaming torches. His tunic, cloak, leggings and shoes are hung with bells and ribbons, and a pair of haloed angels are placing a crown of gold and pearls on his head. Much of the ceremony of Conrad's coronation stayed with Cnut as symbolic of power and greatness. The Viking's seal no longer exists, but it is believed to have been copied from Conrad's. The drawing of Cnut endowing the cross to the New Minster shows him in an imperial crown, and facially he resembles Henry II, if not Conrad. His message to all and sundry was clear – he was the Emperor of the North, Conrad's equal in all but name. After the coronation ceremony, the three greatest rulers of Europe, Conrad, Cnut and Rudolf of Burgundy, left the church side by side. Cnut wrote:

> Be it known to you, that a great crowd of nobles was there at the very Easter celebration with the Lord Pope John and the Emperor Conrad, to wit all the princes of the peoples from Mount Garganus[11] to the nearest sea,[12] who have both received me with honour and honoured me with precious gifts. However, I was honoured most by the Emperor with various gifts and priceless presents, both in gold and silver vessels and in cloaks[13] and extremely precious garments.[14]

The success of Cnut's meeting with the Emperor covered a wide range of activity. His skalds wrote poetry about it – Sighvat's *Knútsdrápa* ending its tenth stanza with the couplet: 'kaeor keisara/kelúss Pétrúsi' – 'dear to the Emperor, close to Peter'.[15] The alliterative repetition of k – for Knutr – speaks for itself. Cnut's relationship with St Peter was perhaps a matter for his own salvation, although a king close to God could expect to rule over a happy kingdom – the now dead Wulfstan would have been proud of him. His relationship with Conrad was more practical, however, as Cnut's letter, written on his way back from Rome, via Denmark, shows.

The letter itself was probably written in English by one of the king's scribes, but its only surviving form is in Latin. Like that of 1019, it was addressed to his bishops and earls and has come to light in the chronicles of John of Worcester. Its tone is very like that of Wulfstan's eight years earlier, but Wulfstan died in 1023, so either Cnut himself had a greater input into both letters than has been assumed or someone was deliberately copying Wulfstan's style and attitude. That someone may have been Lyfing, the abbot of Tavistock, who, for all his pluralism and grasping nature, may have been an accomplished writer.

The letter is a list of considerable achievements, as befitted an important European ruler at the height of his power. As Frank Stenton wrote sixty years ago, 'As king of the Danes he controlled the narrow entry from the Cattegat into the Baltic . . . As king of England he was ruler of a people for whom the freedom of the North Sea was a necessity of life.'[16] But the North was one thing. His presence at Conrad's coronation and his private transactions with the pope and other heads of state mark his arrival as a foremost player on the European scene.

Working, presumably though interpreters, with Pope John, Cnut secured a huge reduction in the cost to his archbishops of the pallium they received from the papacy. Perhaps John was as impressed by him as Fulbert of Chartres had been, though it is not recorded what gifts he left in the church of St Peter. The Emperor Henry II had hung his crown there and it is likely that Cnut saw it on his visit. In his letter, Cnut refers to 'great gifts of gold and silver and other precious objects'.

Of greater importance in the commercial sense were the deals that Cnut struck with Conrad and William of Aquitaine, through whose territory his merchants had to pass. This seems to have cost the king considerably. John of Worcester says:

> and at great price he abolished the many barriers along the way where tolls were extorted from pilgrims.[17] The king sent his message back delivered by that most prudent man, Lyfing, the abbot of Tavistock, but soon after, in the same year, successor to the episcopacy at Crediton of Eadnoth [who was his travelling companion] and by the hands of other ambassadors.

The letter was addressed to Archbishop Aethelnoth and Aelfric, Archbishop of York 'and to all the bishops and leading men and to all the English people, both earls and ceorls'.[18] Cnut told them that he prayed at Rome for the redemption of his sins and for the safety of the people of his kingdoms: 'I had vowed to God to make this journey long ago now, but I could not accomplish it earlier because of the affairs of the kingdom and other sources of obstruction.'[19] We need not doubt that this actually was what Cnut had in mind. Rome was the heart of Christianity because of the Petrine succession in the way that Jerusalem was not, although how long he had wanted to go is unknown. He was of course familiar with similar pilgrimages in England, but the chance to be *seen* at St Peter's cannot have escaped him.

Cnut's shrewd bartering extended from mere pilgrims to merchants too:

> . . . I spoke with the Emperor himself and the Lord Pope and the princes who were there about the needs of all people of my entire realm, both English and Danes, that a juster law and securer peace might be granted to them on the road to Rome and that they should not be straitened by so many barriers along the road, and harassed by unjust tolls; and the Emperor agreed and likewise King Robert who governs most of these same toll gates. And all the princes confirmed by edict that my people, both merchants and the others who travel to make their devotions, might go to Rome and return without being afflicted by barriers and toll-collectors, in firm peace and secure in a just law.

'Robert' in Cnut's text is almost certainly a clerical error for Rudolf III, the last king of an independent Burgundy who would die in 1032.

The solemn word of the Pope, the Emperor and Rudolf was confirmed under oath and witnessed by a large gathering – four archbishops, twenty bishops and 'innumerable multitude of dukes and nobles' – which suggests that all this was achieved soon after Conrad's coronation before any of them had gone home. There is no hint of any quid pro quo in all this, although England, as one of the richest states in Europe, had much to offer in commercial terms. The Pope, however, expected that in lieu of the pallium charges, the tax called Peter's Pence should be paid regularly. There is a smugness about paragraph nine: '. . . I give thanks to Almighty God because everything I desired, as far as I had conceived it in my mind, I have successfully carried out and I have fulfilled my vows completely.' There is something of Benjamin Disraeli in Cnut – perfectly competent as a ruler at home, but enjoying life most when he strutted his stuff on the European stage.

And in the middle of his letter, Cnut spells out his remaining foreign policy, the unfinished business of the Holy River:

So I, as I wish to be made known to you, returning by the same route that I took out, am going to Denmark to arrange peace and a firm treaty, with the counsel of all the Danes, with those races and peoples who would have deprived us of life and rule if they could, but they could not, God destroying their strength. May he preserve us by his bounteous compassion in rule and honour and henceforth scatter and bring to nothing the power and might of all our enemies! And finally, when peace has been arranged with our surrounding peoples and all our kingdom here in the east has been properly ordered and pacified, so that we have no war to fear on any side or the hostility of individuals, I intend to come to England as early this summer as I can to attend to the equipping of a fleet.[20]

We do not know what 'firm treaty' the king made with his own people in Denmark, but it may have involved the use of his bishops, his jarls and perhaps even his towns.

In England, towns were already an important part of the politics and economics of the country, long before Aethelred's time. Cnut had his favourite – he lived in and built up Winchester considerably. And he had his petty hatreds – London, which had resisted him in 1016–17, was heavily hit by the Danegeld and lost, in Aelfheah, its favourite and most popular saint. But essentially, he left them to their own devices under the control of ealdormen, thegns and shire reeves. In Denmark, the situation was different. It is not coincidence that Danish towns developed rapidly in Cnut's reign. Clearly, there was a great deal of English influence, despite the fact that towns like Ribe and Hedeby had long histories as centres of international trade and may even have had their own mints by the late ninth century. The other administrative system of *syssels* underwent extensive changes in Cnut's reign to become *herreds*, more or less the English Hundreds by another name. By the early 1030s, there were new mints at Ribe and Hedeby, as well as Roskilde, Lund, Viborg, Slagelse, Ringsted and Ørbaeck, implying substantial urban growth and the extension of royal control. Where there were mints, there were moneyers, royal servants who, as we have seen, were seriously rich men with sometimes noble status. These were the men with whom Cnut made his firm testimony and in whose hands, ultimately, he left Denmark.

Only one text of the *Anglo-Saxon Chronicle* covered Cnut's homecoming:

> As soon as he arrived in England, he gave into Christ Church in Canterbury the harbour at Sandwich and all the rights that arise there from either side of the harbour, so that whenever the tide is at its very highest and the very fullest [and] a ship is floating as close to the land as it might closest be, and a man stands on that ship and has a [small] axe in his hand, the dunes from within the area as far as the axe can be thrown from the ship shall go to the monastery.[21]

In his letter, Cnut gave similar instructions to those he sent by Wulfstan four years earlier:

> Therefore I adjure and command my councillors whose advice concerning the kingdom I have trusted that they do not henceforth in any way, either from fear of me or favour of some powerful person, consent to any injustice, to suffer it to flourish in all my kingdom. Also I command all the shire reeves and reeves of my entire kingdom, if they desire my regard or their own safety, that they use no unjust compulsion on any man, rich or poor, but that impartial justice may be enjoyed by all, noble and common, rich and poor. Let there be no deviation from this, either because of royal favour or because of any influential person or for the purpose of amassing money for me, for I have no need of money accumulated by iniquitous exaction.[22]

This is an important document. It ranks with that other great medieval soul-baring, John's Magna Carta, Clause XI of which famously reads: 'To no one will we sell, to no one will we refuse right or justice'. The crucial difference is that Magna Carta, in reality a list of sixty-three grievances by the barons and the Church, was wrenched from the king by force – and John never intended to keep one word of his promises. If his barons' war of 1216 had gone his way, the document would no doubt have been destroyed and we would not have the widely held and ludicrous notion that it somehow heralds the birth of democracy. Cnut made his impartiality statement of his own free will and there is no reason to doubt that he meant it. This, after all, was the man who had executed the over-mighty ealdorman Eadric Streona and spared the life of Eadwig, king of the ceorls. It may have been the case, however, that his conscience was troubling him:

> And so be it known to you all now that, because I have humbly vowed to Almighty God himself to lead my life henceforth justly in all things, and to rule justly and devoutly the kingdoms and peoples subject to me and to observe equitable justice in all matters, if anything has been done hitherto other than what was just and through the intemperance of my youth, or through my negligence, I intend henceforth, with God's help, to amend it entirely.[23]

Cnut had taken care to cover all the angles. Perhaps with the whispered advice of Lyfing in his ear, he had written:

> Now, therefore, I command and adjure all my bishops and the reeves of the kingdom, by the faith you owe to God and to me . . . that, before I come to England, all those dues which we owe to God according to ancient laws are settled, such as the alms for the ploughs and the tithes on livestock born in the same year and the pence which we owe to St Peter at Rome, either from the cities or from the townships; and in mid-August the tithe of fruits and on the feast of St Martin [11 November] the first fruits of the grain to the church in the parish where one lives, which are called church scot in English.[24]

And there was the threat that no man doubted when it was made by Cnut: 'If, when I come, these and others like them have not been paid, the royal dues shall be exacted according to the laws appropriate to the crime strictly and without remission from him who is at fault.'[25]

The king now had to turn his attention to Norway. In 1028 Haraldsson had invaded the country during Cnut's absence in England and Cnut needed to reassert his claim to the throne. It is unlikely that all fifty of his ships were the thirty-four-oar sea-serpent size, but perhaps half of them were. He would probably have taken between four and five thousand men with him, mostly the tall warriors who were his *huscarls* and the battle-hardened troops who had fought with him from Ashingdon to the Holy River. He probably bought the services of other fighters in Norway itself, because Haraldsson was old and losing popularity fast. The king who would become St Olaf had alienated his people by forcing Christianity on them and, largely deserted, fled over the mountains into Sweden and beyond to Kiev, to the welcoming arms of his brother-in-law, King Jaroslav.

Cnut sailed home, leaving Norway in the hands of Hákon, son of Yric of Lade, Earl of Northumbria. This was the man who possibly ruled Norway briefly after his father sailed to rule the north of England for Cnut. He was an earl in Worcestershire and may have succeeded Yric in Northumbria in the mid-decade. The Abingdon manuscript of the *Anglo-Saxon Chronicle* records, 'and before that in this year [1030] the brave Earl Hakon died at sea'. According to legend, he was drowned in the treacherous waters of the Pentland Firth taking his new bride back from England. The chronicler John of Worcester states that she was 'the noble lady Gunnhilde, daughter of [Cnut's] sister and of Wyrtgeorn, king of the Wends'.[26] Hákon's loss would be a major blow, because Cnut now sent his son Swein and his first wife/mistress Aelfgifu of Northampton to govern his newly won territory. It would not be a success. Then, in 1031, the king rode to Scotland.

The Worcester manuscript of the *Anglo-Saxon Chronicle* gives the fullest details: 'The Scottish king, Malcolm, bowed to him and two other kings, Maelbeth and Iehmarc.'[27] Malcolm was Maol Callum Mac Coinneach (which translates from the Gaelic as the follower of St Columba and son of the handsome), High King of Scotland. His capital was at Sgàin (Scone) in the modern area of Perthshire, but he was not a powerful, centralist king like Cnut. Scotland was divided into six provinces, inhabited by two peoples, the Picti (the Romans called them 'the painted ones' because of their use of woad in battle) and the Scotti. Its boundaries were constantly shifting, depending on the personalities of the high king and the mór-mhoar (the high stewards) who ran each province. In the inevitable power struggles between these 'stewardries' two powerful rivals emerged – Moray, stretching across the country east to west, and Atholl, centring on Scone but extending as far west as the islands of Mull, Jura, Islay, Arran and Iona. South of the rivers Clyde and Forth, petty kings rather than high stewards ruled, in territories that came, by Cnut's day, to be Strathclyde and Cumbria.

To the north, the landscape and the weather were every bit as bleak as Cnut's Norway. The population was small, semi-nomadic and reliant on their flocks of sheep and herds of long-coated, long-horned cattle. Around the coasts, men lived by fishing and no doubt trade, although by the late eighth century, their seamanship had been eclipsed by the Vikings. Unlike the far richer England to the south, there were no actual towns in Malcolm's Scotland, merely scattered settlements of timber, wattle and thatch clustered around *duns*, the Gaelic name for a fort.

What dominated society in eleventh-century Scotland was the clan system, variants of which still survived in Wales and Ireland, too. It was not the bagpipe-playing, kilt-wearing fancy dress clan system we know today. Like that other half-survival of the Celtic way of life, the Druids, the clans were reinvented in the late eighteenth century and owe a great deal to the new romanticism of novelists like Walter Scott. Lairds or clan chiefs were elected, rather as kings were among the Vikings. Even in Saxon England, succession depended on the will of the witan in the absence of any real right of primogeniture. This system spoke volumes for common sense and avoided the nightmare of infant kings which was to haunt England in the fourteenth and fifteenth centuries.[28] Clan chiefs were adults, and usually adults of proven wisdom and military ability.

Via the clans, a surprisingly liberal legal system operated, albeit not codified like Cnut's. The death penalty was rare and was never carried out in the case of women. Typically in Celtic society, even murderous women could only be banished and honest ones could own property, head a clan and lead their troops to battle. In Celtic legend and Celtic history, Mab the battle-goddess fused with Boudicca the warrior queen in this context.[29]

What complicated 'Scotland' in the early eleventh century was the existence of a Viking settlement in the Orkneys and the Shetlands, certainly from the ninth century, possibly earlier. The *Orkneyinga Saga* details its history and, with the usual caveats about poetry as a historical source, gives us a great deal of information about the raiders who settled here, as their cousins did further south in the Danelaw.

In a mixture of conquest and assimilation, the settlers took over the Pictish farmsteads and probably used the natives as slave labour, at least at first. Birsay became the central stronghold of the Vikings by Cnut's day, the foundations of Jarl Thorfinn the Mighty's fortress still visible on the bleak tidal island. Jarlshof on the southern tip of the Shetlands is equally impressive, boasting buildings that have been identified as a smithy, barn and even bath house.

Christianity came late to the Vikings of Orkney. In 995, when Cnut was born, Olaf Haraldsson – made into a saint by 1040 because of his muscular Christianity – forced the new religion onto Jarl Sigurd the Stout, although, as in England, Christianity and paganism probably coexisted for some time.

Relations between the Scots and the Vikings were stormy. Crinan, the fearsome abbot of Dunkeld, known to the Vikings as *Jarl Hundi*, the Hound Earl, fought against Sigurd Hlodversson in 990. Sigurd's conversion five years later led him to divorce his pagan first wife and marry again. He already had sons by his previous marriage, the most vicious of them Einar Wry-mouth, and his second family produced offspring that led to the same complications facing both Aethelred and Cnut in England.

The arrival of Olaf Tryggvason and Swein Forkbeard close to the millennium galvanised Malcolm to action. He seems not unlike Aethelred in that he had a streak of cruelty and ambition, but he was either a better general or considerably luckier than his English counterpart. Malcolm's initial plan was to annex the Orkneys and leaving the sons of Sigurd to squabble among themselves, Malcolm put the young Jarl Thorfinn, his grandson, to rule Caithness and Sutherland. Arnor the skald describes Thorfinn in language very reminiscent of Ottar the Black's *Knútsdrápa*:

> Reddened the sword's edge.
> Did the Prince in the helmet storm.
> Reddener of raven's claws
> Yet of fifteen winters,
> No man under Heaven,
> Younger than Einar's brother
> Ready has shown himself –
> Valiant and stout of heart –
> To defend and conquer.[30]

The potential war between the half-brothers was averted by mediation, but not before Einar had made an enemy for life of Olaf Haraldsson, whose friend he had murdered. Throughout the 1020s, an uneasy peace existed between Malcolm, his clansmen and Thorfinn on the one hand, and Einar on the other.

Given this chronology, what took Cnut north to Scotland in 1031? Peter Beresford Ellis[31] infers quite rightly that the king did not fight a pitched battle with Malcolm, otherwise the *Anglo-Saxon Chronicle* would have mentioned it, but he is absolutely wrong when he contends that 'Canute [*sic*] went to see Malcolm on an equal footing, one ruler to another . . .' The fact was that Malcolm was king of a tiny kingdom, not even extending to the size of Scotland as it is today. Cnut was king of the larger and vastly richer England to the south, of all Denmark, all Norway and part at least of Sweden. He was an emperor in all but name and Malcolm must have realised this. This is why he bowed to Cnut – he could hardly do otherwise. And it is unlikely that their meeting was one of cordiality. If Cnut did not march north with an army, it is certain that he took a sizeable retinue – his grim-helmeted *huscarls* in coats of mail.

The chronicler Ralph Glaber, in *Historiarum Libri Quinque*, written before 1030, says that Cnut and Malcolm had long been enemies. Again, dates, in both English texts and other sources like the eleventh-century *De Obsessione Dunelmi*, contradict each other, but it is also likely that Malcolm took advantage of the murder of Uhtred of Northumbria to expand south into Bernicia, the area of Lothian south of the Tweed. It is likely that the Scots won a victory at Carham in 1018 against Northumbrian forces and this would, in effect, have counted as a victory against Cnut in that he was king of England by this time. The events of 1031 seem to be the Viking drawing a final line under all this and if he did it without the use of force, it speaks volumes for his reputation and his power by this stage in his reign. Sighvat the skald's contemporaneous lines – 'The most famous princes in the North from the midst of Fife have brought their heads to Knutr; that was to buy peace'[32] – merely underline how humiliating all this was for Malcolm and the Scots.

The minor kings to whom Cnut was introduced by Malcolm were Iehmarc, who was probably Echmarrach Ragnallson, who ruled Galloway and the Isle of Man; and Maelbeth – Macbeth, Shakespeare's 'dread butcher' with the 'fiend-like queen'. The prince was about twenty-five by the time he met Cnut and his destiny lay in the future. Contrary to the Shakespearian tradition, Macbeth was an excellent king. There was no murder of the ancient Duncan (defeated in fact in battle by Macbeth when Duncan was in his thirties), no charmed life and no Burnham Wood marching to Dunsinane. The real Macbeth, before Shakespeare and the Scots antiquarian Hector Boece got at him, ruled Scotland in peace for seventeen years and, alone among kings of Scotland, went on a pilgrimage to Rome.

In all that, he was simply copying a man he must have considered a far greater role model – Cnut.

TWELVE

The Last Day

Days of great glory
In the kingdom of earth are
gone forever.

Beowulf

The last five years of Cnut's reign saw him at the zenith of his power. He kept his head while all around him were losing theirs. In 1030, according to the Worcester and Peterborough manuscripts of the *Anglo-Saxon Chronicle*, 'King Olaf came back to Norway and that people gathered themselves together and fought him. And he was there killed.'[1] Olaf had been heartened by the death of Hákon in the Pentland Firth, rather as Aethelred had been by that of Swein Forkbeard years before, and secured Anund Jakob's backing before sailing back. It is likely that Hákon had been popular, however, and perhaps Cnut too, because a fleet was waiting for him in Trondheim Fjord and Olaf was cut down in the high ground at Stiklestad on 29 July.

He had chosen the field himself according to the saga writer Snorri Sturluson and perhaps had 2,000 men with him. In a vision, says Sturluson's saga, the king saw all Norway ranged against him. In practice, he was probably outnumbered three to one, facing competent military commanders like Thori Hund and Kald Arnason in what was the first recorded fully land battle in Norway's history. Olaf led a charge in person that nearly broke the enemy's ranks, but he found himself surrounded and was hacked to pieces under his banner. His skald, Thormod, dying from wounds later in the day, pulled an arrow from his chest with the words 'Well has the king fed us; I still have fat round the roots of my heart'.[2] With Olaf was his fifteen-year-old half-brother Harald, later called Hardrada, the hard

ruler, who would become the last of the Viking kings. He would die
before Harold Godwinesson's *huscarls* at Stamford Bridge near York
thirty-six years later. According to the skald Sighvat, a total eclipse
brought darkness to the land during the battle of Stiklestad. In fact,
the phenomenon occurred at the end of August. Larson conjectures
that the two domestic events were fused later in the quest for
miracles associated with the life of 'St' Olaf.

Cnut now had no one to rule Norway for him so he sent his son
Swein and, more bizarrely, Aelfgifu of Northampton. At Nidaros
(Trondheim), Cnut called a great council of the *Things* of the
Scandinavian countries of which he was now master. Denmark was
to be ruled by Harthacnut who was almost certainly present with his
father and underwent a coronation ceremony. The boy was probably
seventeen by this time and considered old enough to rule. His name,
as we know, means 'hard Cnut' and although he was tough enough,
and with a streak of cruelty, he had inherited none of his father's
wisdom. He would be directly responsible for the collapse of Cnut's
empire by 1042. At Nidaros, the wily Cnut had taken hostages from
the leading Norwegian families to ensure their good behaviour as he
probably had in England before and after Ashingdon.

Norway was not a success. Later Norwegians would refer to the
five years up to Cnut's death as 'Aelfgifu's time' and the woman
was detested. Her sudden emergence as regent is decidedly odd.
Clearly, and probably despite protestations from the Church, Cnut
had not abandoned her when he took Emma as his queen. It may
be that she lived until 1030 on her estates in Northampton, perhaps
as some kind of royal ambassador in the Danelaw. We know that
she was high born and immensely useful, with local family
connections. Cnut knew her better than we do; perhaps he thought
she could rule Norway as well as anybody. It was not to be. What
is even more odd is why Swein Knutsson needed his mother as
regent. He must have been older than Harthacnut and had already
fought at least one battle by the time of the regency. Again, perhaps
Cnut knew best.

Aelfgifu was a foreigner and the strain of holding a kingdom
together for her husband was too great. Imperious and touchy, she
committed the cardinal sin (of which her husband was almost

wholly innocent) of introducing new ideas to a people at once proud and conservative. She brought in Danish forms of taxation – the Danegeld – and demanded semi-feudal dues which no earlier ruler had done. Against this foreign court, a nostalgic cult grew up with alarming speed around the dead Olaf Haraldsson. Within a year of Stiklestad, Olaf the Stout had become St Olaf, endowed with a few dozen miraculous cures. Nowhere could there be found a more cynical canonization. The Norwegian Christian Church, anxious to make headway, needed a saint and a *royal* one had a cachet all his own. So the legend was born of Olaf dying a martyr to the Christian cause, fighting against the pagan peasants of Trondheim. His son, Magnus, later the Good, was brought back from the safety of the Polish court of Jaroslav the Wise in Kiev. For two years, Magnus, under the careful tutelage of the skald, Sighvat, bided his time, watching Aelfgifu's regency crumble until she only held authority in the south. Olaf's miraculously uncorrupted body was exhumed and a shrine built to him at Nidaros. Weeks after Cnut's own death, Magnus became the undisputed king of Norway.

We do not know whether Norway ever formed part of Cnut's dream or even, precisely, what that dream was. It is reasonably apparent from the skaldic poems that he regarded England as his principal kingdom – everything else was a bonus. And in England, if Cnut's early years were dominated by Thurkil the Tall, his last years belonged to Earl Godwine.

The father of a future king of England, Godwine first appears to history in a charter of Cnut's from 1018. The name is common in the Saxon period and he may or may not be the thegn described in various records in the troubled last years of Aethelred. Most of what we know about Cnut's right-hand man in the 1030s comes from the *Vita Aedwardi Regis*, a chronicle written by a Flemish monk at about the time of the Norman Conquest:

When, however, some fitting business of the kingdom called Cnut to his own people – for in his absence some unbridled men, putting off his authority from their necks, had prepared to rebel – Godwine was his inseparable companion on the whole journey. Here the king tested more closely his wisdom, here his perseverance, here his courage in war, and here the strength of this great nobleman.[3]

There are problems in deciding exactly how, where and when Godwine was employed by Cnut. The implication is that he fought with him, perhaps even at the Holy River, or went with him to Scotland or Rome. The author of the *Vita Aedwardi* also implies that Godwine was useful to Cnut early on: 'He also found out how profound he was in eloquence, and what advantage it would be to him in his newly acquired kingdom if he were to bind him more closely to him by means of some fitting reward.'[4] In fact, two rewards came Godwine's way. The king appointed him 'totius pene regni . . . dux et baillus',[5] ruler and steward through virtually the whole kingdom, and gave him his sister as wife. The exact timing is unclear. Henry of Huntingdon says that Godwine fought in Denmark with Cnut in 1019, but if the king gave Godwine the grand title (and accompanying power) then, what about Thurkil, not banished until 1021? There is certainly no mention of Godwine in Cnut's letter of 1019, whereas Thurkil is the only nobleman referred to by name. Until 1023, Wulfstan occupied a central position in Cnut's government, as witnessed by the collaboration over the king's laws, and a number of Danish jarls may have taken precedence over Godwine.

· Godwine's marriage to Gytha probably took place in 1023. She was not technically Cnut's sister (the only actual sister whose name we know was Estrith) but her brother, Ulf, was married to Estrith. Even so, it forged a family link with the royal house and placed Godwine one step nearer to the seat of power. There is no doubt that Godwine was extremely ambitious. When in England, he bought up land and established a huge power base in Wessex which rivalled and probably surpassed that of Eadric Streona in Mercia. Where Godwine differs is that he was fiercely loyal to Cnut, but that was because he hitched himself to the Viking's star at a time when it was certain to rise. Streona came out of the dark days of Aethelred, Ironside and uncertainty. 'In the reign of this King Cnut,' wrote the author of the *Vita Aedwardi*, 'Godwine flourished in the royal palace, having first place among the highest nobles of the kingdom;

and, as was just, what he wrote all deemed should be written, and what he erased, erased.'[6] By 1023 it is likely that Godwine ran Wessex, an area previously the specific concern of Cnut. This proves that the Viking was perfectly willing to favour English nobility, all part of his clever assimilation process.

In the north in the last years of Cnut's reign, the blood feud continued in the sons of Uhtred and his killer Thurbrand. Because of the high-ranking nature of these men, it is not unreasonable to see it all as a mini civil war, more limited geographically than the Roses conflict of four centuries later, but potentially as devastating. We do not know what happened to Yric of Lade. Governing Northumbria for Cnut from 1017, his name vanishes from the record after 1023. In his *Gesta Regum*, William of Malmesbury believed that Yric returned, willingly or otherwise, to Denmark, but various Norse authorities claim that he died in England. The skald Thord Kolbeinsson had already sung the man's praises: 'The brave warrior, who frequently gave swollen flesh to the raven, marked men with the print of the sword's edge . . .'[7] By 1033 his place had been taken by another Viking, Sigvardr (Sigurd) who ruled from the old Jorvik, Viking York. In the borderlands to the north of that, Uhtred's youngest son Eadulf ruled, although the position of all of them was to change on Cnut's death.

In the Midlands, the dominant earl in the 1030s was Leofric, Cnut's '*comes et princeps*' from Worcester to Scotland. His name appears regularly in the king's charters from 1032 as a man 'very wise in divine and temporal matters',[8] operating largely from his base at Coventry.

The last three years of Cnut's life are the most obscure of all. He signed eight, perhaps nine charters, giving lands mostly to the Church and to individuals like Godwine, Bishop Eadsige and the otherwise unknown Bori. After 1031, no version of the *Anglo-Saxon Chronicle* makes mention of him. In 1032, 'there appeared the wildfire such as no man ever remembered before and also it everywhere did damage in many places'.[9] If superstitious ceorls interpreted this as an omen of change and foreboding, it is not recorded anywhere. We have no idea of the extent of the forest fire that swept the country or where it started. In a climate far warmer than ours, the risk of fire in the height of summer must have been great. There was no organised system to fight it and nothing but beaters and wooden or leather buckets of water to combat the problem. In Cnut's Winchester, Bishop Aelfsige died to be replaced by Aelfwine, 'the king's priest', who presumably benefited from the cheaper pallium finessed by Cnut's visit to Rome five years earlier. The man had been a monk and dean of the New Minster and his prayer book, probably half-written by Aelfsige in a tiny format, still survives.

Churchmen shuffled off the mortal coil in 1033 and 1034 and so did Malcolm, king of Scots. He was eighty years old and despite rumours to the contrary, died of natural causes in Glamis on 25 November 1034. His death paved the way for a power struggle between rivals Duncan and Macbeth which became the stuff of Shakespeare's drama. 'In this year [1035]', wrote the Abingdon Anglo-Saxon Chronicler, 'King Cnut died on 12 November at Shaftesbury and he was taken from there to Winchester and there buried, and Aelfgifu the lady then stayed there . . .' The Peterborough manuscript gives the following year for his death, but this seems to be a mistake. It adds, however, that he was buried in the Old Minster, 'and he was king over all England very nearly twenty summers' – no mean achievement for a 'Viking thug' who had come to the Humber all those years before to raid and pillage. The Encomiast must have heard it from the queen herself:

The lady Emma . . . mourned together with the natives; poor and rich lamented together, the bishops and clerics wept with the monks and the nuns; but let the rejoicing in the kingdom of Heaven be as great as was the mourning in the world! These wept for what they had lost, but let those rejoice over his soul, which they take to themselves. These buried his lifeless body, but let those lead his spirit aloft to be rejoiced in everlasting rest. Mortals above wept for his departure, but for his spirit, let the Heavenly citizens as well as mortals intercede. Let us earnestly pray God that his glory may increase from day to day; and since he has deserved this by his benevolence, let us pray every day: 'May the soul of Knutr rest in peace. Amen.'[10]

We have no clues at all as to the cause of Cnut's death. M.K. Lawson infers from the charter called S975, drawn up in 1035, that the man may have known he was dying. Many charters follow the same kind of official patter, rather as centuries later parliamentary acts used the same form of words, but 975 talks of the monks of Sherborne Abbey in Dorset saying daily prayers and singing psalms for the soul of Cnut. It may be in this context that Harthacnut's striking of coins in Denmark styling himself *Rex* meant that he, too, knew his father was dying. The *Knytlingasaga* specifically mentions symptoms which are probably jaundice, but whether this would give Cnut several months to put his house in order in the way that Lawson implies, is debatable. What Cnut was doing in Shaftesbury, or whether he was taken ill nearby and the abbey, which he had endowed and perhaps partially rebuilt on its windy ridge, was simply the nearest 'hospital' is unknown. Perhaps it happened on one of the many progresses the king made in his lifetime. By our reckoning, he was forty years old, probably younger than his own father, Swein Forkbeard, when he died. There were no stories of a terrible passing. No ghost of a former Saxon king come to pierce the Viking's soul with his lance. Cnut died a Christian king, accepted and perhaps even loved by his people. The Valkyrie did not, in the end, come for him on some blood-spattered battlefield. As Dr D.M. Hadley recounts it, 'the eye mists, hearing fails, the nose gets cold, the tongue curls back, the face falls in, the lips blacken, the mouth gapes, spittle runs, hair stands on end, the heart trembles, the hands shake and the feet go stiff'.[11] The friend of Peter met him face to face.

We have no detailed account of Cnut's funeral. That of Edward the Confessor in January 1066 is shown on the Bayeux Tapestry in stark clarity. In the same scene, the king is shown on his deathbed being given the last rites by his priests, and being carried in his coffin, his earls walking bareheaded behind the corpse while lesser officials ring solemn handbells on the melancholy progress. Cnut's retinue would have carried out a similar ritual, commending the king's soul to God before, perhaps, removing his heart. We know that this was common practice in the medieval period, but it is not until the nineteenth century that we have details. Cnut's chaplain would have given him the last words of comfort he heard in this world, making the sign of the cross over all parts of the king's body from the head to the feet. The nuns of Shaftesbury would have stripped the body and wrapped it in a simple woollen shroud, a memory of the baptism which most Christians had undergone soon after birth, but which 'Lambert' had experienced in his teens. At some point, it may be that Cnut was embalmed, which necessitated the removal of his internal organs and his brain. It was because of this that William of Malmesbury reported seeing the king's heart 'still beating' in its glass jar at Shaftesbury two centuries later.

From Shaftesbury, the retinue made its solemn way east to Winchester, gallopers no doubt racing to the corners of the kingdom with the news. Someone of status would have been sent further, to Harthacnut in Denmark, to Aelfgifu and Swein in Norway (assuming they were still there by then). The king's nearest, the second Aelfgifu (Emma) and his son by the first Aelfgifu, Harold Harefoot, were waiting in the wings to assume centre stage.

It was probably in that month of November that Cnut was buried in the Old Minster, attended by the great and good of his kingdom. First and foremost, Godwine would have come with his large retinue from Wessex, Leofric from Mercia, Sigurd from Northumbria and the whole bevy of thegns who ruled England under them, the sheriffs of their estates, the successors of Aethelred's ealdormen. Churchmen came too, to ease the final passing of the man who had given most of them so much – the bishops, the abbots, the priests. The *huscarls* would have marched behind the king's coffin, at a respectful distance, his warriors from Ashingdon, his veterans of the Holy River. Some of them no doubt were still Vikings at heart and would have preferred their lord to lie in the wooden casket of his dragon-ship than in some cold and still alien Christian church; but those days had gone forever. Ragnarok, the pagan last battle in which Odin and his warriors would fight the Ice Giants and all things would end, came and went to the tolling of English bells.

An anonymous fifteenth-century chronicle[12] is specific about where Cnut was buried – 'according to royal custom before the high altar'. This was certainly customary by 1460, but there is no evidence for it in Cnut's day. The position of the atheling Edward's shrine at

Shaftesbury is based on assumption not fact, and we have no clear
idea where Edmund Ironside and his ancestors were buried in the
context of Glastonbury. Historian John Crook[13] makes a strong case
for Cnut being buried close to the shrine of the Old Minster's
principal saint, Swithun, so that the dead king could reap, even in
death, some of the saint's power. He would not lie there for long.

'The king is dead, long live the king.' The problem for Cnut's
posterity – discussed in detail in the next chapter – is that he left no
clear heir to his throne; a situation every bit as disastrous as that
surrounding Edward the Confessor's death thirty-one years later. As
Frank Stenton put it sixty years ago: 'The period immediately
following the death of Cnut forms a miserable anti-climax to a reign
which, for all its weakness in constructive achievement, can fairly be
regarded as a brilliant age.'[14] There is little doubt that Cnut intended
his only legitimate heir – Harthacnut – to inherit both Denmark and
England. According to Stenton, the Anglo-Scandinavian earls were
waiting to accept him, but if Cnut really had weeks or even months
to prepare for his own death, why did he not make this inheritance
crystal clear? The problem, in any case, was that 'St' Olaf's son,
Magnus, had, by the end of 1035, won back Norway from Aelfgifu
and Swein and posed an obvious threat to Harthacnut's Denmark.
In times when personal leadership and command in the field was all,
Cnut's warlike son obviously felt that to sail for England now would
invite invasion and the possible loss of Denmark.

Viking law, as well as the law of England of course, demanded that
the king be elected and the witan was now faced with an agonizing
choice – opt for the rightful, but absent Harthacnut or go with the
choice of Harold Harefoot, the other son of Cnut and Aelfgifu of
Northampton. The tortuous marriages of Cnut had simply produced
too many heirs for safety and the right of primogeniture lay years in
the future. Emma, waiting at Winchester in Godbegot House, for
news of events, was backed by the ever-faithful Godwine, but
opposing them were Leofric, the liðsmen of London and probably the
majority of thegns from the Midlands and the North.

A great council was held at Oxford, perhaps in January 1036, at
which a kind of uneasy compromise was reached. Harold was to be

regent until Harthacnut could extricate himself from Denmark and Emma was to stay in Winchester with a huge force of her husband's *huscarls* and the royal treasury. In the event, Harold entered the city, probably at the head of a body of troops, and helped himself to most of the dead king's cash. Materially, as well as symbolically, the treasure was vitally important. There is no equivalent of it today, but a kind of parallel would be a usurper seizing all the houses and art collections of Elizabeth II and somehow freezing the assets of her government. It was a bold move of which Cnut would probably grudgingly have approved.

By the summer of 1036, Aelfgifu of Northampton was back in England (and probably had been for some time) and was networking among her son's party for support in making Harefoot king. There is no mention in the *Anglo-Saxon Chronicle* of her other son Swein, but William of Malmesbury says he died shortly after leaving Norway. However grief-stricken Aelfgifu may have been, she was a tough woman, used to playing politics in a man's world and she threw herself whole-heartedly into backing Harefoot's cause. 'Some said of Harold,' wrote the Anglo-Saxon Chronicler incredulously, 'that he was the son of Cnut and Aelfgifu . . . but it seemed incredible to many – yet he was full king over all England.'[15] Legend had it that both Harold and Swein were the sons, respectively, of a shoemaker and a priest. Cnut seems to have had no problem in believing that both boys were his and this slur on Aelfgifu has all the hallmarks of a church-inspired demonisation. It would mean, of course, that neither son had a legitimate right to rule and this would make the selection of either of them by the witan less likely.

It was not until 1037 that this decision was finally ratified and in the meantime, danger came from another direction: 'Alfred, the blameless atheling, king Aethelred's son, came here and meant to go to his mother, who was in Winchester.'[16] The atheling was the younger brother of Edward, later the Confessor, both boys having been brought up in the Norman court. Both the *Chronicle* and Frank Stenton regard this arrival as almost coincidence. Alfred was 'blameless' according to the first and 'came to England in order to visit his mother' according to the second. But the timing surely was crucial. It must have been common knowledge by the summer of 1036, not only that Cnut was dead, but that there were factions in England split over his successor. And Alfred, as the son of Aethelred, had a genuine claim to the throne. He never reached Winchester however. Godwine by this time seems to have thrown in his lot with Aelfgifu and Harefoot and ordered his arrest. According to the *Chronicle*:

> But then Godwine stopped him and set him in captivity and drove off his companions and some variously killed; some of them were sold for money, some cruelly destroyed, some of them were fettered, some of them were blinded, some maimed, some scalped. No more horrible deed was done in this country since the Danes came, and made peace here.[17]

If the *Chronicle* is accurate, this may be the last recorded instance of 'Viking' slavery in England, even though it was carried out by the English. 'The atheling still lived,' the *Chronicle* goes on:

> He was threatened with every evil; until it was decided that he be led to Ely town, fettered thus. As soon as he came on ship he was blinded, and, blind, thus brought to the monks. And there he dwelt for as long as he lived. Afterwards, he was buried, as well befitted him, full honourably, as he was entitled, at the west end, very near at hand to the steeple, in the south side-chapel. His soul is with Christ.[18]

Six years later, the Encomiast was still appalled: 'As I write my pen trembles, and I am horror-stricken at what the blessed youth suffered.' He consoled himself, his readers and the queen, whose son, after all, Alfred was, by reminding all and sundry that Emma may have lost 'her son on earth, [but] she now has a . . . patron in the Heavens'.[19]

We are left with the image of Alfred as an ingénue, naively stumbling into a hornets' nest with some vague hope of picking up some kind of reward. He had reckoned without Godwine and whether the earl actually sanctioned the prince's death, he carried the blame. His brother Edward, the Norman court that had raised him and even Harthacnut, the dead atheling's half-brother, vowed vengeance. Those who believe in such things might say that this was finally exacted when Godwine's son, Harold, was smashed to a bloody pulp on the ridge at Senlac in the October of 1066.

By 1037 in fact as well as name, Harold Harefoot was king of England. The nickname, presumably referring to his athleticism, is not recorded until centuries later, but it has all the hallmarks of an eleventh-century sobriquet. Frank Stenton believed that his mother, the redoubtable lady of Northampton, was the real power in the land, and that may be true, but Harefoot was probably twenty by this time and easily old enough to rule by himself. Not everyone accepted him because of the relationship Cnut had retained with his mother – it is by no means certain that they had gone through any form of Christian marriage. Churchmen in particular found this difficult, though as W.H. Stevenson[20] recorded, at least one bishop, Aelfic of Elmham, referred to Harefoot as 'my royal lord'.

Emma's battle on behalf of Harthacnut had failed and, says the *Chronicle*, 'Here Aelfgifu, King Cnut's widow, was driven out; she was king Harthcnut's mother. And she sought refuge of Baldwin by the south sea and he gave her a dwelling in Bruges and he protected and kept her for as long as she was there.'[21] The Count of Flanders seems a generous man and it was while Emma was in Bruges that the anonymous monk of the monastery of St Omer began work on the *Encomium*, commissioned by her as her side of the story. In this version, Emma chose to leave England, in confusion over the death of Alfred.

It was probably not until 1039 that Harthacnut and Magnus of Norway drew up a treaty which freed Cnut's legitimate son to come to England, belatedly to claim his inheritance. Magnus Olafsson may have gone down in Norwegian posterity as 'the good', but he had an eye to the main chance. Under the terms of the treaty, should either he or Harthacnut die without an heir, all his possessions would pass to the survivor. Technically, therefore, Magnus was heir to the throne of England, as well as Denmark if Harthacnut could secure it. On Harefoot's borders, trouble was brewing. The *Chronicle* records for 1039 that 'the Welsh killed Edwin, brother of Earl Leofric; Tharkil and Aelfyeat and many other good men with them'.[22] This was probably no more than a highly successful raiding party, but its hit rate was impressive and merely added to England's woes. Harthacnut was taking his time to arrive, visiting his mother in Bruges, and to cap it all 'the great gale came'. After twenty years of peace and good government, even the weather seemed to be on the turn. Had Cnut been alive, men must have muttered, he would have driven the Welsh raiders back into their mountains. Some, according to the silly waves story, might have believed he could have calmed the wind too!

On 17 March 1040 Harold Harefoot died at Oxford, one of the most forgotten kings of England. 'He ruled England', recorded the *Chronicle*, 'four years and sixteen weeks and in his days sixteen ships were paid, eight marks a rowlock, just as had been done in king Cnut's day.'[23] The 1040s saw an increasing discussion of the country's economy creeping in – why is unknown. 'In the same year king Harthacnut came to Sandwich seven nights before midsummer.'[24] Sandwich and summer – the old combination of the Viking raids since time immemorial. And Harthacnut came in style, at the head of sixty-two dragon-ships. The Encomiast records a severe storm – a murky tempest of winds and clouds – threatening the arrival. But Harthacnut dreamed in the middle of all this of Harefoot's death 'and the kingdom conquered by his father's strength would return safely by most rightful succession to himself, the rightful heir'.[25] Not surprisingly, says the *Chronicle*, 'he was quickly accepted by Danes and English'.[26] But Harthacnut was not his father. And despite the presence of men of substance like Godwine and Leofric, he learned no lessons, took no advice. Godwine presented him with an expensive ship, probably to buy his place at the new king's side and attempt to wash his hands of the blood of Alfred. But there was no Thurkil the Tall now to lead his troops, no loyal follower like Yric of Lade, no wise old churchman like Wulfstan. Instead, Harthacnut raised heavy taxes to pay his battle fleet – 'they determined', according to the *Chronicle*, 'that men pay sixty two ships of his at eight marks a rowlock; in this year the sester[27] of wheat went to fifty five pence and higher. Then they were disloyal who had striven for him.'[28] The disloyalty came from Worcester. Harthacnut had sent his *huscarls* to collect the taxes, rather as

William of Normandy would do thirty years later. A mob in the town had refused to pay and hacked two of the taxmen to death. The new king led an army in person and burned Worcester, ravaging the countryside for five days. Men had seen nothing like this for more than twenty years; a whole generation had grown up knowing nothing but the stability of Cnut and the turn of the seasons.

'He never did anything kingly while he lived,' muttered the *Chronicle* and that included having the body of Harefoot dug up. The king had been buried in the abbey at Westminster, the old building before it was effectively rebuilt in the Norman style by the Confessor. The decomposed corpse was thrown into a ditch before being recovered by Thames fishermen and quietly reinterred nearby at the aptly named church of St Clement Danes. Harthacnut sought to exact revenge for the murder of Alfred – Godwine and Lyfing, the Bishop of Worcester and Crediton, were in the firing line. John of Worcester records that Godwine got away with it not merely with his bribe of the ship and eighty armed warriors but his appearance in court before the king with a vast array of thegns as oath-helpers to swear he was innocent of the atheling's death. Lyfing was not so powerful or so lucky – he lost the bishopric of Worcester. In 1041, the *Chronicle* tells us, 'Harthacnut betrayed earl Eadwulf, under his safe conduct; and then he was a pledge-breaker'.[29] To a Viking – or to an Englishman – there could be no greater condemnation. Eadwulf was the Earl of Northumbria, the son of Uhtred, and the likelihood is that he was murdered on a visit to Harthacnut's court, perhaps at Winchester, while under the king's safe conduct. On his removal, Sigurd took his inheritance up to the Scots border.

Only in his behaviour to Aethelred's remaining son, Edward, did Harthacnut show any fellow-feeling: 'Soon after that year [1041] came Edward, his brother on his mother's side, from beyond the sea . . . who had for many years been driven from the land . . . He lived thus in his brother's [sic] court as long as Harthacnut lived.'[30] The Encomiast saw this as a fitting moment to bring his/Emma's version of events to an end: 'Here there is loyalty among sharers of rule, here the bond of motherly and brotherly love is of strength undestructible.' Had he lived, history may have recorded a more balanced view of the last surviving son of Cnut, but as it was, fate struck him down. On 8 June 1042, at the wedding feast of his father's man, Tovi the Proud, 'Here Harthacnut died as he stood at his drink and he suddenly fell to the earth with an awful convulsion; and those who were close by took hold of him and he spoke no word afterwards . . .'[31] It was a heart attack, it was a seizure, it was a stroke, we do not know. Both of Cnut's sons were dead before their twenty-fourth birthdays. To most men at the time, it was a visitation from the hand of God. The weather matched the mood: 'all this year was a very heavy time in many and various ways; bad weather, crops – and many cattle died this year, more than men ever remembered . . .'[32]

On the first day of Easter 1043, 'Edward was hallowed king in Winchester . . . with much celebration'.[33] So records the *Anglo-Saxon Chronicle*. In England, the line of Cnut had come to an end.

THIRTEEN

The Destiny of Cnut

In these wondrous ways the Guardian of Hosts
has shaped and assigned the skills of men,
on this middle-earth, and ordained the destiny
of every man and woman in this world.
Wherefore let each of us now thank Him,
for all that He, in His mercy, allots to men.
                                      The Fortunes of Men

In the year of Cnut's birth, an anonymous Saxon poet wrote *The Battle of Maldon*; cane sugar was brought into Europe for the first time, probably via traders from Egypt passing through Venice. The Arab traveller al-Biruni brought the Indian game of chess to a fascinated Europe; circumstantial evidence makes it the king's favourite game.

When he was five, Vikings from Greenland landed at what today is L'Anse aux Meadows in Newfoundland and although the settlement lasted for only a few years, links with a brave New World had been established. In Snorri Sturluson's Iceland, the *Althing* decided by a very modern-sounding majority vote that Christianity be adopted as the religion of the state. In the scattered Frisian islands to the south-west, farmers for the first time in recorded history began to build dykes and ramparts to reclaim land from the sea. Sheet glass was invented by an otherwise unknown philosopher called Theophilus. Coffee was already being drunk as a medicine along the Gulf of Persia, warmly recommended by the great physician ibn Siva, whom an awestruck Europe would come to know as Avicenna.

By the time Cnut was reddening the Humber with his father's invasion fleet, Bindforth, a monk of Romsey not far away, had

already written his *Handboc*, a superb astronomical work in Latin
and Old English, and more ominously, in Henry II's German states,
the first trial for heresy took place.

As the Viking established his position as king in both England and
Denmark, the first recorded epidemic of dancing mania erupted
across Europe: rheumatic fever? ergotism? the devil's work?
Terrified peasants ran screaming from it, churchmen muttered holy
incantations, noblemen locked their gates and their men-at-arms
stood to their weapons. Norwegian skalds were arriving at the court
of Richard of Normandy, to find their audience Frenchmen in all but
name. Not far away, in Orleans, a synod of the Church condemned
the sect who would one day be guilty of the Cathar heresy and
whose members would be hacked down in the Albigensian crusade.

In the year that Cnut was laid to rest in his Old Minster, ten
thousand religious manuscripts and images were walled up for
safety in the fortress of Tun-Huang in the Xixia province of China;
they would lie there, undisturbed, for nearly nine centuries.

The world turned more slowly in the eleventh century, but Cnut
lived and reigned at a time when the nation state was coming of age
and when the frontiers of Europe were taking on a shape we would
recognise even today. Cnut and his Empire of the North were very
much part of all that.

A certain consensus among historians past and present is that
with the succession of Edward, whom men later called the
Confessor, England reverted to a Saxon government as though the
reigns of Forkbeard, Cnut and both his sons had not existed. This is
not quite true. The Viking language survived – and survives – in a
plethora of place names in the Danelaw. Four of our seven weekdays
bear Viking origins – Tuesday, Wednesday, Thursday and Friday.
The laws of Cnut lived on until at least 1066 and in many senses for
centuries more: the Whig politician and philosopher Edmund Burke
was still writing about them in the 1770s.

Like Cnut, Edward was shrewd enough to realise that an
acceptance of the status quo was the best way to win friends and
influence people. And if slowly, Edward began to introduce new
ideas from his upbringing in Normandy, it was not without
opposition. When he began to build a castle (a specifically Norman

structure) at Dover, there was open rebellion and nineteen followers of Count Eustace of Boulogne were killed in the fighting. In 1052, the king was obliged to bow to public (Anglo-Scandinavian) opinion and banish his Norman favourite, Robert of Jumiéges, Bishop of London. It should be noted too that exile was the worst punishment in *Viking* society.

In many ways, Cnut's government lived on in the form of Earl Godwine of Wessex and his son, Harold, who was elected king by the witan in January 1066 on the Confessor's death. Rather than 1035 or 1043 marking the end of Cnut's personal influence, it should perhaps be under October 1066 that a line should be drawn. That misty day, on the hill at Senlac, a new power hacked its way into English history and William of Normandy, with his castles and his cavalry, his shaven head and his harsh voice, ushered in either a new greatness or the end of civilization, depending on one's view.

William seems to have gone out of his way to erase the memory of Cnut. In his great Domesday survey, carried out at the end of his reign, there is reference only to lands in the past as far back as *tempus Regis Edwardii*, in the time of King Edward, as though there *was* no time before him. Edward had grown up an exile in the Norman court and his banishment was a direct result of Cnut's seizure of the throne in 1016. And whereas Cnut was little more than a usurper, the otherwise very ordinary Edward became a saint, canonised by a brilliant propaganda exercise among the monks of the new abbey at Westminster which he founded.

William deliberately abandoned Winchester (despite enlarging the palace there) and chose London instead as his capital – the very city which had held out against Cnut and which he had punished with a huge Danegeld. And when the men of the north rose belatedly against the new usurper in 1069, William punished the Danelaw with a ferocity certainly not seen since 1016 and possibly not even then. In Domesday nearly twenty years later, there are hundreds of parishes that are described as 'waste', most of them burned beyond recovery by William's mail-clad soldiers.

By 1066 too, most of those who had known Cnut – his jarls, his thegns, his queens, the ceorls who had probably stood silent in awe as his retinue clashed past them on his way to a meeting of the witan or to endow a chapel or to sail to Denmark – were dead. Godwine, of whom the chronicler Walter Map wrote, 'I do not say he was a good man, but a mighty and an unscrupulous one',[1] was dining with King Edward on Easter Monday 1053 when, according to the Abingdon manuscript of the *Anglo-Saxon Chronicle*, 'he suddenly sank towards the foot-stool, bereft of speech and all of his strength'.[2] He was buried near Cnut in the Old Minster. His son Harold, who was probably about nine when Cnut died, went down under his banner, the Fighting Man, at Senlac, the last king of the English. Stigand, the priest of Ashingdon who became Cnut's chaplain, was an extraordinary survivor, being chaplain to Edward, Bishop of Elmham and Winchester and finally, Archbishop of Canterbury. He probably crowned Harold Godwinesson and certainly crowned William – his likeness and name 'Stigand Archieps' are stitched in the Bayeux Tapestry. He fell foul of the Norman regime, however, and became another casualty of the new broom; the Norman Lanfranc replaced him and he died in prison at William's new castle at Winchester in 1070.

From 1043, her attempts to fight for her chosen son having come to nothing, Emma of Normandy, Cnut's second wife, spent her life in relative quietness in Winchester. Probably she was allowed to retain her house at Godbegot and she would have watched the Confessor and his Norman cronies occupying the palace that she and her husband had made their own. She died, the survivor of four kings, on 14 March 1052 and was buried beside Cnut in the Old Minster; her little bones are there still. She was probably nearly seventy. The last record we have of the other Aelfgifu, Cnut's first wife and very probably his on-and-off mistress, comes from the brief reign of Harold Harefoot; a will of Bishop Alfric refers to two gold marks to the king and one 'to my lady'.[3] Harefoot had neither wife nor mistress that we know of, so this is probably history's farewell to Aelfgifu of Northampton. Did she, like her namesake, embittered, go back home to her Midland shire to live out the rest of her life? Perhaps, but there is an intriguing footnote to the story of the lady from Northampton. In an unexplained and out of context scene in the Bayeux Tapestry, a priest appears to be stroking the cheek of a woman. She is one of only four females in the entire work and the

Latin inscription above the figures reads 'Ubi unus clericus et Aelfgyra' (Where a priest and Aelfgifu). The lack of the rest of the sentence – no verb – is suggestive of some sort of scandal and this is reinforced by the naked man squatting in the border design, apparently gesturing up Aelfgifu's dress.

It draws on John of Worcester's take that neither Swein nor Harefoot was actually Cnut's son and that the priest was involved in a cover-up whereby Swein, at least, was smuggled into her bedchamber to be passed off as a prince. The fact that the *Anglo-Saxon Chronicle* also casts doubt on Harefoot's parentage makes it clear that some people, at least, accepted the bastardy of Aelfgifu's children as fact.

Why does she appear in the Bayeux Tapestry at all? Andrew Bridgeford, in his recent work on the subject,[4] finds subversive elements stitched into the linen and contends that Eustace of Boulogne, not Odo of Bayeux, is the central character and may well be the tapestry's patron. Since Harefoot was largely responsible for the murder of many men from Boulogne along with the atheling Alfred in 1036, this, Bridgeford contends, explains his slur on Harefoot's parentage. The theory is tortuous and Aelfgifu not an uncommon name in eleventh-century England, so it may be no more than coincidence. Another possibility of course is that the lady from Northampton was still alive in 1070 when the tapestry was made (she need only have been eighty years old; not an impossible situation) and that her inclusion may refer to something else entirely, now lost to time.

In 1093, the hammers of King William Rufus' stonemasons began to smash the Old Minster in Winchester to rubble. There had long been contention between the two churches, the bells of one drowning out those of the other. Now, one church would rise in their place – the huge Norman cathedral with its tell-tale arches and massive columns. We have no clear idea of what happened to the bones of Cnut and Emma for well over a century. It is possible that they were removed from their original site near Swithun's shrine to a free-standing position in the crypt. Equally, they could have been placed in the so-called 'Memorial Court' discovered by archaeologist Martin Biddle in the 1960s. Swithun's body was 'translated' for a second or possibly third time on 15 July 1093 and it is possible that soon after this, Cnut's body followed it, along with that of his queen. Alternatively, it may not have been until much later that this happened. The Cartulary of Winchester Cathedral reads:

> In the year of Our Lord 1158 Henry, Lord Bishop of Winchester, caused the bodies of kings and bishops to be brought from the Old Minster into the new church, which were removed from an unseemly place and placed together in a more respectful manner around the high altar of the blessed Apostles Peter and Paul.[5]

The Bishop was Henry of Blois, an energetic rebuilder, whose great-great-great aunt by marriage was Emma. It may be that the movement of her bones and those of her second husband was motivated as much by this family link as by piety.

By the fourteenth century, a huge Gothic screen had covered the Romanesque apse of Henry of Blois's time and niches along its front probably housed statuettes of a number of kings and bishops of Winchester, including 'Emma Regina . . . Cnutus Rex; Hardecnutus Rex, fillius eius' (Queen Emma, King Cnut, King Harthacnut, his son). The Winchester Chronicle of 1460 – a decade in which kings' lives and reputations were held cheaply indeed – records in Latin: 'His bones are now enclosed in a lead coffer around the door of the small crypt and on either side of the coffer is inscribed this verse: "Full of good works, here lies one Cnut by name".'[6] Interestingly, his name is given the Danish spelling of Knutr in the original.

A century and a half later, the bones seem to have been moved again, this time into mortuary chests on top of new screens in the presbytery. Lieutenant Hammond of the Norwich Militia visited the cathedral in the summer of 1635 while the king of his day, Charles I, was taxing his people illegally with the ship money Cnut had raised as a matter of course and taxing the patience of his parliament by refusing to summon it:

> [The] monuments are many, fayre and ancient especially 10 in little wooden gilt coffers are wrapt and shin'd in lead, the bones of 4 Saxon Kings, 2 Danish Kings and 4 Bishops and a Queen . . .

vizt. King Canutus and his son Hardicanute both in one . . . On the North side is Queen Emma, and her sonne and 4 Saxon Bishops with the Miters thereon.[7]

There is some confusion here. If Cnut and Emma were buried separately, who is the 'sonne' in her coffin? It can only be Harold Harefoot, who we know was buried at St Clement Danes, London. But other sources claim eight chests, not the ten referred to by Hammond, so he seems rather a casual observer.

Extraordinarily, Cnut's bones seem to have survived the organised iconoclasm of the Reformation. St Swithun's tomb was smashed and robbed in the 1530s as part of Henry VIII's determined break with Rome. Perhaps Cnut's great gilded cross was melted down in the process. His tomb would not survive the next attack however. On Thursday 14 December 1642, the parliament's troops under General William Waller marched into the cathedral's west door, 'their colours flying, their drums beating, their matches fired'. His lobster-helmeted cavalry clattered up the aisles of the nave. An eye witness, Bruno Ryvers, calling himself Mercurius Rusticus, described what happened:

But these monsters of men, to whom nothing is holy, nothing is sacred, did not stick to prophane and violate these cabinets of the dead, and to scatter their bones all over the pavement of the church; for on the North side of the Quire, they threw down the Chests, wherein were deposited the bones of the bishops, the like they did to the bones of William Rufus, of Queen Emma, of Hardecanutus and Edward the Confessor [*sic*].[8]

The troopers' officers came in to stop them, but much of the damage had been done: 'those windows which they could not reach with their Swords, Muskets and Rests,[9] they broke to pieces by throwing at them the bones of Kings, Queens, Bishops . . . and Saints'.[10] The diarist John Evelyn was a 'before and after' witness of this desecration. He went to the cathedral before the storm broke in 1642: 'I visited . . . the Church and its Saxon kings Monuments, which I esteemed a worthy antiquity.'[11] On 16 September 1685, an older and wiser man was back:

There is still the Coffines of the 6 Saxon Kings, whose bones had
been scatter'd by the sacriligeous Rebells of 1641 [*sic*] in
expectation (I suppose) of finding some valuable Reliques and
afterwards gather'd up againe and put into new chests, which
now stood above the stalls of the Quire.[12]

The eight chests (or ten according to Hammond) had now become six
and a revolution in its own way just as important as that of the mid-
seventeenth century had taken place before they were opened again.

The eighteenth century saw the first real attempt to assess the
past, to interpret and evaluate evidence. It was mostly carried out by
amateurs, enthusiasts whose antiquarian interests led them to amass
without analysis, to note down and draw without circumspection.
But at least the drawings and the notes were made and the great
Cnut became a subject for investigation. In 1797, when there was a
run on the banks in the face of William Pitt's unpopular
introduction of paper money and in the summer when the fleets at
the Nore and Spithead refused to sail against the French as the
liðsmen might have done in Cnut's time, officers of the West
Yorkshire Militia obtained permission to open the mortuary chests
and examine the contents. Officers of the militia were country
gentlemen, products of the Enlightenment and the Age of Reason;
they looked at the world in a way that Cnut would not have
understood and they wanted answers. One of them, Henry
Hammond of Corby Castle, left a report of their findings: '. . . 3rd
and 4th chests, bearing the names of Canute, Rufus, Emma, Wina,
Alwin and Stigand. Neither of these contains any skull, but they are
full of leg and thigh bones, one set of which, in the third chest, is
much smaller and weaker than the rest.'[13] Howard speculated that
these belonged to Emma and that her skull was in another chest.
There were twelve skulls in all, which tallied with the number of
names written on the chests, so at least none had been lost by
Waller's sacrilegious troopers in 1642.

The next time the chests were opened was in the 1890s. Science
and history had both moved on by this date and local antiquarian
Francis Baigent discovered two fifteenth-century chests, one inside
the other. In 1932, these inner chests were replaced and a certain

'sorting' of the bones took place. The 1930s is an infuriating decade for modern historians and archaeologists. Howard Carter's legendary finds in the Egyptian Valley of the Kings in the previous decade had unleashed an avalanche of digs, professional and amateur, all over the world. In Romania, the floor of the church at Snagov monastery was cracked open in search of the body of Vlad the Impaler, Dracula. In London, the bones of the 'Princes in the Tower' were studied minutely. In both cases, wrong deductions were drawn and false assumptions made. In July 1959, a further act of desecration took place when the bones in Winchester were 'cleaned' and tins were found, presumably from 1932, containing, among other things, teeth, zinc and what appeared to be cherry stones. The number of femurs would indicate that at least five adults still lie in the chests, but it is likely that Cnut's head was long ago separated from his body.

Somewhere between the investigations of Henry Howard and Francis Baigent, the Georgians reinvented the Vikings. John Pinkerton wrote in 1789, 'we, misled by a puerile love of the Romans, revile the ruder Goths [Saxons and Vikings] our fathers, as despisers of learning and the arts . . .'[14] Out of this was born the concept of the Dark Ages, a time of dismal barbarism across Europe which had eclipsed the grandeur that was Rome and replaced it with smoky huts, pillage and endless drink-fuelled carousing. Paintings of the Old Norse gods became popular, fancy dress parties were held, horns appeared on helmets!

The Christian Socialist, novelist and wife beater Charles Kingsley claimed loftily in his *Hereward the Wake* (1866) that Alexandra, Princess of Wales, was a direct descendant of Harald Bluetooth and therefore of Cnut. The second half of the nineteenth century was awash with novels recalling the sagas, the halls of Valhalla, Kipling's 'shouts and slaughters', and Andrew Warn records that to the Victorians, the Vikings were all things to all men, they were 'buccaneering, triumphant, defiant, confused, disillusioned, unbiddable, disciplined, elaborately pagan, austerely pious, relentlessly jolly or self-destructively sybaritic. They are merchant adventurers, mercenary soldiers, pioneering colonists, pitiless raiders, self-sufficient farmers, cutting-edge naval technologists, primitive democrats, psychopathic berserkers, ardent lovers and complicated poets.'[15] So they were.

The Viking myth was gaining ground everywhere. British imperialists appropriated their exploratory success, their indomitable courage, their navigational cutting edge. Socialist William Morris, fascinated by Old Norse and early medieval art, became a staunch supporter of this, as of so many, causes. The Germans, too, despite invading Denmark in 1864, made a great deal of their common mythology and Richard Wagner saw his *Ring des Nibelungen* performed at Bayreuth in Bavaria in 1876. It still goes on today – and in that context, what are J.R.R. Tolkien's Riders of Rohan but Cnut's *huscarls* in a magical setting?

As we have seen, earlier generations had put tentative toes into the dangerous waters of the North Sea research and if only one novel on Cnut emerged – *The Word of King Canute* in 1903[16] – serious study was not far behind. Archaeology has added vastly to the knowledge of the Viking era. The discovery of the Gokstad ship in 1870 sent shivers of delight through intellectual and patriotic circles – the reality was every bit as impressive as the tales of the sagas. When Laurence Marcellus Larson went into print in 1912 with what is the first English biography of Cnut, he witheringly dismissed the un-named 'eminent writer' who scoffed at Cnut – 'the Dane contributed nothing to English civilization, for he had nothing to contribute'. It was clearly time for a reassessment and Larson's work is excellent. Allowing for the spelling of Canute (Larson admitted himself he would rather have spelt it 'Cnut') and the fact that he believed the *Anglo-Saxon Chronicle* to be written by one hand, the book had a remarkably modern feel to it. Larson was writing at a time when a great deal of research had been carried out by Scandinavians. Gudbrand Vigfusson was an Icelander working in England in the 1860s in parallel with the Norwegian philologist Sophus Bugge. Before that J.J.A. Wirsaae, a Danish antiquarian, was working specifically on Viking place names. Dwarfing them all was J.C.H.R. Steenstrup, whose masterpiece *Normannerne*, written between 1876 and 1882, set a pattern of Scandinavian scholarship that has endured to the present.

It is in the watering down of history that Cnut's story changes. Charles Dickens, well-meaning and with a novelist's eye for a good story, wrote his *Child's History of England* in 1868 and taught a whole generation that Canute had refused single combat with Edmund Ironside because he was 'a little man', whereas Ironside was 'a big man'. I have no idea of his sources, if any. The only physical description of Cnut is that he was very tall, but the myth has endured into the modern pantheon. Dickens had to concede, however, that Cnut was a poet and musician and his take on the wave story would have accorded with the king's view of an all-powerful God: 'It is not the sea alone that is bidden to go "thus far and no further". The great command goes forth to all the kings upon the earth and went to Canute in the year one thousand and thirty five and stretched him dead upon his bed.'[17]

Cassell's *History of England*, published in 1873, continued the moralizing disapproval apparent in David Hume nearly a century earlier. Cnut used bribery and avoided battle when he could, whereas Edmund Ironside was a true hero in the fine old English mould. Ashingdon is set at Ashdon and as well as a church, Cassell's tells us, Cnut had four tumuli erected, known in the 1870s as the Bartlow Hills. Some archaeology had obviously been carried out, because two of the 'barrows' were found to contain stone coffins, skeletons, iron chains and cavalry harness. Cnut's 'small stature' and 'sickly disposition' were given, à la Dickens, as the excuse not to mix it personally with Ironside. In Cassell's, the much-accused Eadric Streona stands committed of Ironside's murder, at the hands of the Mercian's chamberlains; and Olaf Haraldsson was 'just and unwarlike'. Six London churches were, incomprehensibly, dedicated in the Middle Ages to this aggressive and pushy former ally of Aethelred.

But Cnut's reputation had further to fall. Sellar and Yeatman went into print with the immortal *1066 and All That*, in which, with excruciating puns, they portray Cnut as a 'Bad King' (a running gag throughout the book). Clever satirists like these wrote more than a kernel of truth in their tongue-in-cheek sideswipes at the king, but their non-historian readership saw only the humour and so Cnut became a figure of fun, a subject, along with Henry VIII, fit for ridiculous music hall songs.

In a bizarre twist on the skaldic poetry of his own day, Marriott Edgar, famous for his stage soliloquies, wrote 'Canute the Great', in which the king's hobbies are 'roving and raiding'. Once again, a curious vein of truth ran through the poem, but once again, the public only saw the ribald humour and not the very real man behind it.

Today's satirists do it better. Usborne Books' *The Viking Invader*, written in the form of a tabloid, has Dr John Haywood as historical consultant and is considerably funnier than Sellar and Yeatman. Under a banner headline 'Son of Unready Loses Throne' the article covers the history of 1016–20 as though written by the *Sun*.

'Thus far shalt thou go and no further.' As Dickens wrote a century and a half ago, the power of any king is limited by circumstance, by personality and by time. Nearly a century ago, Laurence Larson summed up Cnut with a phrase no one has bettered: 'Slavic ancestry, Christian culture, Anglo-Saxon ideas'.[18] All three moulded the man who was Cnut and made his reign what it was. '. . . Deep in his strong soul', Larson went on, 'lay unconquered the fierce passions that ruled the Viking age – pitiless cruelty, craving for revenge, consuming hatred and lust for power.'[19] Such things make great kings – William the Bastard, Henry II, Richard I, Edward I, Edward III, Henry V, Edward IV; the list is long. And cruelty, revenge, hatred and the lust for power are relative terms. They must be seen against the background of the age. When Laurence Larson was writing, Adolf Hitler was a failed artist struggling to make a living in the back streets of Vienna; Josef Stalin was a yet-little-known revolutionary in Nicholas II's Russia, about to join the Bolshevik party. The dictatorship of these men and the lesser monsters who have peopled our own time, dwarf the supposed cruelties of men like Cnut. Even Larson conceded that the hostages Cnut had mutilated represented broken oaths, the most serious of crimes in the Viking world; Ulf, whom he may or may not have had murdered, was a patent traitor; the men he executed in 1018 or banished in 1020 were enemies and a threat to the stability and peace of his reign. The most damning charge against him, that he attempted to engineer the deaths of Aethelred's younger sons, has no hard evidence to prove that it ever happened.

We are left with a man who does not deserve the dismissals of the twentieth century. If he was, to quote historians from Laurence Larson to Michael Wood, 'a pirate' and a 'Viking thug', he 'developed into a statesman'[20] and became a great king. How can we measure him? The Encomiast, admittedly paid to be nice in 1042, did not get it far wrong:

> He indeed became a friend and intimate of churchmen . . . He diligently defended wards and widows, he supported orphans and strangers, he suppressed unjust laws and those who applied them, he exalted and cherished justice and equity, he built and dignified churches . . . he enjoined peace and unanimity upon his people . . .[21]

The nature of the historical record in his day and in the two or three centuries that followed, means that we have no personality traits with which to wrestle. The historians of a thousand years from now will still be able to write authoritatively of Adolf Hitler and Joseph Stalin because of the sheer weight of evidence surrounding them. They have been scrutinised and analysed by an army of experts from psychoanalysts to media gurus and it is difficult to know what else remains to be said. Against them, a leader of the Western World in the misty eleventh century is a blank canvas. We do not know exactly when or where Cnut was born, precisely who his mother was or what kind of upbringing he had. His first campaigns as a boy are recorded only in the tortuous phraseology of the skaldic poems. His first marriage is shrouded in secrecy – where? when? why? We can answer none with certainty. His conversion to Christianity – taking the saint's name Lambert – is a footnote, yet it coloured his life. He gave freely to the Church, along with his second wife, the redoubtable Emma Aelfgifu, and almost the only personal touch we have of the man, as opposed to the king, is his response to the chanting of the monks of Ely as he rowed to their abbey in the Fenlands; and the possibility that he had a short temper and did not like losing a game of chess.

Tangible reminders are few. Three runic inscriptions from Denmark mention him, a relative handful of charters survive. Even the *Anglo-Saxon Chronicle* is infuriatingly terse. His laws, once so important and so comprehensive, have been subsumed by others, more pertinent if not always so wise. The navy he built has vanished – expensive, high-tech gadgetry long ago replacing the craftsmanship, the courage, the sinew that drove the tough fir-blades through the foaming North Sea. Today's pampered army, with its women soldiers, its camouflage and its stress counselling bears little resemblance to the one he led, over England, Scotland, Denmark, Norway and Sweden, the fierce thegns and *huscarls*, standing behind their shield walls, bristling with the spears of the swine-array, spitting their guttural insults at their enemies, be they Englishman, Scot, Dane, Swede or Norwegian. Where is the gold cross he and Emma gave to Winchester? Melted down by successive robbers from Thomas Cromwell to his namesake Oliver. Where is the peacock cloak he left draped over the tomb of Edmund Ironside? Rotted in the ravages of time. Where is the crown that legend says he wore no longer after the waves incident? Vanished into that great Lost Property receptacle which we call history.

The Normans did their best to obliterate the achievements and the memory of Cnut; perhaps because Duke William, only a boy when the king died, knew that the Viking was a man too much like himself. Edward the Confessor was putty by comparison, more like the 'redeless' Aethelred than most men cared to admit. And after time, with the Old and New Minster gone and Winchester no longer the capital of England, even old men forgot.

Today, Cnut's reputation is grudgingly being restored. He was a lawgiver, a warrior, a statesman, an emperor, a benefactor of the Church; and in the quieter moments we cannot see, a lover, husband and father.

The last words should come from Cnut's own time:

What has become of the steed? What has become of the warrior? What has become of the giver of treasure? What has become of the seats of banquet? Where are the joys of the hall? O, for the bright cup! O, for the mail-clad warrior! O, for the glory of the prince! Now that time has passed away and grown dark under the cover of night, as if it had never been.[22]

AETHELRED'S FAMILY TREE

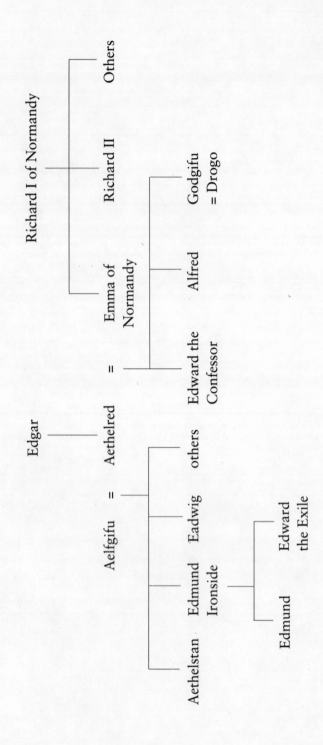

CNUT'S FAMILY TREE

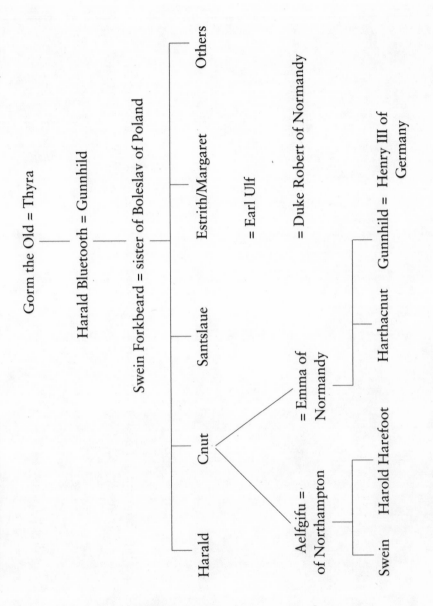

Gorm the Old = Thyra

Harald Bluetooth = Gunnhild

Swein Forkbeard = sister of Boleslav of Poland

Harald

Cnut

Santslaue

Estrith/Margaret

Others

= Earl Ulf

= Duke Robert of Normandy

Aelfgifu =
of Northampton

= Emma of
Normandy

Swein

Harold Harefoot

Harthacnut

Gunnhild = Henry III of
Germany

Notes

One

1. Hume, David, *History of England*, vol. 1 (T. Cadell, 1792), pp. 152–3.
2. Swanton, Michael (tr.), *Anglo-Saxon Chronicle*, 5th edn (Phoenix Press, 2003), p. 124 (Abingdon (C) text).
3. Swanton (tr.), *Anglo-Saxon Chronicle*, Canterbury (F) and Peterborough (E) text, pp. 55–6.
4. No actual examples of horned helmets have been found by archaeologists in any area where the Vikings lived, raided or settled. There are one or two ambiguous portrayals of horned helmets in carvings and other artwork, but these are usually ascribed to lofty deities like Odin. The Victorians virtually invented the common misconception that horns were traditional Viking headgear, sadly continued today in the otherwise historically excellent Playmobil toys!
5. A hide was a unit of land used extensively in Saxon England as a means of measurement. Its size varied depending on the quality of the land itself, but by the early eleventh century, it was usually the equivalent of 120 acres; 'small hides' were half that. Commonly expressed in the Burghal Hideage, a list of English forts, and in Domesday Book, the term could still be found in rural areas into the nineteenth century.
6. Swanton (tr.), *Anglo-Saxon Chronicle*, Abingdon (C) text, p. 124.
7. Topographical Preface to the *Anglo-Saxon Chronicle* (C text) but also found in D and F.
8. Swanton (tr.), *Anglo-Saxon Chronicle*, Abingdon (C) text, p. 124.
9. Ibid.
10. Ibid., Winchester (A) text, p. 80.
11. Ibid., p. 126. By now we have one of the common errors that cause chaos in writing a narrative of events. In the Winchester text, dates were written into the margin of the pages in anticipation of single-line entries. Where, inevitably, the text ran on for longer entries, dates were obliterated or copied over, so that we cannot be sure whether Tryggvason's raid was in 991 or 993.
12. Swanton (tr.), *Anglo-Saxon Chronicle*, Peterborough (E) text, p. 146.
13. Hume, *The History of England*, vol. 1, p. 145.
14. All quotations from *The Battle of Maldon* are from Kevin Crossley-Holland, *The Anglo-Saxon World* (Boydell Press, 1982), pp. 10–17.
15. Given the circumstances described in *The Two Towers*, the 'goodies' could never have won at Helm's Deep!

16. *The Fortunes of Men* from the Exeter Book, trans. K. Crossley-Holland, *Anglo-Saxon World*, pp. 273–5.
17. Tacitus, *Germania*, quoted in Kevin Crossley-Holland, *The Anglo-Saxon World*, p. 2.
18. Swanton (tr.), *Anglo-Saxon Chronicle*, Winchester (A) text, p. 126.
19. Kipling, Rudyard, Danegeld (AD 980–1016) from Songs Written for C.R.L. Fletcher's *A History of England*, 1911.
20. Swanton (tr.), *Anglo-Saxon Chronicle*, Peterborough (E) text, pp. 127–8.
21. Ibid., p. 128.
22. Revelation 20: 2–3, King James edn, 1611.

Two

1. Swanton, Michael (tr.), *Anglo-Saxon Chronicle*, Peterborough (E) text, 5th edn (Phoenix Press, 2003), p. 131.
2. Stenton, Frank, *Anglo-Saxon England* (Oxford University Press, 1965), p. 384.
3. Ibid.
4. Swanton (tr.), *Anglo-Saxon Chronicle*, Winchester (A) text, p. 132.
5. 'The Cartulary of St Frideswide', I Peter 2–3 in D.Whitelock (tr.), *English Historical Documents*, p. 591.
6. Ibid.
7. Swanton (tr.), *Anglo-Saxon Chronicle*, Peterborough (E) text, p. 135.
8. Ibid. – and an unusually poetic phrase from the *Chronicle*, clearly 'lifted' from skaldic poetry.
9. Swanton (tr.) *Anglo-Saxon Chronicle*, Peterborough (E) text, p. 135.
10. Ibid., p. 136.
11. Ibid., Abingdon (C) text, p. 136.
12. *Historia Anglorum*: Henry, Archdeacon of Huntingdon.
13. Swanton (tr.), *Anglo-Saxon Chronicle*, Peterborough (E) text, p. 138.
14. Ibid., p. 142.
15. Ibid., p. 143.
16. Campbell, Alistair (tr.), *Encomium Emmae Reginae* (Royal Historical Society, Camden edn, 1949), bk 1, ch. 3.
17. Ibid.
18. Swanton (tr.), *Anglo-Saxon Chronicle*, Peterborough (E) text, p. 144.
19. And would be for centuries. 'Revolts of the North' are a recurrent theme in English history.
20. Swanton (tr.), *Anglo-Saxon Chronicle*, Peterborough (E) text, p. 143.
21. Ibid.
22. Ibid., p. 144.
23. Ibid., p. 144.
24. Ibid., p. 144.

Three

1. The master Danish storyteller (1805–75) was a failed writer and singer who reached fame as a poet and received a pension from the king. His most famous stories for children – *The Ugly Duckling*, *The Tinderbox* and *The Emperor's New Clothes* – reached a huge audience and still delight children today.

2. The famous 'bog bodies' such as Tollund Man and Grauballe Man are among the most important finds in Western Europe. The chemicals in the peat have preserved skin, nails and hair to the extent that fingerprints can be taken, stomach contents examined and last meals identified.

3. Larson, Laurence, *Canute the Great*, 'The Heroes of the Nations' series (G.P. Putnam's Sons, 1912), p. 3.

4. The Jellinge style takes its name from a silver cup found in the royal mounds at Jellinge, characterised by writhing mythical beasts with open jaws. The Mammen style grew out of this, with bodies more substantial and studded with beading. Both forms (which are very similar) grew out of the Borre style from southern Norway, with its tangled and complicated ring-chain patterns. What dominated in Cnut's time was the flowering of Viking art, Ringerike, also from south Norway, with weather vanes, grave stones, memorials and much else laced with fearsome, beautiful monsters such as that which provides the chapter heads in this book.

5. The Emperor's guard in Byzantium, the east's equivalent of Rome, took its name from the Old Norse *varan* 'to swear'. The unit was founded in 988 by Vladimir of Kiev and a century later contained Normans and Englishmen as well as Scandinavians. This elite corps was finally destroyed in the capture of the city by the Turks under Mehmet II in 1453.

6. Larson, *Canute the Great*, p. 3.

7. *Beowulf* in Kevin Crossley-Holland (tr.), *The Anglo-Saxon World* (Boydell, 1982), pp. 71–142.

8. Saxo Grammaticus, *Gesta Danorum* (Deeds of the Danes), p. 318.

9. The death of the Danish king in 1863 reopened the 'Schleswig-Holstein question' about who owned what. The combined armies of Prussia and Austria made short work of Danish military opposition to their invasion. Neither country would have risked it in the reign of Cnut!

10. Richards, Julian, *Blood of the Vikings* (Hodder & Stoughton, 2001).

11. Campbell, Alistair (tr.), *Encomium Emmae Reginae*, 3rd series (Royal Historical Society, Camden edn, 1949), vol. LXXII, p. 9.

12. Ottar the Black, *Knútsdrápa*, *c.* 1017, trans E.H.D. Whitelock.

13. *The Fortunes of Man* in Crossley-Holland (tr.), *Anglo-Saxon World*, p. 273.

14. Quoted in Brian Bates, *The Real Middle Earth* (Pan, 2002), p. 177.

15. Ibid., p. 178.

16. *Beowulf*, quoted in Crossley-Holland (tr.), *Anglo-Saxon World*.

17. The Exeter Book, quoted in Crossley-Holland (tr.), *Anglo-Saxon World*.
18. *Beowulf*, quoted in Crossley-Holland (tr.), *Anglo-Saxon World*.

Four

1. Campbell, Alistair (tr.), *Encomium Emmae Reginae*, third series (Royal Historical Society, Camden edn, 1949), vol. LXXII, p. 15.
2. Swanton, Michael (tr.) *Anglo-Saxon Chronicle*, Peterborough (E) text, 5th edn (Phoenix Press, 2003), p. 145.
3. Not all historians follow this view, arguing that allegiance was given personally, one man to another. It had to be earned (or bought) on an individual basis.
4. Swanton (tr.) *Anglo-Saxon Chronicle*, Peterborough (E) text, p. 145.
5. Ibid.
6. William of Jumièges, *Historia Normannorum* v, chapters 11–12.
7. Swanton (tr.), *Anglo-Saxon Chronicle*, Abingdon (C) and Worcester (D) texts, p. 145.
8. Lavelle, Ryan, *Aethelred II* (Tempus, 2002), p. 131.
9. Campbell (tr.), *Encomium*, p. 19.
10. Ibid.
11. Swanton (tr.), *Anglo-Saxon Chronicle*, Peterborough (E) text, p. 154.
12. Ibid.
13. Ibid., p. 142.
14. Ibid.
15. Ibid., p. 153.
16. Campbell (tr.), *Encomium Reginae* ii, ch. 4, p. 21.
17. Swanton (tr.), *Anglo-Saxon Chronicle*, Peterborough (E) text, p. 153
18. Ibid., p. 146.
19. Larson, Laurence, *Canute the Great* (G.P. Putnam's Sons, 1912), p. 75.
20. Swanton (tr.), *Anglo-Saxon Chronicle*, Worcester (D) text, p. 153.
21. Fletcher, Richard, *Bloodfeud* (Penguin, 2003), p. 4.
22. Swanton (tr.), *Anglo-Saxon Chronicle*, Worcester (D) text, p. 153.
23. Ibid.
24. 'The Liðsmen's Song' from *Corpus Poeticum Boreale* ii, in Larson, *Canute*, p. 108.
25. *Knutsdrápa* in D. Whitelock (ed.), *English Historical Documents*, p. 335.
26. Swanton (tr.), *Anglo-Saxon Chronicle*, Peterborough (E) text, p. 150.
27. Campbell (tr.), *Encomium*, p. lviii.
28. Swanton (tr.), *Anglo-Saxon Chronicle*, Worcester (D) text, p. 150.
29. Ibid.
30. Ibid. On the legality of the situation, Laurence Larson points out that neither man could legally claim to be king at this stage because the *complete* witan had voted for neither of them.

31. Swanton (tr.), *Anglo-Saxon Chronicle*, Peterborough (E) text, p. 151.
32. Campbell (tr.), *Encomium*, p. 25.
33. Swanton (tr.), *Anglo-Saxon Chronicle*, Peterborough (E) text, p. 151.
34. Swanton (tr.), *Anglo-Saxon Chronicle*, Worcester (D) text, p. 152.
35. The Exeter Book, in Kevin Crossley-Holland (tr.), *The Anglo Saxon World* (Boydell Press, 1982).
36. Swanton (tr.), *Anglo-Saxon Chronicle*, Peterborough (E) text, p. 152.
37. Campbell (tr.), *Encomium*, p. 27.
38. Howard, Ian, *Swein Forkbeard's Invasions and the Danish Conquests in England, 991–1017* (Boydell Press, 2003), p. 140.
39. Campbell (tr.), *Encomium*, p. 27.
40. Swanton (tr.), *Anglo-Saxon Chronicle*, Worcester (D) text, p. 152.
41. From *The Battle of Brunanburh*, Anon.
42. 'Bald's Leechbook', in Crossley-Holland (tr.), *Anglo Saxon World*, p. 246.
43. Swanton (tr.) *Anglo-Saxon Chronicle*, Peterborough (E) text, p. 152.
44. Swanton (tr.), *Anglo-Saxon Chronicle*, Canterbury (F) text, p. 152.
45. In a series of Deerhurst lectures, given at the church since the late 1980s.
46. Sturluson, Snorr, *Saga of Magnus the Good*, ch. 6.
47. Swanton (tr.), *Anglo-Saxon Chronicle*, Canterbury (E) text, p. 153.
48. Campbell (tr.), *Encomium* ii, p. 31.
49. Ibid.

Five

1. Swanton, Michael (tr.), *Anglo-Saxon Chronicle*, Worcester (D) Text, 5th edn (Phoenix Press, 2003), p. 154.
2. Vansittart, Peter, *Green Knights, Black Angels* (Macmillan, 1969), p. 19.
3. Swanton (tr.), *Anglo-Saxon Chronicle*, Peterborough (E) text, p. 85.
4. These laws were reiterated in Cnut's time (see Chapter 6).
5. Sturluson, Snorri, *Olafsaga*.
6. In the 1960s, the phrase 'aks at robots' in Manchester, meant to 'ask at the traffic lights'! In the Isle of Wight, a 'gurt mallyshag in me nammet' is a large caterpillar in one's packed lunch.
7. Gildas was a Romano-British monk from Strathclyde who wrote *De Excidio et Conquesta Britanniae*, a history of the Celts between 516 and 547.
8. Bede was a Saxon scholar and monk of Jarrow whose writings were prodigious on all sorts of topics. His *Historia Ecclesiastica Gentis Anglorum* written in 731 has been called 'the single most valuable source for early English history'.
9. Both words are Saxon dialect terms for 'horse'.
10. For further details of Viking burials, see D.M. Hadley, *Death in Medieval England* (Tempus, 2001).

11. Both quoted in S. Lapidge (ed.), *Encyclopaedia of Anglo-Saxon England* (Blackwell, 2001), p. 460.

12. Bede, quoted in Robert Lacey and Danny Danziger, *The Year 1000* (Little, Brown, 1999), p. 56.

13. A practice which continued until George II decided (quite rightly) to dispense with such nonsense.

14. Crossley-Holland, K., *Anglo-Saxon World*, p. 254.

15. Quoted in Dorothy Whitelock, *The Beginnings of English Society* (Penguin, 1952), p. 99.

16. The name has no link with copper, but is derived from the Old Norse meaning a cup.

17. III Aethelred ch. II – quoted in Simon Keynes (contrib.) in S. Lapidge (ed.), *Encyclopaedia of Anglo-Saxon England*, p. 444.

Six

1. Swanton, Michael (tr.), *Anglo-Saxon Chronicle*, Worcester (D) text, 5th edn (Phoenix Press, 2003).

2. Quoted in John Haywood, *The Penguin Historical Atlas of the Vikings* (Penguin, 1995), p. 122.

3. According to various chroniclers, their battle cry at Hastings was 'Dieu nous aidez' (God help us).

4. Lavalle, Ryan, *Aethelred II* (Tempus, 2002), p. 98.

5. The change of name of the royal family from Battenburg to Mountbatten in 1914 is a similar example.

6. Quoted in 'Medieval Kingship' by Janet L. Nelson in M. Lapidge (ed.), *The Blackwell Encyclopaedia of Anglo-Saxon England* (Blackwell, 2001), p. 383.

7. Campbell, Alistair (tr.), *Encomium Emmae Reginae*, 3rd series (Royal Historical Society, Camden edn, 1949), vol. LXXII, p. 33.

8. Campbell (tr.), *Encomium*, p. 33.

9. Victoria was supposed to marry Albert's elder brother Ernst of Saxe-Coburg Gotha, but when she met Albert she was so smitten that she chose him instead.

10. Larson, Laurence, *Canute the Great* (G.P. Putnam's Sons, 1912), p. 126.

11. Campbell (tr.), *Encomium*, p. 33.

12. John of Worcester, *Chronicon* i.

13. Larson, *Canute the Great*, p. 126.

14. The son of Alfred the Great (899–924).

15. Egbert was king of Wessex and perhaps *bretwalda* (overlord) of much of England. He died in 839.

16. Jonsson, K., 'The Coinage of Cnut', in Rumble, A.R. (ed.), *The Reign of Cnut* (Leicester University Press, 1999).

17. Campbell (tr.), *Encomium*, p. 35.

18. Sturluson, Snorri, *Olafsaga.*
19. *Chronicon*, p. 182.
20. The legend of Lady Godiva (Godgifu) is that to prevent the people of Coventry from having to pay her husband's extortionate taxes, she rode naked through the town's streets. All the townspeople demurely closed their shutters and stayed indoors to spare the lady's blushes, except the voyeuristic Tom, who was immediately struck blind by God's intervention. Like Queen Emma, Godgifu was a frequent benefactress to the Church and outlived her husband by several years, possibly dying in 1086.
21. Swanton (tr.), *Anglo-Saxon Chronicle*, Peterborough (E) text, p. 154.
22. Swanton (tr.), *Anglo-Saxon Chronicle*, Worcester (D) text, p. 154.
23. Swanton (tr.), *Anglo-Saxon Chronicle*, Canterbury (F) text, p. 155.

Seven

1. Fulbert, *Lettres*, ed. Behrends, pp. 66–8, quoted in M.K. Lawson, *Cnut – The Danes in England in the Early Eleventh Century* (Longman, 1993), p. 158.
2. Alcuin, *Letters*, quoted in D. Whitelock, *The Beginnings of English Society* (Penguin, 1952), p. 148.
3. *Voluspá* II, 133–4.
4. Sturluson, Snorri, *Heimskringla.*
5. Larson, Laurence, *Canute the Great* (G.P. Putnam's Sons, 1912), p. 55.
6. Ibid.
7. Lawson, M.K., *Cnut*, p. 130.
8. 'The Law of the Northumbrian Priests' in D. Whitelock (ed.), *English Historical Documents*, vol. 1, p. 474.
9. In *The Canterbury Tales*, a satire written by the poet Geoffrey Chaucer about 1386, only one of his several ecclesiastical pilgrims is a good man – the parson. All the others exhibit every kind of corruption known to man.
10. Quoted in Wendy Davies, *From the Vikings to the Normans* (Oxford University Press, 2003), p. 150.
11. Ibid., p. 152.
12. Larson, *Canute the Great*, pp. 176–7.
13. *Historia Dunelonensis Ecclesiasiae*, quoted in M.K. Lawson, *Cnut*, p. 133.
14. Hicks, Carola (ed.), *England in the Eleventh Century*, Harlaxton Medieval Studies vol. 2 (Paul Watkins, 1992), p. 221.
15. A mancuse was the equivalent of thirty Saxon shillings (there were forty to the pound in Cnut's reign).
16. *Vita St Editha*, ii, 13, ed. Wilmot, quoted in M.K. Lawson, *Cnut*, p. 135.
17. St George was probably tortured and executed by the Emperor Diocletian at Nicomedia in April 303. As such, he became a martyred saint of the Eastern Roman Empire in Byzantium. His cult as a slayer of dragons and chivalrous hero

dates from the crusades and post-dates Cnut's reign by two centuries. It is hardly surprising that Englishmen today are virtually unaware of their patron saint's day as his links to this country are virtually non-existent. In fact, Cnut's acquisition of the man's finger may have been the start of the link, however tenuous.

18. Swanton, Michael (tr.), *The Anglo-Saxon Chronicle*, Winchester (D) text (Phoenix Press, 2000), p. 156.
19. 'Mene Sungen de Muneches binnen Ely, / da Cnut ching reu der by' (*Liber Eliensis*), quoted in L. Rumble (ed.), *The Reign of Cnut* (Leicester University Press, 1999), p. 124.
20. Unnamed poem by Hallvarðr Háreksblesi.

Eight

1. Usually a cattle disease, something like brucellosis or foot and mouth.
2. Crossley-Holland, Kevin, *The Anglo-Saxon World* (Boydell Press, 1982), p. 262.
3. 'of the Norwegians' is a later addition. Cnut could not legitimately lay claim to Norway until 1030.
4. Bald's *Leechbook*, quoted in Crossley-Holland, *Anglo-Saxon World*, p. 248.
5. Lawson, M.K., *Cnut – The Danes in England in the Early Eleventh Century* (Longman, 1993), p. 63.
6. Quoted in Dorothy Whitelock, *The Beginnings of English Society* (Penguin, 1952), p. 136.
7. Whitelock, *Beginnings of English Society*, p. 140.
8. Quoted in Patrick Warnald (ed.), *The Anglo-Saxon Encyclopedia*, p. 338.
9. Quoted in Whitelock, *Beginnings of English Society*, p. 142.
10. In one of the Hood poems, the outlaw hacks off the head of Guy of Gisborne and impales it on the end of his longbow, a far cry from the happy-go-lucky giver to the poor of the later stories.
11. Fletcher, Richard, *Bloodfeud* (Penguin, 2003), p. 103.
12. Hume, David, *The History of England* (T. Cadell, 1792).

Nine

1. 'Winchester – the rise of an early capital' in Boris Ford (ed.), *The Cambridge Cultural History of Britain* (Cambridge University Press, 1995), vol. 1, pp. 195–205.
2. *Corpus Poeticium Boreale* ii quoted in Laurence Larson, *Canute the Great* (G.P. Putnam's Sons, 1912), pp. 135–6.
3. Sturluson, Snorri, *Olafsaga*, quoted in Larson, *Canute the Great*.
4. *Histriola Legum Castrensium Regis Canuti Magni*, quoted in Larson, *Canute the Great*.
5. *Gesta Danorum*, quoted in Larson, *Canute the Great*, p. 351.
6. *Scriptores* iii, quoted in Larson, *Canute the Great*, p. 151.

7. Hooper, N., 'Military Developments in the Reign of Cnut', in A. Rumble, *The Reign of Cnut* (Leicester University Press, 1999).

8. John of Worcester, *Chronicom ex Chanscis*.

9. The use of cavalry as a shock force on battlefields always had its risks. Prince Rupert's horsemen galloped too far too fast and Wellington complained that his cavalry were 'always getting him into scrapes'.

10. The Kolstad stone, quoted in Larson, *Canute the Great*, p. 134.

11. Quoted in Larson, *Canute the Great*, p. 135.

12. Thietmar of Merseburg, *Chronicon* vii, 41, quoted in Larson, *Canute the Great*, pp. 448–9.

13. John of Worcester, *Chronicon* i, quoted in Larson, *Canute the Great*, p. 195.

14. In that sense only, the liðsmen may be seen as proto-Marines.

15. S950 quoted in M.K. Lawson, *Cnut – The Danes in England in the Early Eleventh Century* (Longman, 1993), Appendix IV.

16. Ibid.

17. 'An Iron Reverse Die', in Alexander R. Rumble (ed.), *The Reign of Cnut* (Leicester University Press, 1999), p. 237. Isn't it encouraging that the ceorls are still out there!

18. A silver penny of Cnut was offered for sale recently by a coin dealer for £310.

19. Jonsson, K., 'The coinage of Cnut' in Rumble (ed.), *The Reign of Cnut*.

20. 'Continuity and Change in English Monetary History Part 2', *British Numismatics Journal*, 1981.

21. Larson, *Canute the Great*, p. 283.

22. 'Cnut's Secular Laws', ch. 8, quoted in D. Whitelock (ed.), *English Historical Documents*.

23. 'The Fortunes of Men' quoted in Kevin Crossley-Holland (tr.), *Anglo-Saxon World* (Boydell Press, 1982), p. 275.

24. Flack, Roberta, 'King Cnut in the verse of his skalds' in Rumble (ed.), *The Reign of Cnut*.

25. Flack, Roberta, in Rumble (ed.), *The Reign of Cnut*.

26. Mail-shirted.

27. Aella was the 'unnatural king' of Northumbria killed in York by a raiding party of Vikings under Ragnar Hairybreeks in 867. The term 'Aella's kin' was often used to mean the English. The plot of Kirk Douglas's film *The Vikings* is loosely based on these events.

28. Quoted in Christopher Page, 'Music' in *The Cambridge Cultural History of Britain*, vol. 1, pp. 247–53.

29. Flack, Roberta, in Rumble (ed.), *The Reign of Cnut*.

Ten

1. Swanton, Michael (tr.), *Anglo-Saxon Chronicle*, Abingdon (C) and Worcester (D) texts, 5th edn (Phoenix Press, 2003), p. 154.

2. Campbell, Alistair (tr.), *Encomium Emmae Reginae*, 3rd series (Royal Historical Society, Camden edn, 1949), vol. LXXII, p. 19.

3. All extracts from Cnut's letter of 1020 are quoted in Kevin Crossley-Holland, *The Anglo-Saxon World* (Boydell Press, 1982), pp. 28–9.

4. Sturluson, Snorri, *Olafsaga*, quoted in Martin Windrow, *Warriors and Warlords: The Art of Angus McBride* (Osprey, 2002), pp. 62–3.

5. Wimmer, *De danske Runemindesmaerker* I, ii, 133, quoted in Laurence Larson, *Canute the Great* (G.P. Putnam's Sons, 1912), p. 35.

6. The island's inlets have changed drastically over the centuries. St Helens harbour or even the now land-locked Brading are possibilities.

7. Crossley-Holland, *Anglo-Saxon World*, p. 63.

8. Ibid., p. 64.

9. Adam of Bremen, *Chronicon*, quoted in Larson, *Canute the Great*, p. 154.

10. Swanton (tr.), *Anglo-Saxon Chronicle*, Peterborough (E) texts, p. 157.

11. Sturluson, *Olafsaga*, quoted in Larson, *Canute the Great*, pp. 156–8.

12. Rumble, A. (ed.), *The Reign of Cnut* (Leicester University Press, 1999), p. 229.

13. Quoted in Larson, *Canute the Great*, p. 99.

14. Sturluson, *Olafsaga*, ch. 150.

Eleven

1. Swanton, Michael (tr.), *Anglo-Saxon Chronicle*, Worcester (D) text, 5th edn (Phoenix Press, 2003), p. 155.

2. The letter of 1027 extracts are taken from Dorothy Whitelock (ed.), *English Historical Documents*, vol. 3, pp. 476–80.

3. Campbell, Alistair (tr.), *Encomium Emmae Reginae*, 3rd series (Royal Historical Society, Camden edn, 1949), vol. LXXII, p. 37.

4. *Fagrskinna*, ch. 33, quoted in Laurence Larson, *Canute the Great* (G.P. Putnam's Sons, 1912), pp. 225–6.

5. Matthew 16:18, King James edn, 1611.

6. With the famous line, taken from Voltaire, that it was 'not Holy, nor Roman nor an Empire'.

7. Quoted in Robert Laffont (ed.), *A History of Rome and the Romans* (Macdonald, 1963) p. 131.

8. Duffy, Eamonn, *Saints and Sinners: A History of the Popes* (Yale University Press, 1997), p. 86.

9. Otto von Bismarck, the 'Iron Chancellor' of Prussia, engineered a war with Denmark in 1864 in order to bring Schleswig-Holstein under German control.

10. This area, between the Jura Mountains and the North Sea, was created at the redistribution of lands on the dissolution of the Carolingian Empire. The name later became corrupted to Lorraine.

11. Now named Monte St Angelo, in Southern Italy, 'in the kingdom of Naples'. See Edward Gibbon, *Decline and Fall of the Roman Empire*.

12. The Adriatic.

13. Possibly the peacock cloak he left draped over the tomb of Edward Ironside at Glastonbury in 1032.

14. Cnut's letter of 1027, in Whitelock (ed.), *English Historical Documents*.

15. Quoted in Rumble, A. (ed.), *The Reign of Cnut* (Leicester University Press, 1999), p. 118.

16. Stenton, Sir Frank, *Anglo-Saxon England* (Oxford Uuniversity Press, 1965), p. 401.

17. Cnut's letter of 1027, in Whitelock (ed.), *English Historical Documents*.

18. Ibid.

19. Ibid.

20. Ibid.

21. Swanton (tr.), *Anglo-Saxon Chronicle*, Winchester (A) text, p. 158.

22. Cnut's letter of 1027 in Whitelock (ed.), *English Historical Documents*.

23. Ibid.

24. Ibid.

25. Swanton (tr.), *Anglo-Saxon Chronicle*, Worcester (D) text, p. 159.

26. John of Worcester, *Chronicon*.

27. Swanton (tr.), *Anglo-Saxon Chronicle*, Worcester (D) text, p. 159.

28. So the military successes of Henry V were rendered the weaker because his heir, in 1422, was nine months old!

29. See my *Boudicca the Warrior Queen* (Sutton Publishing, 2003).

30. Berresford Ellis, Peter, *Macbeth* (Frederick Muller, 1980), p. 31.

31. Ibid., p. 36.

32. Sighvat the Skald, *Occasional Verses*, verse 15.

Twelve

1. Swanton, Michael (tr.), *Anglo-Saxon Chronicle*, Peterborough (E) text, 5th edn (Phoenix Press, 2003), p. 157.

2. Quoted in Johannes Brøndsted, *The Vikings* (Penguin, 1960), p. 104.

3. *Vita Edwardi Regis* quoted in Simon Keynes, 'Cnut's Earls' in A. Rumble (ed.), *The Reign of Cnut* (Leicester University Press, 1999), p. 71.

4. Ibid.

5. Ibid., p. 72.

6. Ibid.

7. Kolbeinsson, Thord, *Eiriksdrápa*, verse 12, quoted in D. Whitelock (ed.), *English Historical Documents*, p. 334.

8. Hearne, *Hemingi Chartularium* I, pp. 259–60.

9. Swanton (tr.), *Anglo-Saxon Chronicle*, Peterborough (E) text, p. 159.

10. Campbell, Alistair (tr.), *Encomium Emmae Reginae*, 3rd series (Royal Historical Society, Camden edn, 1949), vol. LXXII, p. 39.
11. Hadley, D.M., *Death in Medieval England* (Tempus, 2001), p. 70.
12. CCCC Ms 110, p. 359, quoted in Rumble (ed.), *The Reign of Cnut*, p. 171.
13. In 'Cnut's Bones', quoted in Rumble (ed.), *The Reign of Cnut*.
14. Stenton, Frank, *Anglo-Saxon England* (Oxford University Press, 1965), p. 413.
15. Swanton (tr.), *Anglo-Saxon Chronicle*, Peterborough (E) text, p. 161.
16. Ibid., p. 159.
17. Swanton (tr.), *Anglo-Saxon Chronicle*, Abingdon (C) text, p. 158.
18. Swanton (tr.), *Anglo-Saxon Chronicle*, Peterborough (E) text, p. 160.
19. Campbell (tr.), *Encomium*, p. 47.
20. *English Historical Review*, vol. XXV, iii, pp. 115–16.
21. Swanton (tr.), *Anglo-Saxon Chronicle*, Peterborough (E) text, p. 161.
22. Ibid., p. 160.
23. Ibid., p. 161.
24. Ibid.
25. Campbell (tr.), *Encomium*, p. 47.
26. Swanton (tr.), *Anglo-Saxon Chronicle*, Peterborough (E) text, p. 161.
27. A sester was the equivalent of sixteen bushels of wheat.
28. Swanton (tr.), *Anglo-Saxon Chronicle*, Peterborough (E) text, p. 161.
29. Ibid., p. 162.
30. Ibid.
31. Ibid.
32. Ibid.
33. Ibid., p. 163.

Thirteen

1. Quoted in Larson, p. 145.
2. Swanton, Michael (tr.), *Anglo-Saxon Chronicle*, Abingdon (C) text, 5th edn (Phoenix Press, 2003) p. 162.
3. Kemble, *Codex Diplomaticus* quoted in Laurence Larson, *Canute the Great* (G.P. Putnam's Sons, 1912), p. 333.
4. Bridgeford, Andrew, *1066: The Hidden History of the Bayeux Tapestry* (Fourth Estate, 2004).
5. Quoted in 'Cnut's Bones' in A. Rumble (ed.), *The Reign of Cnut* (Leicester University Press, 1999), p. 181.
6. Ibid., p. 187.
7. Ibid., p. 188.
8. Ibid., p. 189.
9. Linstocks, forked sticks used to support the weight of musket barrels.
10. 'Cnut's Bones', in Rumble, *The Reign of Cnut*, p. 189.

11. 'Cnut's Bones', in Rumble, *The Reign of Cnut*, p. 190.

12. de Beer, E.S. (ed.), *The Diary of John Evelyn*, vol. II, p. 79 and p. 472.

13. Mihauer, *History of Winchester*, III, 49–50 footnote.

14. Quoted in Wawn, Andrew, *The Vikings and the Victorians* (D.S. Brewer, 2000), p. 3.

15. Wawn, *Vikings and the Victorians*, p. 4.

16. Written by the Scandinavian American Ottilie Lijencrantz.

17. Dickens, Charles, *A Child's History of England*, p. 138.

18. Larson, Laurence, *Canute the Great* (G.P. Putnam's Sons, 1912).

19. Ibid.

20. Ibid.

21. Ibid.

22. Old English poem *The Wanderer*, Anon.

Bibliography

Bates, Bryan, *The Real Middle Earth*, Pan, London, 2002

Bennett, Matthew (ed.), *Hutchinson Dictionary of Ancient and Medieval Warfare*, Helicon, Oxford, 1998

Berresford Ellis, Peter, *Macbeth*, Frederick Muller, London, 1980

Bridgeford, Andrew, *1066: The Hidden History of the Bayeux Tapestry*, Fourth Estate, London, 2004

Brøndsted, Johannes, *The Vikings*, Penguin, London, 1960

Brook, G.L., *Harley Lyrics (Cnut's Song)*, Manchester University Press, 1948

Campbell, Alistair (trans.), *Encomium Emmae Reginae*, Camden, Royal Historical Society, London, 1949

Cannon, John (ed.), *Oxford Companion to British History*, Oxford University Press, 1997

Chesterton, G.K., *Ballad of the White Horse*, Methuen, London, 1911

Clout, Q., (ed.), *The Times London History Atlas*, BCA, London, 1991

Cohen, M.J. and Major, John, *History in Quotations*, Cassell, London, 2004

Cotterell, Arthur, *Encyclopaedia of Mythology*, Lorenz Books, London, 1999

Crossley-Holland, Kevin, *The Anglo-Saxon World*, Boydell Press, Woodbridge, 1982

Darlington, R.R. (ed.), *Vita Wulfstani – William of Malmesbury*, Offices of the Society, London, 1928

Darlington, R.R., McQuirk, P. and Bray, J. (eds), Clarendon Press, London, 1995

Darville, Timothy, Stamper, Paul and Timby, Jane, *England – An Archaeological Guide*, Oxford University Press, 2002

Davies, Wendy, *From the Vikings to the Normans*, Oxford University Press, 2003

Duffy, Eamon, *Saints and Sinners: A History of the Popes*, Yale University Press, 1997

Fleming, Fergus, *The Viking Invader*, Usborne Publishing, London, 2004

Fletcher, C.R.L., *A History of England*, London, 1911

Fletcher, Richard, *Bloodfeud*, Penguin, London, 2003

Ford, Boris (ed.), *The Cambridge Cultural History of Britain Vols 1 & 2*, Cambridge University Press, 1995

Frantzen, Allen J. and Niles, John D., *Anglo-Saxonism and the Construction of Social Identity*, University Press of Florida, 1997

Gearey, Patrick J. (ed.), *Readings in Medieval History*, Broadview, Peterborough, Ontario, 1991

Gore, Terry L., *Neglected Heroes*, Praeger, Westport, 1995

Graham-Campbell, James (ed.), *Cultural Atlas of the Viking World*, Andromeda, Oxford, 1994

Graham-Campbell, James, *The Viking World*, Frances Lincoln, London, 2001

Green, J.R. and A.S., *Conquest of England*, Harper & Bros, 1884

Greenwood, Douglas, *Who's Buried Where in England*, Constable, London, 1982

Hadley, D.M., *Death in Medieval England*, Tempus, Stroud, 2001

Hammond, Norman (ed.), *Wonders of the Ancient World*, National Geographic Society, Washington DC, 1994

Harrison, Mark, *Anglo-Saxon Thegn*, Osprey, Oxford, 1993

Harrison, Mark, *Viking Warrior*, Osprey, Oxford, 1993

Haywood, John, *The Penguin Historical Atlas of the Vikings*, Penguin, London, 1995

Heath, Ian, *The Vikings*, Osprey, Oxford, 1985

Hicks, Carola (ed.), *England in the Eleventh Century*, Harlaxton Medieval Studies Vol. 2, Paul Watkins, Stamford, 1992

Higham, N.J., *The Death of Anglo-Saxon England*, Sutton Publishing, Stroud, 1997

Hinde, Thomas (ed.), *The Domesday Book*, Salamander Books, London, 2002

Hollister, W., *Anglo-Saxon Military Institutions*, Clarendon Press, London, 1962

Howard, Ian, *Swein Forkbeard's Invasions and the Danish Conquests in England, 991–1017*, Boydell Press, Woodbridge, 2003

Howarth, David, *1066 The Year of the Conquest*, Penguin, London, 1978

Hume, David, *History of England*, Vol. 1, T. Cadell, 1792

Joliffe, G., *Constitutional History of Medieval England*, A&C Black, 1937

Kean, Maurice, *Medieval Warfare*, Oxford University Press, 1999

Knightly, Charles, *The Perpetual Almanack of Folklore*, Thames & Hudson, London, 1987

Lacey, Robert and Danziger, Danny, *The Year 1000*, Little Brown, London, 1999

Laffont, Robert (ed.), *History of Rome and the Romans*, Macdonald, London, 1965

Lang, Sean, *British History for Dummies*, John Wiley & Sons, Chichester, 2004

Langford, *Writings of Edmund Burke*, Vol. 8, Clarendon Press, London, 1981

Lapidge, Michael (ed.), *The Blackwell Encyclopaedia of Anglo-Saxon England*, Blackwell Publishing, Oxford, 2001

Larson, Laurence, *Canute the Great*, G.P. Putnam's Sons, New York, 1912

Lavelle, Ryan, *Aethelred II*, Tempus, Stroud, 2002

Lawson, M.K., *Cnut – The Danes in England in the Early Eleventh Century*, Longman, London, 1993

Leyser, Henrietta, *Medieval Women*, Phoenix, London, 1995

Loyn, H.R., *Anglo-Saxon England and the Norman Conquest*, Longmans, London, 1962

McLynn, Frank, *1066 – The Year of the Three Battles*, Jonathan Cape, London, 1998

Newark, Tim, *Warlords*, Brockhampton Press, London, 1996

Parker Pearson, Mike, *The Archaeology of Death and Burial*, Sutton Publishing, Stroud, 1999

Porter, Roy, *London – A Social History*, Penguin, London, 1994

Ramsay, James H., *Foundations of England*, Swan Sonnenschein & Co, 1898

Richards, Julian, *Blood of the Vikings*, Hodder & Stoughton, London, 2001

Rumble, Alexander R. (ed.), *The Reign of Cnut*, Leicester University Press, London, 1999

Saint, Andrew and Darley, Gillian, *The Chronicles of London*, Weidenfeld & Nicolson, London, 1994

Savage, Ann, *The Anglo-Saxon Chronicles*, Guild Publishing, London, 1983

Sellar, W.C. and Yeatman, R.J., *1066 and All That*, Methuen & Co, London, 1930

Starcke, *Denmark in World History*, University of Pennsylvania Press, 1963

Stenton, Doris, *English Women in History (Aelfgifu of Northants)*, Allen & Unwin, London, 1957

Stenton, Sir Frank, *Anglo-Saxon England*, Oxford University Press, 1965

Swanton, Michael (trans.), *The Anglo Saxon-Chronicles*, Phoenix, London, 2000

Vansittart, Peter, *Green Knights, Black Angels*, Macmillan, London, 1969

Vinogradoff, *English Society in the 11th Century*, Clarendon, London, 1908

Watkins, L. and Chibnall, M., *The Waltham Chronicle*, Oxford University Press, 1994

Wawn, Andrew, *The Vikings and the Victorians*, DS Brewer, Cambridge, 2000

Weir, Alison, *Britain's Royal Families*, Pimlico, London, 2002

Whitelock, Dorothy, *The Beginnings of English Society*, Penguin, London, 1952

Whitelock, Dorothy (ed.), *English Historical Documents*, Oxford University Press, London, 1955

Williams, Ann (ed.), *Domesday Book*, Penguin Books, London, 2003

Windrow, Martin, *Warriors and Warlords: The Art of Angus McBride*, Osprey, Poole, 2002

Wood, Michael, *Domesday – A Search for the Roots of England*, BBC Books, London, 1986

Wood, Michael, *In Search of the Dark Ages*, BBC Books, London, 1981

Periodicals

BBC History, Vol. 1, No. 3, July 2000

BBC History, Vol. 2, No. 11, November 2001

BBC History, Vol. 3, No. 8, August 2002

Index